YEARS

SIMON &
SCHUSTER

Sociopath

A MEMOIR

Patric Gagne, PhD

Simon & Schuster

NEW YORK   LONDON   TORONTO
SYDNEY   NEW DELHI

This publication contains the opinions and ideas of its author. It is intended to provide helpful and informative material on the subject addressed. It is sold with the understanding that the author and publisher are not engaged in rendering medical, health, or any other kind of personal or professional services in the book. Readers should consult their own medical, health, or other professional before adopting any of the suggestions in this book or drawing inferences from it.

1230 Avenue of the Americas
New York, NY 10020

Copyright © 2024 by Patricia Gagne

First Simon & Schuster hardcover edition April 2024

SIMON & SCHUSTER and colophon are registered trademarks of Simon & Schuster, LLC

Simon & Schuster: Celebrating 100 Years of Publishing in 2024

For information about special discounts for bulk purchases, please contact Simon & Schuster Special Sales at 1-866-506-1949 or business@simonandschuster.com.

The Simon & Schuster Speakers Bureau can bring authors to your live event. For more information or to book an event, contact the Simon & Schuster Speakers Bureau at 1-866-248-3049 or visit our website at www.simonspeakers.com.

Interior design by Paul Dippolito

Manufactured in the United States of America

1   3   5   7   9   10   8   6   4   2

Library of Congress Cataloging-in-Publication Data has been applied for.

ISBN 978-1-6680-0318-3
ISBN 978-1-6680-0320-6 (ebook)

For David

Contents

PART III

EPILOGUE

Every saint has a past, and every sinner has a future.

—Oscar Wilde

The story you are about to read is true. Though I did my best to present the information as accurately as I remember it, some timelines have been condensed, some dialogue has been reconstructed, and some characters have been presented as composites. Certain names, dates, and details have been changed to protect the identities of the innocent (and the not so innocent).

Introduction

My name is Patric Gagne and I am a sociopath. I am a passionate mother and wife. I am an engaging therapist. I am extremely charming and well-liked. I have lots of friends. I am a member of a country club. I throw parties for every occasion you can imagine. I live in a nice house. I am a writer. I like to cook. I vote. I make people laugh. I have a dog and a cat, and I wait in carpool lines next to other women with dogs and cats.

On the surface I resemble almost every other average American woman. Social media confirms my existence as a happy mommy and loving partner whose posts are borderline narcissistic. Your friends would probably describe me as nice. But guess what?

I can't stand your friends.

I'm a liar. I'm a thief. I'm emotionally shallow. I'm mostly immune to remorse and guilt. I'm highly manipulative. I don't care what other people think. I'm not interested in morals. I'm not interested, period. Rules do not factor into my decision-making. I'm capable of almost anything.

Sound familiar?

If you picked up this book, I'm willing to bet it might. You, too, could be one of the estimated fifteen million people in America believed to be sociopaths. Or you could know one of the millions more whose personalities are thought to reside on the sociopathic spectrum. And we're not talking strictly criminals. Doctors, lawyers, teachers, mail carriers . . . Sociopaths are hiding everywhere, in plain sight. All you need to do is start looking.

The looking started early for me. As a child, while other kids in my neighborhood were riding bikes and having playdates with friends, I was reading mysteries. True crime, mostly. I was fascinated by the darkness in people. What *is* it that makes them evil? What is it that makes them capable? I wanted to know.

So when I stumbled across the word "sociopath," I thought I had my answer. I'd heard the term before. But what did it mean? What exactly *is* a sociopath? I assumed the dictionary would tell me. Yet when I reached for my battered, yellowing 1980 Funk & Wagnalls copy, I discovered the word wasn't there.

Thinking it was a mistake, I went into my mother's office and opened another dictionary. Hers was a newer edition. "Sociopath" was sure to be there. Except it wasn't. I saw the place where it *should* have been—right between "sociology" and "sock"—but the word was missing. It was as if it didn't exist. But I knew better. I had read it in books. I had seen it on the news. I had heard it at school. I had written it in my journal. I knew the definition of "sociopath" was out there somewhere. I just had to find it.

In retrospect, it all makes sense. As a doctor of psychology, I can't help but marvel at the cunning genius of the subconscious mind, why we're drawn to certain subjects and indifferent toward others. According to Freud, nothing happens by accident. But you don't need a PhD to know why I chose this field. You don't have to understand Freud to grasp the connection. You don't have to believe in fate to see my path could never have led anywhere else.

The red flags were there from the beginning. I knew as early as seven that something was off. I didn't care about things the way other kids did. Certain emotions—like happiness and anger—came naturally, if somewhat sporadically. But social emotions—things like guilt, empathy, remorse, and even love—did not. Most of the time, I felt nothing. So I did "bad" things to make the nothingness go away. It was like a compulsion.

Had you asked me back then, I would have described this

compulsion as a *pressure*, a sort of tension building in my head. It was like mercury slowly rising in an old-fashioned thermometer. At first it was barely noticeable, just a blip on my otherwise peaceful cognitive radar. But over time it would get stronger. The quickest way to relieve the pressure was to do something undeniably wrong, something I knew would absolutely make anyone else feel one of the emotions I couldn't. So that's what I did.

As a child, I didn't realize there were other options. I didn't know anything about emotion or psychology. I didn't understand that the human brain has evolved to function empathically, or that the stress of living without natural access to feeling is believed to be one of the causes of compulsive acts of violence and destructive behavior. All I knew was that I liked doing things that made me feel something, to feel *anything*. It was better than nothing.

Now that I'm an adult, I can tell you why I behaved this way. I can point to research examining the relationship between anxiety and apathy, and how stress associated with inner conflict is believed to subconsciously compel sociopaths to behave destructively. I can postulate that the pressure I experienced was almost certainly a negative reaction to my lack of feeling, that my urge to act out was most likely my brain's way of trying to jolt itself into some semblance of "normal." But none of this information was easy to find. I had to hunt for it.

I am still hunting.

"Sociopath" is a mysterious word. Its origin is based in century-old science, but it's since been misappropriated to cover all manner of sin. There is no singular definition for the term, not anymore. The word, much like the people it represents, has become something of a paradox. A shape-shifting modifier whose meaning is often assigned via vitriol and grievance, "sociopath" is a word that evokes far more emotion than it does analysis. And why is that?

Why does the word "sociopath" make people *feel* more than it makes them think? Ironically, it's what I wanted to know long before I was diagnosed. So I made it my mission to find out.

This book is the story of that mission, one that I was driven to write because the lived experience of sociopathy deserves to be illustrated. To be clear, I don't want to minimize the severity of this disorder. Nor do I want to romanticize it. Sociopathy is a perilous mental condition, the symptoms, causes, and treatments for which need research and clinical attention. But this is precisely why I wanted to share my story: so individuals affected by sociopathy might receive the help they have needed for far too long. And—perhaps more importantly—that other sociopaths might see themselves reflected in a person who has more to offer than just darkness.

Of course, not everyone will relate to my experience. It is by pure luck that I am able to tell it. It was luck that I was born into a world where I would be afforded almost every privilege imaginable. The truth, I am well aware, is that my life would have gone very differently if my race, my class, or my gender were otherwise. It was luck that, in part, set me on a course to unpack the mystery of my condition and build a life where I have been fortunate enough to help others. Indeed, it is lucky that this book exists at all. And it is lucky that I have come to understand the value of relatability and representation.

Most sociopaths aren't like the characters in movies. They don't resemble the serial murderers in *Killing Eve* or *Dexter*, and they aren't similar to the one-dimensional antagonists many crime novels suggest. They're more complex than the fictionalized examples presented in *The Sociopath Next Door*. Diagnosing them requires more than the twenty-question "sociopath tests" in glossy magazines, and understanding them cannot be done using "sociopath tutorials" on YouTube.

Think you know a sociopath? I'll bet you're right. But I'll also bet it's the last person you suspect. Contrary to popular belief, sociopaths are more than their personality markers. They are children seeking understanding. They are patients hoping for validation. They are parents looking for answers. They are human beings in need of compassion. But the system is failing them. Schools aren't recognizing them. Professionals aren't treating them. They quite literally have nowhere to go for help.

Representation matters. I offer my story because it illustrates the truth no one wants to admit: that darkness is where you least expect it. I am a criminal without a record. I am a master of disguise. I have never been caught. I have rarely been sorry. I am friendly. I am responsible. I am invisible. I blend right in. I am a twenty-first-century sociopath. And I've written this book because I know I'm not alone.

PART I

CHAPTER 1

Honest Girl

Whenever I ask my mother if she remembers the time in second grade when I stabbed a kid in the head with a pencil, her answer is the same: "Vaguely."

And I believe her. Because so much about my early childhood is vague. Some things I remember with absolute clarity. Like the smell of the trees at Redwood National Park and our house on the hill near downtown San Francisco. God, I loved that house. I can still remember the forty-three steps from the ground floor to my room on the fifth, and the chairs in the dining room I would climb to steal crystals from the chandelier. Other things, however, aren't so clear. Like the first time I snuck into my neighbor's house when they weren't home. Or where I got the locket with the "L" inscribed on it.

The locket contains two black-and-white photos I've never bothered to remove, and I still can't help staring at them. Who were these people? Where did they come from? I wish I knew. I guess it's possible I found the locket on the street, but it's far more likely that I stole it.

I started stealing before I could talk. At least, I think I did. I don't remember the first time I took something, just that by the time I was six or seven I had an entire box full of things I'd stolen in my closet.

Somewhere in the archives of *People* magazine there is a photo of Ringo Starr holding me as a toddler. We're standing in his backyard—not far from my birthplace in Los Angeles, where my father was an executive in the music business—and I am literally stealing the glasses off his face. Certainly, I was not the first child to ever play with a grown-up's glasses. But based on the spectacles currently perched on my bookshelf, I'm pretty sure I was the only one to swipe a pair from a Beatle.

To be clear: I wasn't a kleptomaniac. A kleptomaniac is a person with a persistent and irresistible urge to take things that don't belong to them. I suffered from a different type of urge, a compulsion brought about by the discomfort of apathy, the nearly indescribable absence of common social emotions like shame and empathy. But, of course, I didn't understand any of this back then. All I knew was that I didn't feel things the way other kids did. I didn't feel guilt when I lied. I didn't feel compassion when classmates got hurt on the playground. For the most part, I felt nothing. And I didn't like the way that "nothing" felt. So I did things to replace the nothingness with . . . something.

It would start with an impulse to make that nothingness stop, an unrelenting pressure that expanded to permeate my entire self. The longer I tried to ignore it, the worse it got. My muscles would tense, my stomach would knot. Tighter. Tighter. It was claustrophobic, like being trapped inside my brain. Trapped inside a void.

My conscious reactions to apathy started out trivial. Stealing wasn't something I necessarily *wanted* to do. It just happened to be the easiest way to stop the tension. The first time I made this connection was in first grade, sitting behind a girl named Clancy.

The pressure had been building for days. Without knowing exactly why, I was overcome with frustration and had the urge to do something violent. I wanted to stand up and flip over my desk. I imagined running to the heavy steel door that opened to the playground and slamming my fingers in its hinges. For a minute I thought I might actually do it. But then I saw Clancy's barrette.

She had two in her hair, pink bows on either side. The one on the left had slipped down. *Take it*, my thoughts commanded suddenly, *and you'll feel better.*

The idea seemed so strange. Clancy was my classmate. I liked her, and I certainly didn't want to steal from her. But I wanted my brain to stop pulsing, and some part of me knew it would help. So, carefully, I reached forward and unclipped the bow.

The pink clip was hardly attached. Without my help, it probably would have fallen out on its own. Except it didn't. With it in my hand, I felt better, as if some of the air had been released from an over-inflated balloon. The pressure had evaporated. I didn't know why, but I didn't care. I'd found a solution. It was a relief.

These early acts of deviance are encoded in my mind like GPS coordinates plotting a course toward awareness. Even now, I can recall where I came across most of the things that didn't belong to me as a child. But I can't explain the locket with the "L." For the life of me, I don't remember where I got it. I *do* recall the day my mother found it in my room and demanded to know why I had it.

"Patric, you absolutely must tell me where you got this," she said. We were standing next to my bed. One of the pillow shams was crooked against the headboard, and I was consumed with the urge to straighten it. But Mom was not letting up.

"Look at me," she said, grabbing my shoulders. "Somewhere out there a person is missing this locket. They are missing it right now and they're so sad they can't find it. Think about how sad that person must be."

I shut my eyes and tried to imagine what the missing-locket person was feeling. But I couldn't. I felt nothing. When I opened my eyes and looked into hers, I knew my mother could tell.

"Sweetheart, listen to me," she said, kneeling. "Taking something that doesn't belong to you is stealing. And stealing is very, very bad."

Again, nothing.

Mom paused, not sure what to do next. She took a deep breath and asked, "Have you done this before?"

I nodded and pointed to the closet, where I showed her my stash of contraband. Together we went through the box. I explained what everything was and where it had come from. Once the box was empty, she stood and said we were going to return every item to its rightful owner, which was fine with me. I didn't fear consequences, and I didn't suffer from remorse, two more things I'd already figured out weren't "normal." Returning the stuff actually served my purpose. The box was full, and emptying it would give me a fresh space to store things I had yet to steal.

After we'd gone through everything, Mom asked me, "Why did you take these things?"

I thought of the pressure in my head and the sense that I needed to do bad things sometimes. "I don't know," I said. It was true. I had no idea what prompted the sensation.

"Well . . . Are you sorry?" she asked.

"Yes," I said. Also true. I *was* sorry. But I was sorry I had to steal to stop fantasizing about violence, not because I had hurt anyone.

Mom seemed to want to put the matter behind us. "I love you so much, sweetheart," she said. "I don't know why you took all these things, but I want you to promise that if you ever do something like this again, you'll tell me."

I nodded. My mom was the best. I loved her so much that it was easy to keep that promise. At least, it was at first. We never did find the owner of the locket, but over the years I got better at imagining what it must have felt like once they realized it was gone. It's probably a lot like how I would feel now if someone took it from me, only I don't know for sure.

Empathy, like remorse, never came naturally to me. I was raised in the Baptist church. I knew we were supposed to feel bad about committing sins. My teachers talked about "honor systems" and something called "shame," but I didn't understand why these things mattered. I got the concepts intellectually, but they weren't things I *felt*.

As one can imagine, my inability to grasp core emotional skills made the process of making and keeping friends somewhat of a challenge. It wasn't that I was mean or anything. I was simply different. And others didn't always appreciate my unique attributes.

———

It was early autumn and I'd just turned seven. I'd been invited—along with all the girls from class—to a friend's slumber party. Her name was Collette and she lived a few blocks away from us. I arrived at her house wearing my favorite pink-and-yellow skirt. It was her birthday and I insisted on carrying her present, the convertible Barbie car wrapped in iridescent paper.

Mom gave me a big hug when she dropped me off. She was anxious about our first night apart. "Now, don't you worry," she said, handing me my backpack and Holly Hobbie sleeping bag. "If you need to come home, you can."

But I wasn't worried. In fact, I was excited. A whole night in another place! I couldn't wait to get started.

The party was fun. We gorged on pizza, cake, and ice cream before changing into our pajamas. We had a dance party in the living room and played games in the yard. But around bedtime, Collette's mom announced it was "quiet time." She started a movie in the living room, and all of us pulled our sleeping bags into a circle. Then, one by one, the girls fell asleep.

When the movie ended, I was the only one awake. There, in the dark, I was again acutely aware of my lack of feeling. I looked at my motionless friends. It was unsettling, seeing them with their eyes closed. I sensed my mounting tension in response to the emptiness and felt the urge to hit the girl next to me as hard as I could.

That's weird, I thought. I didn't *want* to hurt her. At the same time, I knew it would make me relax. Shaking my head against the temptation, I inched out of my sleeping bag to get away from her. Then I got up and began to roam around the house.

Collette had a baby brother named Jacob. His second-floor nursery had a balcony overlooking the street. I quietly climbed the stairs and let myself into the room. He was asleep, and I stared at him. He looked so tiny in his crib, much smaller than my little sister. A blanket was balled up in the corner. I picked it up and adjusted it around his tiny frame. Then I turned my attention to the balcony doors.

The deadbolt made a tiny *click* as I opened the doors and stepped out into the darkness. From there I could see most of the city. I stood on tiptoes and leaned forward to look up the street, eyeing the intersection at the next block. I recognized the street name and knew it was one over from mine. I bet it would take just a few minutes to walk home.

Suddenly, I knew I didn't want to be there anymore. I didn't like being the only one awake, and I *really* didn't like being so unrestricted. At home I always had Mom to keep me in line. But here? Who would stop me? And from what? I was uneasy.

It was dark when I walked out the front door, and I loved it. It made me feel invisible, and the pressure I'd been sensing instantly evaporated. I stepped onto the sidewalk and began the trek home, staring at the houses as I strolled. What were the people like who lived inside them? What were they doing? I wished I could find out. I wished I *was* invisible so I could watch them all day.

The air was crisp, and fog blanketed the streets as I made my way home. "Witching weather," my mother liked to call it. At the intersection I pulled my sleeping bag from my backpack and wrapped it around me like a huge scarf. The distance was longer than I'd expected, but I didn't mind.

I looked across the street and noticed a house with its garage door open. *What's inside?* I wondered. Then it occurred to me, *I can go find out.*

I marveled at the change in atmosphere as I stepped off the curb. The rules, it seemed, had disappeared along with the daylight. In the darkness, with everyone else asleep, there were no restrictions. I could do anything. I could go anywhere. At Collette's house that idea had made me uncomfortable. But now the same potential had the opposite effect. I felt powerful and in control. I wondered why there was a difference.

Moonlight illuminated my path as I made my way toward the open garage. Stepping inside, I paused to look around. A beige station wagon was parked to one side, leaving room for a vast assortment of toys and knickknacks. *Children must live here*, I thought. My ankle brushed against the deck of a skateboard. It felt like sandpaper.

Resisting the urge to take it, I crossed instead to the car and opened the rear passenger door. A soft glow from the dome light brightened the garage, so I jumped inside, pulling the door closed behind me. I paused and waited for something to happen.

The silence inside the vehicle was deafening, but I liked it. It reminded me of the movie *Superman* and Christopher Reeve's visit to the Fortress of Solitude. "It's like my chamber," I whispered. I imagined myself getting stronger with each passing second.

Outside a flash of movement caught my eye and I saw a car driving by. It was a dark sedan, and my eyes narrowed as I watched it pass. "What are *you* doing here?" I decided the car was an enemy.

Quickly opening the door, I tiptoed outside just in time to see the sedan round the corner. *General Zod*, I thought, defiantly. Then I ran back across the street to where I'd left my things. As I bent down to collect them, I caught the familiar scent of laundry detergent and decided it was time to go home. I hugged the side of the walkway closest to the trees. Picking up speed, I found myself happily zigzagging between the safety of shadows. *How could anyone be afraid of the night?* I wondered happily as I walked. *It's the best part of any day.*

By the time I reached the base of the hill to my house, I was exhausted. I trudged up the steep incline, pulling the backpack behind me like a sled. The side door was open, so I was able to enter the house without knocking. I walked quietly up the stairs to my room, trying not to wake my parents. But moments after I crawled into bed, my mother barged through the door.

"PATRIC!" she yelled, slamming on the light switch. "WHAT ARE YOU DOING HERE?!" Her reaction startled me, and I began to cry. Hoping she'd understand, I explained everything I'd done, but that only seemed to make things worse. She began crying, too, her eyes wide with fear as tears spilled down her cheeks.

"Sweetheart," she said finally, pulling me close. "You must never, *ever* do something like that again. What if something happened? What if you couldn't get home?" I nodded in agreement, though I wasn't genuinely troubled by either of those concerns. More than anything,

I was confused. Mom had said I could come home anytime I wanted. So why was she so upset?

"Because I meant I'd come get you," she explained. "Promise me you'll never do something like that again."

I promised, but I wouldn't have the opportunity to prove it for several years. Parents, I soon discovered, typically frowned on play-mates who came over for slumber parties only to get listless in the middle of the night and decide to walk home on their own. Collette's mom was not happy when she discovered what I'd done, and made no secret of her disdain. Once she'd told the other parents about my disappearing act, party invitations stopped coming. But it wasn't just parents who were leery. Other kids also sensed that something about me was off.

"You're weird," said Ava.

It's one of my few memories of first grade. There was a child-sized dollhouse in the corner of the room, and a bunch of us were playing "house." Ava was a classmate of mine. She was friendly and fair, and everyone liked her. It's one of the many reasons why she naturally assumed the position of "mom" anytime we played house. I, however, preferred a different role.

"I call butler," I said. Ava looked at me, confused.

Butlers, from what I'd gathered watching television, had the best job in the world. They could disappear for extended lengths of time without explanation. They had unrestricted access to everyone's coats and bags. No one ever questioned their actions. They could walk into a room and not be expected to interact with anyone. They could eavesdrop. It was the ideal profession; at least it was to me. But my explanation didn't resonate with everyone.

"Why are you so weird?" Ava asked.

She hadn't said it to be nasty. It was more a statement of fact, a question I knew I didn't really need to answer. But when I looked at her, I noticed a most peculiar expression on her face, one I hadn't seen before.

It was a very specific look—equal parts confusion, certainty, and fear. She wasn't alone. The other kids were staring at me the same way. It made me wary. As if they could see something about me that I couldn't.

Eager to change the subject, I smiled and bowed. "Forgive me, madame," I said in my most butler-like voice. "But if I'm acting weird, it's only because someone has murdered the cook!"

It was a distraction I'd already perfected: shock with a hint of humor. Everyone laughed and screamed as the game took on a thrilling—albeit gruesome—tone, and my "weirdness" faded into the background. But this, I knew, was only a temporary fix.

My penchant for thievery and disappearing aside, something about me made other kids uncomfortable. I knew it. They knew it. And though we could peacefully coexist as classmates, I was rarely included in after-school activities. Not that I minded; I loved being alone. But after a while, my mother grew concerned.

"I don't like that you spend so much time by yourself," she said. It was a Saturday afternoon and she'd come upstairs to check on me after several hours of alone time.

"It's okay, Mommy," I said. "I like it."

Mom frowned and sat on my bed, pulling a stuffed raccoon absent-mindedly into her lap. "I just think it might be good for you to have some friends over." She paused. "Do you want to invite anyone from school? What about Ava?"

I shrugged and looked out the window. I'd been trying to determine how many bedsheets I needed to knot together to make a rope long enough to reach the ground from my room on the top floor. Earlier in the week I'd seen something called an "emergency ladder" in a Sears catalogue and had become fixated on the idea of making my own. I wasn't sure what I wanted to do with it, just that I knew I had to have it. Only now Mom was distracting me.

"I don't know," I said. "I mean, Ava's nice. Maybe we can invite her over next month."

Mom tossed the raccoon aside and stood. "Well, we're having the Goodmans over for dinner," she said brightly. "So tonight, I guess you'll just play with the girls."

The Goodmans lived on our block and were casual friends of my parents. Their two daughters were neighborhood terrors and I hated them. Sydney was a bully and Tina was an idiot. They were constantly in trouble, usually because of something Syd instigated, and I found their behavior infuriating. Granted, I was in no position to judge. But at the time I justified my revulsion. From my perspective, it all came down to intent. Whereas my actions might have sometimes been questionable, I wasn't breaking rules because I enjoyed it; I acted out because I felt I had no choice. It was a means of self-preservation, of keeping worse things from happening. The Goodmans' actions, on the other hand, were reckless, attention-seeking, and mean. The bad things they liked to do served no purpose other than cruelty for cruelty's sake.

My sister, Harlowe, was four years younger than me and still a toddler. We shared the top floor of the house with our nanny, a lovely woman from El Salvador named Lee. Nanny Lee stayed in the room next to ours. When the Goodmans visited, she'd typically be in Harlowe's room putting her to bed. And rarely did a visit pass without Syd trying to do something heinous to them.

"Let's sneak into Lee's room and dump water in her bed!" Syd hissed later that night while we sat in my room.

I was already annoyed. "That's dumb," I said. "She's going to know it was us and then what? What do you get out of it? She'll tell our parents, and then you'll just have to go home."

The barrette I'd stolen from Clancy was attached to one of my braids. I began to tug on the clasp as I realized, *Maybe the water dump isn't the worst idea after all.*

Syd had cracked open the door and was peeking outside. "Yeah, well, it's too late anyway because she's already in her room. She must have gotten Harlowe to sleep." She whirled around. "Let's wake her up!" Tina looked up from her magazine and snorted approval. I was perplexed.

"Why?"

"Because then Lee will have to put her back to sleep! And every time she does, we'll wake her up, over and over! It'll be so funny!"

It didn't sound funny to me. For starters, no one was messing with my sister. I wasn't sure how far it was between the fifth and fourth floors, but I was prepared to "accidentally" shove both Syd and her sister down the stairs, if needed. As for Nanny Lee, I didn't want her coming out of her room. I knew that the second my sister went to sleep, Lee would call her family and talk for hours. That meant I could listen to my Blondie records undisturbed.

At the time I'd developed something of a fixation with Debbie Harry. I was transfixed by anything and everything Blondie, especially *Parallel Lines*. On the album cover Debbie Harry stands in a white dress with her hands on her hips and a fierce look on her face. I loved this picture and wanted to look just like her. So much so that if you look in my mother's photo albums, you will find more than a year's worth of pictures in which I am clearly attempting to re-create this iconic stance.

Debbie Harry wasn't smiling on her album cover, so I decided I wouldn't, either—for anything. Unfortunately, following a spectacularly disastrous episode with the school photographer that resulted in me kicking over a tripod, Mom decided that Debbie Harry was a "bad influence" and threw away all of my Blondie albums. That I'd fished them out of the dumpster and listened to them at night hadn't yet registered with Nanny Lee.

I decided to switch tactics. "How about this," I offered. "Let's sneak into the backyard and spy on our parents through the windows."

I could tell Syd was irritated. My plan didn't involve torturing anyone and was therefore comparatively lackluster. All the same, the thought of eavesdropping on our parents was more exciting than even she could resist. Tina, too, seemed thrilled.

After some negotiations, Syd agreed. We snuck out of my bedroom and crept single-file past Nanny Lee's room. Eventually we made it all the way downstairs to the laundry room. I unlocked the door that opened to the side of the house. The California air was both chilly and sweet.

"Okay," I said. "You two go this way, and I'll meet you on the back deck." They looked nervous. The yard was not only pitch-black but also essentially nonexistent, as most of the house was supported by wooden stilts that plunged a hundred feet down a hill. One ill-placed step and they'd tumble to the bottom. "You're not scared, right?" I put on my most concerned face.

Tina responded first. "Get me a Coke," she said, and then disappeared along the side of the house with Syd reluctantly following.

As soon as they were out of sight, I stepped back into the house and locked the door. Then I crept upstairs to my room, turned off the lights, got into bed, and turned on my record player. I was calm and quite satisfied with myself. I knew I should have felt bad about what I'd done, except I didn't. I got to listen to Blondie uninterrupted.

It was nearly an hour before I saw my mother's shadow on the walls of the stairwell. I threw my headphones to the floor and managed to kill the volume just before she walked through the door. "Patric," she asked, "did you lock Syd and Tina outside?"

"Yeah," I replied honestly. I could tell Mom wasn't sure what to say next.

"Well, the Goodmans are very upset," she said, as she sat on the bed next to me. "They got lost in the dark and didn't know how to get back inside. They could have gotten hurt, honey." She paused and added, "I don't think they're ever going to come over again."

"Great!" I replied, thrilled. "Tina always takes a bath in my tub with all the lights off—which is *crazy*—and Syd always sneaks food upstairs and spills it everywhere. They're both really annoying!" My mother shook her head and sighed.

"Well, thank you for telling me the truth, sweetheart." She kissed the top of my head. "But you're grounded. No going outside and no television for a week." I nodded, quietly accepting my fate. It was a small price to pay.

Mom got up and had made it to the stairs before I called out, "Mommy?" She turned around and came back to my room.

I took a deep breath. "I got the Blondie records out of the trash after you threw them away and listen to them every night even though I know I'm not supposed to." Mom stood still, her glamorous shape backlit against the lights from the hall.

"You have them . . . here? In your room?"

I nodded. Mom walked to my record player, where *Parallel Lines* still spun silently. She looked at me and shook her head. Then, one by one, she collected the albums and tucked them under her arm before kissing me once more. She pushed the hair out of my face and across my forehead.

"Thank you for telling me, my honest girl," she said. "Now good night."

Mom walked out of my room and down the stairs as I rolled over and nestled deep into my pillows. I rubbed my feet together underneath the blankets like a cricket. I felt safe and content. The record player continued to run and the repetitive sound was soothing. I watched the empty turntable spin round and round, and for a second I questioned the wisdom of giving up my secret and losing my Blondie records. Nevertheless, I found myself smiling as I drifted off to sleep.

CHAPTER 2

Layers

There are few things my father loves more than a chocolate layer cake. When he was a boy in Mississippi, my grandparents' house-keeper, Lela Mae, used to make him one from scratch every week. When we'd visit for Christmas, I was mesmerized by the smell of those cakes—and by Lela Mae in her white uniform and apron, tow-ering in the doorway of the kitchen, guarding the entrance as if it was her own fiefdom.

My mother was also from the South. Born and raised in Virginia, she understood the importance of ritual and placed tremendous value on Southern-style housekeeping. As soon as she learned about the cakes, she adopted the tradition as her own.

I used to watch her at our dining room table in San Francisco, slicing each layer into identical halves by tying sewing thread around them and pulling the ends through the center into a knot. "This way it's perfectly even," she'd say.

I loved hanging out with her in that room. I would lie under the table and read books while she cut and iced the cakes. Over time, it became something like a confessional. I would tell her about all the stuff going on at school and admit to any behavior I thought might be questionable. She'd let me know if my actions (or reactions) were out of line and explain how to make things right. Since my judgment wasn't exactly dependable, Mom and I found it best for me to run things by her.

"Did you thank the Patels for the sugar?" she asked. Mom had sent me to our neighbors' house with a measuring cup earlier that morning.

"No. They weren't home," I said.

Mom stopped mid-slice to look at me. "Then how'd you get the sugar?" she asked.

"Out of the container."

I knew the Patels weren't home as soon as I reached their driveway. For some reason they refused to use the garage, so if they were home, their pea-green station wagon would always be there. But on that day, it wasn't.

Confident the sliding glass door would be unlocked, I went to the side of the house and gave it a tug. It slid open, as I knew it would. I stepped inside and helped myself to the sugar container on the counter, stopping on the way out to play with their dog, Moses.

"I know you said we couldn't, but can we please get a dog?" I continued. "It could play with Moses if it got bored." Mom stared at me, horrified.

"If the Patels weren't home when you went to their house," she asked slowly, "then how did you get inside?" I recounted my expedition to Mom. When I finished, she buried her face in her hands. "No, honey," she said, finally looking up. "No. You can't just go inside someone's house if they aren't there."

I was confused. "Why not? They wouldn't care. We go over there all the time. It's fine as long as you don't take anything."

"But you *did* take something," she said, clearly upset. "You took the sugar."

Now I was really confused. "But you *told* me to take the sugar."

Mom exhaled sharply. "I told you to *ask* them for sugar. Not just go over and help yourself without their permission. You are not to do anything like that again. That is very, very wrong. Do you understand me?"

"Yes," I lied. Because I didn't understand. I assumed that asking the Patels for the sugar was a formality. They didn't care. I'd saved them the hassle of having to answer the door and make small talk.

Who wanted to do that? I knew I didn't. But I also knew I couldn't explain any of this to my mom. She was big on honesty. "When in doubt, tell the truth," she liked to say. "The truth helps people understand." Only I wasn't sure I agreed.

As a child, I lived in a constant state of doubt. I had doubts about the way I was supposed to feel and the way I didn't. Doubts about the things I did. Doubts about the things I wanted to do. Telling the truth about these uncertainties sounded like a good idea in *theory*, but in practice I found it often made things worse. I could never tell what information was going to cause a negative reaction. It seemed like I was constantly oscillating between the poles of honesty and dishonesty, and I never knew where I would land. This was particularly true when it came to Mom. Angering her was never something I wanted to risk. She was my emotional compass, and I trusted her to guide me. With Mom on my side, I didn't have to worry about feeling or not feeling, or choosing right from wrong. But when she was angry, I felt like I was on my own. And back then, on my own wasn't a safe place to be.

Mom sighed again and tied a new piece of thread around another layer of cake. "Bottom line, we can only go to the Patels' when they're home. And no, it's not okay even if you don't take anything."

I nodded and decided against confessing to all the trips I'd made to their house whenever Mom left my sister and me alone with Nanny Lee. Since this was technically a new rule, I didn't see any reason to apply it retroactively.

Mom looked as if she was about to say something else, but she was interrupted by the stomping of my father's feet on the stairs. We heard kitchen cabinets opening and closing before the door into the dining room swung open and he rushed inside.

"Has anyone seen my briefcase?" he asked. He strode past us and started searching the living room. I heard him stifle a sniffle and wondered if he might be getting a cold. I hoped not. We were supposed to go ice-skating that night.

Since the Blondie embargo, I'd become obsessed with *Ice Castles*, a movie about a blinded ice-skater. I was excited to try some of the moves I'd been practicing blindfolded in socks on our hardwood floors at an actual skating rink, but Dad coming down with a cold would put a serious damper on the plan.

"It's upstairs in your office," Mom told him. "But why do you need it? Dinner's almost ready and it's Saturday. We're taking the girls skating." There was an edge to her voice. Dad looked up and put his hands over his face.

"Oh, honey, I forgot!" he said, walking over to her. "Bruce called, and I need to run to the studio."

My father was a rising star in the music industry, a business that often required long and unorthodox work hours.

Dad looked at me. "I'm sorry, sweetheart." Then he asked Mom, "Can we do it another night?"

Mom looked out the window, not saying a word. I thought it was an odd response, but Dad didn't seem to notice. Instead, he headed for the door, yelling over his shoulder, "I'll make it up to you next week!"

Mom sat still for a moment, then she got up and walked into the kitchen, leaving the cake partially iced on the table. I followed behind her, unsure of what to do. In the kitchen, she stood at the sink and stared into space. Early evening light poured through the sliding glass doors in the family room. Years later Mom would tell me she hated this time of day, and that our time in San Francisco is when the hatred started. But I never shared that perspective. To me the arrival of twilight has always been magical, an overture to darkness. On that day in particular I remember how beautiful my mom looked as the light bounced off the countertops and onto her face. I came up behind her and gave her a hug. I didn't know what to say.

Things continued this way for a while. Dad was almost never home before midnight, and my interactions with him were reduced to brief kisses in the car before school and occasional outings on the weekends. Not that I cared much. In fact, it was almost nice; I loved having my mom and sister all to myself.

I loved having a sister, period. I've heard that parents worry about jealousy and sibling rivalries, but those things were never a problem for us. I didn't like being the center of attention anyway. Once my sister arrived, I had someone to share the focus. And I liked having a buddy who appreciated my penchant for mischief. One-sided rule-breaking was typically at the forefront of any interaction between us, as it remains today. Harlowe would hand me a cup, I would throw it down the center of the stairwell. Harlowe would get in the tub and point to the bubble bath, I would empty the bottle and turn on the Jacuzzi jets. Every action caused a hysterical reaction. Mom loved it. But the frenzied sound of Harlowe's laughter didn't always resonate with my dad.

"What are you guys doing?" he asked one day, walking into my room unexpectedly. He usually liked to play with us, but it seemed like lately he only wanted to sleep when he was at home, which wasn't often.

Dad had started to spend more and more time at work, and after a while my mother became depressed. Some days she'd burst into tears over the tiniest thing. Other times she'd be angry and snap at us for reasons I didn't understand. I was anxious and confused and, for the first time, unable to rely on my mother for guidance. It had been weeks since she'd made one of her cakes, and no time seemed good to talk to her about the stuff I'd been doing. Like stealing.

I'd been taking backpacks from school. I didn't even want them, and almost always eventually returned them. It was more of a compulsion, something I did to ease tension. When I saw an unattended backpack, I took it. It didn't matter where it was or whose it was, it was the taking that mattered. Doing anything I knew wasn't "right" was how I released the pressure, how I gave myself a jolt to counter my apathy. After a while, though, it stopped working. Regardless of how many bags I took, I could no longer generate that jolt. I felt nothing. And the nothingness, I'd started to notice, made my urge to do bad things more extreme.

It was a lot like the last time I ever saw Syd. We were standing on

the sidewalk waiting to go to school when she started to get on my
nerves. She'd wanted to spend the night at our house, only she wasn't
allowed.

"It's all your fault," she whined. "If you hadn't played that stupid
trick on us, we could still come over and I could play with your toys.
You always ruin everything."

"Sorry," I said, even though I wasn't. I was glad she wasn't allowed
to visit. My head was hurting. The pressure had been steadily increasing, yet nothing I did seemed to help. I was emotionally disconnected
but also stressed and somewhat disoriented. It was like I was losing
my mind, and I just wanted to be alone.

Abruptly, Syd kicked my backpack from where it sat at my feet,
knocking everything to the ground. "You know what?" she said. "I
don't care. Your house sucks, and so do you."

The tantrum was meaningless, something she'd done to get my
attention like countless times before. But she'd picked the wrong day
to start a fight. Looking at Syd I knew that I never wanted to see her
again. I figured this message should have been clear after I locked her
outside my house in the dead of night. But evidently I needed to send
a more direct message.

Without a word, I leaned down to collect my things. We carried
pencil boxes back then. Mine was pink with Hello Kitty characters and
full of sharpened yellow #2s. I grabbed one, stood up, and jammed it
into the side of her head.

The pencil splintered and part of it lodged in her neck. Syd started
screaming and the other kids understandably lost it. Meanwhile, I was
in a daze. The pressure was gone. But, unlike every other time I'd
done something bad, my physical attack on Syd had resulted in something different, a sort of euphoria.

I walked away from the scene blissfully at ease. For weeks I'd been
engaging in all manner of subversive behavior to make the pressure
disappear and none of it had worked. But now—with that one violent
act—all traces of pressure were eradicated. Not just gone but *replaced*
by a deep sense of peace. It was like I'd discovered a fast track to

tranquility, one that was equal parts efficacy and madness. None of it made sense, but I didn't care. I wandered around in a stupor for a while. Then I went home and calmly told my mom what had happened.

"WHAT THE HELL WAS GOING THROUGH YOUR MIND?" my father wanted to know. I was sitting at the foot of my bed later that night. Both my parents stood before me, demanding answers. But I didn't have any.

"Nothing," I said. "I don't know. I just did it."

"And you're not sorry?" Dad was frustrated and irritable. He'd just returned from another work trip, and they'd been fighting.

"Yes! I said I was sorry!" I exclaimed. I'd even already written Syd an apology letter. "So why is everyone still so mad?"

"Because you're not sorry," Mom said quietly. "Not really. Not in your heart." Then she looked at me as if I was a stranger. It paralyzed me, that look. It was the same expression I'd seen on Ava's face the day we played house. It was a look of hazy recognition, as if to say, "There's something off about you. I can't quite put my finger on it, but I can *feel* it."

My stomach lurched as though I'd been punched. I hated the way my mother stared at me that night. She'd never done it before, and I wanted her to stop. Seeing her look at me that way was like being observed by someone who didn't know me at all. Suddenly, I was furious with myself for telling the truth. It hadn't helped anyone "understand." If anything, it had made everyone more confused, including me. Anxious to make things right, I stood up and tried to hug her, but she lifted her hand to stop me.

"No," she said. "No." She stared at me long and hard once more, and then she left. I watched as Dad followed her out of my room, their frames becoming smaller as they descended the staircase. I crawled into bed and wished I had someone I could hurt, so I could feel the way I did after stabbing Syd. Settling for myself, I squeezed a pillow to my chest, digging my nails into my forearm.

"Be *sorry*!" I hissed. I continued to claw at my skin and clench my jaw, willing remorse with all my might. I can't remember how long I tried, only that I was desperate and furious once I finally gave up. Exhausted, I collapsed back into the bed. I looked at my arm. It was bleeding.

After the Syd incident Mom withdrew from everyone. For weeks she hardly came out of her room, and when she did, she always seemed sad. Nanny Lee was mostly in charge then. I loved Nanny Lee. She was kind and gentle, and she always read books to us after we should have been asleep. But what I really needed was my mother.

The euphoria I'd felt after stabbing Syd was both disconcerting and tempting. I wanted to experience it again. I wanted to *hurt* again. Only I *didn't* want to. I was confused and scared and I needed my mom to help me. I wasn't sure how things had gone so wrong. I just knew it was all my fault, and I had to find a way to make it better.

I'd been upstairs in my room contemplating this one day when I caught a whiff of a familiar smell.

Chocolate cake.

She must have just taken the layers out of the oven. That meant she would soon put them in the freezer to cool before transferring them to the dining room for slicing and icing. And in that instant, I knew just what to do.

The box inside my closet had once again grown full. Books, candy from the grocery store, albums from my father's office, coffee mugs from the teachers' lounge, a pair of shoes; all sorts of things I'd lifted to release some tension. I pulled the box from its hiding place and set it on top of my dresser. This. *This* was how I could make it all up to my mother.

If she was making cakes again, it must have meant she was feeling better. I would tell her about all the stuff I'd done, and she would help me make it right. She'd give me a big hug and call me her honest girl. My mental box would be empty, and I'd have a clean space to work with. The pressure, the doubt, the stress, the desire to hurt, all of it would go away the second I confessed. I'd sit on the floor next to the table and practice my apology speeches while she finished the cakes, only this time I would try to *really* mean them. She would be so proud of me.

I made my way down the stairs quietly, dragging the box behind me. It took some time, but I finally made it to the ground floor to where I could peer into the dining room without being seen. The smell of chocolate cakes was so strong and sweet, just like my mom.

I tightened my grip on the box as I leaned around the corner. I already had a vision in my head of what I would see: Mom in her peach dress and flats putting the final touches of icing around the first layer of cake. I was so positive about this vision that I gasped when I caught sight of her, sitting at the table, silently sobbing. All the lights were off. Her hands were shaking and the thread was limp as she half-heartedly attempted to slice through a layer of cake. The table was littered with remnants of previous slices, all cut unevenly and tossed to the side. How long had she been sitting there? I'll never know.

Her face was blotchy, her apron wet with tears. She was hyperventilating, her head making tiny jerking movements with each sharp breath. I jumped back behind the corner and froze, not sure what to do next. I'd never seen her like this before. Her sadness seemed to consume her. From the living room, I could hear a stifled scream as yet another layer of cake bit the dust. Then I heard the door open and knew she'd left the dining room. I looked down at my box and knew it needed to disappear.

The sound of a mixer erupted from the kitchen as Mom began to make another cake. I bent down and cautiously picked up the box. Then I made my way back up the stairs to my room, stopping at the landing of my parents' bedroom. I opened the double doors and went to the wooden chest at the foot of their bed. This, I knew, was my mother's hiding place. It only took me a few seconds to find *Parallel Lines* hidden inside a blanket. I shoved the record under my arm and walked upstairs to my room, kicking the door open gently with my foot. I didn't bother with the headphones this time when I turned on my record player. Mom was too distracted to notice anything I was doing.

It's like being invisible, I thought.

The sound of Debbie Harry filled my room as I pushed the box back into the closet. Two days later I got rid of it, dumping the contents into a garbage can in front of Syd's house. Then I walked back home without a shred of remorse.

CHAPTER 3

Florida

"Eyes down, gentlemen!" shouted the guard. "Look up here and you'll find yourself in the hole!"

I held my sister's hand tightly. We were walking through a cell-lined corridor in the nearby state prison at ten thirty on a school night. A few feet ahead, my mother was chatting with our uncle Gilbert, the chief guard. Several officers walked alongside and behind our group as we made our way toward the center tower.

"This is what we call an honor block," said Uncle Gilbert. "The prisoners here have demonstrated good behavior, so they're allowed to roam around this section of the prison. The doors on their cells aren't always locked like the others."

I knew what others he meant. In the hour or so we'd spent inside the prison, my sister, mother, and I had been given a full tour of the facility and its all-male inhabitants, including the "dangerous offenders" section, where the inmates were confined in an interior room behind thick glass walls. Uncle Gilbert didn't want us standing near the glass because lots of the men had been arrested for violent crimes. He didn't specifically explain why, but his tone reminded me of when Dad would insist on covering our eyes during "sexy" parts of movies.

"But if you're curious," he said, "I'll let you look at them through the glass or on the TV next door." The one-way mirror allowed for an up-close and personal perspective; however, the camera gave me a bird's-eye view I preferred. An officer named Bobby sat behind a bank of monitors and showed me how to use the system. I scanned the room, panning and zooming for a good look at each inmate. What had they done to get locked up like this? I knew it had to be something bad. But what? I asked Bobby.

"Rape, murder, arson, that sort of stuff," he responded.

Uncle Gilbert cleared his throat. It was a signal that Bobby needed to tread more carefully. Bobby gave him a quick nod and leaned forward to look me in the eye.

"Here's the thing," he said, gesturing to the men. "These guys have all done some messed-up stuff. But it isn't just what they did. It's that they ain't sorry about it. They weren't scared to do it to begin with. *That's* why they're in here."

"Oh," I said, though I still didn't get it.

"The men in this prison?" Bobby added. "I'd say eighty percent are sociopaths."

It was the first time I'd heard the word.

"Oh," I said again. "What's a sociopath?"

"Somebody who doesn't feel bad about what they do," Bobby said. "No shame. Doesn't scare easy. Never feels guilty. Someone who isn't afraid of getting caught and does the same stupid stuff over and over."

"Huh," I said, looking again at the men. "Really?"

Bobby paused. "Here," he said, taking out his wallet and laying it on the desk. "Let's say I went outside for a few minutes and left my wallet behind."

I nodded, engrossed.

"Would you go through it? Would you take anything out of it while I was gone?"

"No," I lied.

Bobby laughed. "Nah, of course you wouldn't! And if you *did* take something out of it, I bet you'd feel pretty bad about it, right?"

"*So* bad," I replied.

"Right," said Bobby. "That's because you aren't a sociopath! A sociopath *would* take my wallet. Not only that, but he wouldn't feel bad about it. He'd probably come back next week and do it again! He wouldn't be able to help himself because sociopaths aren't afraid of consequences."

I swallowed hard. Did this mean there was a word for someone like me? Somehow, I understood that a graveyard-shift corrections officer was not the best person to ask.

Bobby leaned forward to press a button, then barked over the intercom, "Rogers! Hands off the glass!"

One of the inmates backed away from the one-way mirror, shaking his head and smiling at the camera. "That guy loves to bust chops," said Bobby.

I used the camera to zoom in on Rogers. "Officer Bobby?" I asked. "Do all sociopaths end up in jail?"

"Probably," said Bobby, "unless they're really smart."

I stared at the men behind the glass, all of them living together in a cage. "What if they get into a big fight and kill each other?" I asked.

"Then they will have paid their debt to society," he responded with a satisfied sigh. I wasn't sure what that meant, but I nodded and looked back at the screen.

"Patric," called my mother. "Wrap it up, sweetheart. Your sister needs to use the bathroom."

Mom had come up with the idea to visit the prison a few months earlier. Uncle Gilbert, who worked the night shift during the week, was always telling stories about the Florida Department of Corrections, and it had piqued our interest.

After we left the control room, we were each offered a "lockup experience" in solitary and then given a tour of the honor block. As we walked up the stairs to the central tower, I gazed at the inmates below. There had to be hundreds of men there. That the only thing separating them from us were five middle-aged guards positively blew my mind.

By then I was eleven years old and we'd been living in Florida for two years.

———

"Pack a bag," Mom had said, shortly after the stabbing incident. "We're going to visit Grandma for the weekend." This is how my mother informed us she was leaving my father and moving us to Florida. Not knowing any better, I packed for the weekend.

Things in Florida were weird from the start. For one thing, my mother refused to admit that she'd left my father and that we were now permanent residents of the Sunshine State. This remained the case even after Dad shipped the car (along with the rest of her things) so she could start looking for a new house. Mom, I realized, didn't always tell the truth. And it was frustrating. *I may as well just lie, too, then,* I thought more than once, *since I get in trouble either way.*

After a while, Mom seemed to grasp that her decision to prolong our family "vacation" was not sitting well with my sister and me. To compensate for some of her guilt, she relaxed a few of her steadfast rules. She even let me have my first pet, a ferret named Baby. I adored Baby. Other than my sister, she was my only real companion—a fierce one at that. Baby was a rambunctious rascal with an endearing personality and a penchant for shiny objects. She was a natural-born thief. Indeed, she would often prowl my grandmother's house at night in search of jewelry—earrings, necklaces, anything she could wrap her jaws around—then drag it back to the tiny bedroom I shared with my sister and add it to the trove she kept beneath my bed.

Every morning was like Christmas. I'd wake up and drop to the floor to inspect what my four-legged Santa had brought. The things I liked, I kept for myself. The things I didn't, I left alone.

"Good girl, Baby!" I said one morning, holding up a dangly gold earring.

I gave the ferret a kiss, then buried my nose in her neck and inhaled deeply. I'd been told that ferrets were unpopular pets because of their odor, but I loved the way Baby smelled. Her earthy scent reminded me of books in the public library. Baby gnawed at my hair, signaling she wanted to play.

I attached the earring as I stood and looked at my reflection in the mirror. Then I scooped up the ferret and dropped her into my knapsack. Baby sprawled into a long stretch. "You ready?" I asked her. "Let's go!"

One of the perks of living in Florida was the general lack of supervision. My grandmother was mostly in charge back then, and quite liberal when it came to childhood freedom. As long as my sister and I periodically checked in and promised not to go more than two blocks away from the house, we were basically left to our own devices.

As the "weekend" at my grandmother's turned into months, I returned to familiar ways of dealing with my internal pressure. I stole money from the collection trays at church. I threw roadkill into the yard of a nasty lady who lived down the street. I broke into a vacant house a few blocks away and spent my free time there, soaking up the quiet.

I loved it in that house. Whenever I stepped inside, I was instantly at ease. The blankness of the space matched the way I felt, and I liked the equilibrium. I also liked that, although it was empty, the house seemed full. I'd sit for hours alone in that frenetic stillness. The lack of feeling—which normally stressed me out—had the opposite effect in the vacant house. In a weird way, it reminded me of the Gravitron. The perennial county-fair favorite is a spinning ride that offers no seat belts or even seats. Riders are pinned to the wall through centrifugal force. I used to love it. Over and over again I'd spin, confounded by the machine's operator, who sat in a control booth in the center of the wheel.

Once I asked my mother, "Why doesn't he get dizzy?"

"Because he's in the exact center," she explained. "He's not affected by the spinning."

That's how I felt when I went to the house. Intellectually I knew I was breaking some adult code, and that knowledge made me the operator in the center of the ride. All around me the home was pulsing, aghast at having been violated, yet I was calm in its center, at peace and in control. I'd free Baby from her knapsack so she could roam, then sit in the sunroom and read my books. It was bliss.

Of course I knew I wasn't supposed to go into houses that weren't mine, and that I needed to tell my mom about it. After all, I wanted to be honest. I wanted to be *safe*. But anytime I tried to confess, she seemed so upset. There was never a good time to talk to Mom in Florida. Lately it seemed like she wanted to avoid me. She refused to discuss anything even remotely uncomfortable. And I mean obvious things, like the fact that we were absolutely, positively not living with Dad in San Francisco and were apparently never going back. Even after she finally found a place for us to live—a small townhouse next to the beach—Mom still refused to say anything specific about her long-term plans.

"Mom, why are we going to a new school?" I asked, as she maneuvered her car through a carpool line of strangers a few months after we'd moved into the townhouse.

"I don't know," she said. "I just figured it might be more fun than sitting at home all day while Dad and I try to figure things out."

"Well, who's gonna take care of Baby?" I asked, already missing my ferret. "She's going to be so bored without me."

"I'll make sure she gets lots of attention while you're gone," Mom promised. "In the meantime, maybe you could make some new friends."

"*New* friends?" I said. "I didn't have any *old* friends."

"Well," Mom replied hopefully. "Maybe this time will be better."

Only it wasn't. The school might have been new, but *I* was the same. The other kids were nice enough, but right away I knew they sensed I was different. Granted, my behavioral "tells" weren't exactly subtle.

"Have you ever French-kissed?" a kid named Ryan wanted to know. We were eating lunch in the cafeteria about a month after Mom enrolled us at our new school.

"No," I said.

"Why not?" Ryan pressed.

"Because my mom died."

The second I said it, I started laughing. The response didn't even make sense. I don't recall why I said it, only that I was positive it would end the conversation. And it did, along with any chance of flying beneath the radar. Ryan's expression, along with those of the rest of the kids at the table, quickly changed. They all gave me the same look. I'd seen it before.

Word of my mother's demise soon spread to the principal, who called me to her office.

"Patric," she said, sitting too close to me on her couch. "I heard your mother passed away. Is that true, honey?" Her face was full of concern.

"No," I said, eager to put her mind at ease. "She's not dead."

"Oh," she replied, furrowing her brow. "Well, why did you *say* she was dead?"

I didn't have an answer. It was such a stupid lie and one that was very uncharacteristic of me. I knew that it was a mistake just as I knew it would probably result in a great deal of unwanted attention. But I did it anyway. I wouldn't go so far as to say I didn't *care* about the repercussions; I just knew they wouldn't bother me. Even then, I understood there was a difference.

"Well, we were all talking about the worst thing that could ever happen," I lied. "So that's what I said. My mother dying would be the worst thing."

The principal nodded solemnly and mustered a smile. "That makes more sense," she said. "You and your sister seem like such sweet girls."

She was half right. Harlowe *was* a sweet girl. Although we'd only been in school a few weeks, my sister was already thriving. She'd been on several playdates and was easily the most popular girl in her class. People were naturally drawn to Harlowe. She was like Dorothy in *The Wizard of Oz*, picking up new buddies wherever she went. But I was like a blond, ferret-toting Wednesday Addams, leisurely repelling everyone in my path.

Occasionally I tried to fit in—to act "normal" like the other kids around me—only it never lasted. For one thing, my exposure to conventional behavior and reactions was limited to my immediate family, so I could only fake it for so long. But more importantly, I didn't have anyone who could teach me. My struggles to conform felt a little like those of a kid in my class who had a hard time reading. He was great at things like math and music, but he had a learning disability that made it difficult for him to interpret letters. He'd been assigned a special instructor who worked with him until he got better at it.

Maybe that's what I have, I thought one day. *A* feeling *disability*.

I thought of the men inside the prison and wondered if they experienced something similar. It was as though the full range of emotions was something everyone else just *got*. Some feelings came naturally to me, like anger and happiness. But other emotions weren't so easy. Empathy and guilt, embarrassment and jealousy were like a language I couldn't speak or understand.

Was there a special instructor who could help me? I knew that kids who needed extra help were supposed to go to their teacher. But I couldn't do that. My fifth-grade instructor, Mrs. Ravenel, was the meanest teacher in school. So much so that misbehaving students were sent to *her* instead of the principal for punishment. And she had zero tolerance for kids who were different.

"Well, what do you want?" she once demanded of a Black second-grader who'd been consigned to our classroom for talking too much. "You want me to take you outside and hang you from a tree by your thumbs? Is that what you want?"

The little boy started to shake and cry. All the other kids in class were laughing, but I was furious.

Hung from a tree? I thought. *For* talking? Even though Mrs. Ravenel told us children "like that" needed to be taught a lesson, I didn't think it made sense. I may have been missing an emotional connection to the concepts of right and wrong, but I knew they existed. What this teacher was doing was wrong. She was hurting a kid using emotion. Worse, she was enjoying it.

It's better to be like me, I thought.

It was the first time I realized that fear couldn't be used against me. It wasn't that I was immune to it, per se, just that mine was muted. I understood this wasn't the case for most kids. While my classmates lived in constant terror of Mrs. Ravenel, I was never intimidated by her antics. While my cousins were afraid to leave the house after dark, I had no problem wandering around the neighborhood alone. And while my sister was quietly playing in our room after school, I was breaking into nearby homes. Could I have gotten caught? Sure. Was I worried about the consequences? No. I had decided fear must be a useless emotion. I pitied people who seemed to be afraid of everything. What a waste! I was content to follow my own rules and live with impunity. I saw no purpose in apprehension.

But all that changed when I met the man with the kittens.

"I just found them," he said. "Would you like one?"

It was a late afternoon after school and my sister and I were playing outside. Mom had decided to get her real estate license and was gone a lot in those days, a choice that didn't exactly align with her "we aren't here permanently" narrative. Several days a week, she would send me and Harlowe to my grandmother's after school so she could study. Typically we spent our exile on the back patio, but that day we'd decided to pick flowers in the front yard. With no one paying attention, we could take as many as we wanted, including buds from my grandmother's rosebushes, which we weren't supposed to touch.

"What color are they?" I asked him.

"Well, what color do you like?" He seemed genuinely friendly.

"Black," I said definitively. I'd always wanted a black cat. And Baby would, too! I imagined the three of us having a blast inside the vacant house—my ferret and my cat playing happily in the yard while I lounged in the sunroom watching.

The man asked Harlowe, "And what color do you like?" She grabbed my hand and wouldn't look at him, pulling me gently back toward the house.

"Oh, you don't have to be afraid of me, sweetheart!" he said to her. "Besides," he said, returning his attention to me. "It just so happens that I have two black kittens. One for each of you. They're just around the corner. Wanna come take a look?"

"Sure!" I said without hesitation. But Harlowe wasn't having it. She tightened her grip on my hand and started walking backward.

"No," she said quietly.

No? Was she crazy? This man was offering two black kittens for free, and she wasn't going to take him up on it? I knew why. She was scared. But that wasn't my issue. I pulled my fingers from her vise grip and gave her a kiss on the forehead. "I'll be right back."

"No!" Harlowe said again. Except I wasn't listening. Off I went to follow the man as he led me down the street and toward the intersection.

"They're just over here to the left," he said.

I glanced at my sister as I rounded the corner. She was standing in the middle of the street now, her face full of fear. *Why is she so afraid?* I wondered. The question nagged at me.

I turned back to look at Harlowe again but could no longer see her. We were now on a different street, the one with the house where I liked to hide. I saw a van parked in its driveway. The man waved me to follow as he walked toward it.

"That's my van there," he said, "in front of our house."

That's when it clicked. I knew nobody lived in that house. That was my empty house. He was lying, and I'd made a terrible mistake. I was in danger.

The door to the van was open, and a woman sat in the back next to a cardboard box. "Come look!" she called to me. "They're so cute!" But I didn't have to take another step to know there weren't any kittens inside that box. What I *did* have to do was make sure this couple didn't know I was on to them.

It was too late to run. The man had walked back alongside me and was blocking any escape to the street. Instinctively, I leaned in to my lack of feeling. Faking my friendliest expression, I turned to him with a bright smile.

"Is that your wife?" I asked. "That's so sweet! She's keeping the kittens company so they won't be lonely!" The man tilted his head, unsure of what to think. I waved to her and whispered to him, "What's her name?"

His gut was telling him not to trust me. I could see it on his face. He was giving me the *look*. But despite his instincts he smiled again and turned away from me. "Anna," he called, "will you scoot over so our new friend can get a look at those kittens?"

But I was already gone. I'd started to run the second the man turned his head, the angry sound of his voice as he yelled after me eliminating any doubt of his true intentions.

Fear, I learned that day, could be useful.

At the top of the prison tower, I stared out the windows at the men gathered below. They stared back.

"Uncle Gilbert," I said. "Do sociopaths get afraid?"

He thought for a minute before responding. "I'm sure they probably do," he said. "But I don't think they feel it the way we do."

I was perplexed. "Well, has anyone ever asked them?"

Uncle Gilbert pointed to the men in the yard. "Asked *them?*" he replied. He offered a half chuckle. "Not on my watch," he said. "Why? You wanna go down there and talk to them about their feelings?"

"Yes!" I said, rising from my chair. "Could I do it now?"

"Not a chance!" my mom chimed in.

"Why not?"

"Because it's *dangerous*," she said. "Besides, it's late and we have to get going." Mom smiled, changing the subject. "Remember, it's Paul's birthday tomorrow and we're taking him to the beach. We can get up early and make a picnic basket. How's that sound?"

It sounded boring. I liked Paul, an airline pilot who had a crush on Mom. But I hated the beach. I hoped we wouldn't be there long. The last time we'd gone, a stranger had come up to me and exposed his penis while everyone else was swimming. Remembering *Ice Castles*,

I'd pretended to be blind and acted disoriented until he seemed genuinely disturbed and wandered away.

Giving my mom a limp shrug, I shifted my gaze back to the men below and took one last look. *What separates someone like me from someone like them?* I wondered.

Suddenly I was desperate to find out.

CHAPTER 4

Alert

"Baby died."

I was in the living room watching television when Mom told me. It was several months after our trip to the prison. Harlowe had found our pet cold and lifeless on the floor, and now my little sister was in the upstairs bathroom crying her eyes out.

"Patric, did you hear me?" Mom asked, aggravated.

I had, only I wasn't sure what to do about it. The news of Baby's death was a shock that wouldn't settle. It was just rattling around in my head. I blinked a few times, then nodded to my mother and continued watching television.

After a heavy sigh to convey that my non-reaction was unacceptable, she headed upstairs to comfort Harlowe. And for the first time I could recall, I was jealous. I wanted to be upstairs crying, too. I wished so much I could be in the bathroom, lying on the floor and sobbing next to my sister as waves of authentic grief washed over us. I knew I was "supposed" to be at least as visibly devastated as my sister. So why wasn't I?

I looked at my reflection in the sliding glass door. I closed my eyes and concentrated until I could feel tears welling up behind my lids. Then I looked again. *That's more like it*, I thought.

The girl behind the glass with the tears streaming down her face looked like someone who had just lost a pet. She looked like someone who needed consoling. But I knew the girl on my side of the glass could not look that way, at least not without making a conscious effort. I blinked, and my concentration broke. The tears disappeared. I returned my attention to the television.

To say I felt nothing isn't true. I loved Baby more than almost anything else in the world. That she was now dead was inconceivable to me. And yet here we were, and here she wasn't. When trying to explain this lack of certain emotions, I've likened it to standing next to a roller coaster. I can hear the people on the ride. I can see the dips and curves of the track. I can sense the creeping adrenaline as the train begins its steep ascent. As the first car reaches the top of the hill, I suck the air into my lungs and then exhale forcefully with my hands over my head, watching the coaster rush to the bottom. I *get* it. I'm just not experiencing it for myself.

I could tell that my mother didn't know what to do with a kid like me. Like any decent parent, she expected a normal kid with normal reactions. That I wasn't able to give her what she wanted put me into a state I'd started referring to as "stuck stress." It, too, reminded me of a roller coaster, but it had nothing to do with how I experienced the ride. Rather, it was the sensation *before* launch, when the over-the-shoulder restraints would drop into place. To everyone else, these restraints represented safety. Security. But not to me. I hated the way they trapped me. Unable to hide if I needed to. Unable to breathe. It was the claustrophobia that arose anytime I became aware I wasn't feeling what others expected me to be feeling.

That's how I was the night Baby died. I could hear my sister crying. I could imagine the waves of grief. It's just that I wasn't standing in the ocean with them. It wasn't so much that I was lacking the feeling as it was that I was separated from it, like my reflection in the door. I could see my emotions, but I wasn't connected to them.

I turned off the television. I might not have been able to express (or experience) my feelings the way I thought others did, but I knew that casually watching reruns of *Dallas* while my first pet lay dead in the next room was only going to cause problems. I went to the laundry room, where I presumed Baby's corpse was still. Maybe if I saw her for myself, I would feel more . . . what? I didn't know. Mom had covered the ferret with a holiday-themed dish towel, and cheerful Christmas trees outlined Baby's tiny body.

She must have been cold, I thought. *She was next to the dryer to get warm.* I bent down and slowly lifted the cloth. Baby was still underneath, her eyes slightly open. I hung my head and I exhaled, thinking, *This sucks.*

I looked at Baby again and acknowledged that she seemed both wholly familiar and utterly strange. "That's not you," I said to no one in particular. Not anymore. I knelt down and sniffed Baby's neck, trying to capture her scent one last time. But even that was different. All the things that made Baby unique were gone. Her body, once delightful and spirited, now seemed bereft of meaning. It was like an old item of clothing that had been left behind, or one of the millions of empty seashells scattered on the beach. I felt strangely calm about it.

I left my pet and began the slow climb up the stairs to my room. Baby's death had put me in an impossible situation. I hated that Mom was upset, but I didn't know what I could do to make her understand. I wasn't *choosing* to behave this way. It was just a reaction, *my* natural reaction. I suppose I could have faked it. It would have been really easy for me to pretend to be emotional and produce tears alongside Harlowe. But I didn't *want* to. It would have been a lie. And lying, I'd promised my mom, was something I wouldn't do.

In recent weeks, I'd been on pretty thin ice with Mom. It all started when I'd gone to a sleepover at my friend Grace's house. Initially everything had been fine. I liked being away from home. The independence was exciting and liberating. But when we got into bed and I knew everyone was asleep, everything started to change.

The silence was an inescapable temptation. Usually, something was happening to keep me distracted—an overheard conversation, the sound of Grace's mom puttering around downstairs, the chatter of the television from the bedroom down the hall. But that night there was only stillness. I felt the sensation of pressure as it began its familiar rise. *You can do anything you want*, said the voice in my head.

It was true. In the dark with everyone sleeping, I was completely at liberty. I could get Grace's bike from the garage and take a midnight cruise around the community. I could spy on the neighbors. Without any adults to deal with or my sister to guard, there was nothing to stop me from doing something outrageous. *Only I don't want to do something outrageous*, I thought angrily. I rubbed my feet together beneath the covers. Typically, it helped me relax. But that night it had no effect at all. "This is fucking bullshit," I said aloud.

I grinned at the audacity of the foul language. The words sounded so strange coming from my mouth.

You love it, said the voice inside my head.

It was true. I *did* love it. The voice in my head was not coming from some alternate personality. It was *my* voice—*my* dark side. I felt the warmth of devilish possibility fill me as frustration gave way to excitement. Opportunities like these didn't happen all the time. Even though I wasn't necessarily amped to go on a late-night exploration of God knows where, I also knew I couldn't stop myself. It was a very specific feeling. It reminded me of how I felt when my room was in disarray. Even if I didn't feel like it, I *had* to clean it up. And now I *had* to jump at the chance to feel something.

Is this how those guys in the prison felt before they went to jail? I wondered. Like they *had* to do stuff they weren't supposed to, even when they didn't necessarily *want* to? I thought about them sleeping soundly in their tiny cells. From where I was sitting, it didn't seem that bad. *They've got it easy now*, I thought. Trapped in jail, their dark sides could no longer force them to do things they didn't feel like doing—not like *me*. Not like *now*. In a strange way, they were free. I was almost envious.

My head jolted slightly as a solution popped into focus. I didn't have to do bad things that night, or any other night for that matter. I just needed to go home. There, under Mom's watchful eye, I couldn't get into trouble even if I wanted to. And I *didn't* want to. I just needed to be constrained. I just needed to be *honest*.

Breathing a sigh of relief, I crawled out of bed and snuck over to where I'd stashed my overnight bag. I found a pen and paper and scribbled a note, propping it up on Grace's bedside table. Once she read it, she'd believe I got sick in the middle of the night and gone home. *Selective honesty*, I thought.

I picked up my bag with a satisfied sigh and headed for the door. Grace's house wasn't far from mine, so I didn't think Mom would be upset about it. *I could have done something bad*, I thought, as I stepped into the cool night air. *Instead, I decided to do the right thing. To be a good girl.* I couldn't wait to tell my mom.

She was leaning against the kitchen counter talking to Paul when I walked in. The two of them were laughing, and for a second I thought they were happy I came home. But one look at her face, and I knew I was wrong.

"Why?" Mom said, almost screaming. "WHY ARE YOU HERE?!"

I tried to explain, but the scene quickly devolved into chaos (on her part) and confusion (on mine). Paul tried to mediate, but Mom ended up dropping her wine glass on the floor and racing upstairs to her room, sobbing. Paul followed, shouting after her. Meanwhile I stood frozen, glued to my spot near the front door, unsure what to do next.

"I should have just lied," I whispered. Based on Mom's reaction, it would have been the smarter choice. *The safer choice*, observed my dark side.

I cleaned up the mess while I considered my options. Should I return to Grace's? Should I try to talk to Mom again? By the time I was done, I'd decided that going back to the sleepover would not be a good idea. So I quietly climbed the stairs to my room, hoping I could sneak into bed without anyone noticing. When I reached the second floor, I could hear my mother crying from behind her bedroom door.

"I-don't-know-what-to-do-with-her," I heard her say between gasps. "I-don't-know-what-to-do."

The door was ajar. Through the crack I could see Mom on the side of her bed, rocking herself in desperation. Paul, also unsure of what to do, gently patted the back of her head while she hyperventilated.

I recoiled as if I'd been burned, unable to withstand more than a second of that image. It reminded me of seeing her crying in San Francisco. I went to my bedroom, closed the door, and stood completely still. In the silence I thought I could feel every cell in my body. All five senses were wildly activated, and I noticed that I'd stopped breathing. Was this how normal people felt when they were afraid? I suspected that it was. But I didn't feel afraid in my mind. I didn't feel scared. So what was I? I stood in the dark searching for the right word to describe what I was feeling until suddenly it appeared.

Alert.

It wasn't fear. It was vigilance. I was keenly and eerily alert. I had a serious problem that needed an immediate solution. I couldn't completely surrender the protection and guidance of my mother because I felt like I needed it to control my behavior. But I also knew her guidance came at a price, and that price was trust. If Mom thought I was being dishonest—even if I wasn't—I lost her as my compass.

I closed my eyes and recalled the times in San Francisco when I'd lie under the dining room table and tell her my secrets. When she'd call me her honest girl, I'd know I was safe.

"When in doubt, tell the truth." I recalled my mother's mantra from San Francisco. "The truth helps people understand."

The next day, after Paul left, I walked into Mom's room. Although it was after noon, the curtains were still drawn and the lights were off. In the corner, the television was on, but the volume was muted. Its silent images threw daggers of light across the darkened room. I walked to the bed where my mother lay awake and staring. She appeared to have been up all night crying. Her face was red and blotchy, and there were dark bags around her eyes.

"Mommy . . ." I started to say before she interrupted me.

"Listen to me, Patric," she said, her voice raspy. "Listen to me carefully." She looked scared. "You must never ever sneak out of the house again, *any* house," she said. "And you must never, ever tell me a lie."

I nodded, desperate for her to understand. "But I didn't lie!" I said with a squeal.

Mom looked at her hands. I could tell she was searching for words. "Look," she continued, unable to meet my imploring gaze. "I know you're . . . different," she said.

"I know," I whispered. "I know I shouldn't do stuff, but I do it anyway. I know I'm supposed to care, but I don't. I *want* to but I just . . . can't help it. I don't know what's wrong with me."

We sat for a few seconds in silence, the light of the television turning the white pillows different pastel colors. I stared at them and became momentarily hypnotized by the flickering hues. *I wish I was a pillow*, I thought.

"I can't keep you safe if you aren't telling me the truth." Mom grabbed my hand and stared into my eyes. "So promise me," she said, "promise me you will never lie or break a promise again. Promise me you'll be honest, and not just with your words," Mom continued urgently, "but with your actions, too."

I looked into her eyes, completely understanding what she meant. "Okay," I said. "I promise."

And I meant it. From that day forward, I went to extremes refusing to be dishonest about anything. I even started counting the number of bites I consumed at dinnertime, just in case Mom wanted to know how much I'd eaten. I worked so hard to be perfect. I went out of my way to tell the truth, just like I'd promised. My reaction to Baby's death was the honest one. So why was I standing in my bedroom alone and in trouble once again?

The next morning, I was glad to be at school for once. Similar to the peace I'd felt in my room, it was nice to be around people who weren't expecting me to be sad. None of my classmates or teachers knew that

Baby had died, so I didn't have to force myself to look upset. I went about my day as if nothing was wrong, because—as far as I was concerned—nothing was.

In the carpool line that afternoon, I was relieved to see my grandmother's car rounding the corner. Mom was probably still mad, so time in the car with my grandmother was a reprieve. We chatted happily on the way home. I assumed my grandmother hadn't heard about Baby, so everything was normal. But when we turned the corner onto our street, I noticed something strange: Mom's car was parked in the driveway. Why had Grandma picked me up if Mom was home?

I got out of the car and ran up the pathway to our townhouse. Before I could push it open, the door swung briskly inward. My sister stood smiling on the other side, a Popsicle in her hand. She gave it to me.

"Welcome home, Kaat!" she said, using the nickname she'd inexplicably assigned me the previous summer. "Wanna play Barbies?"

I smiled at her and accepted the Popsicle. Over her shoulder, I could see Mom in the kitchen, making something to eat. She had yet to acknowledge me.

"Mommy," I said, walking inside. "Why didn't you pick me up today?"

Mom didn't turn from the counter where she was carefully slicing a tomato. "Because I was busy with your sister," she replied.

"Doing what?" I said, looking at Harlowe. "Making Popsicles?"

Mom shook her head, transferring the tomato to a bowl. "We buried Baby, actually."

I froze. Cold rage rose from the ground and into my stomach. I set the Popsicle on the counter, its red dye instantly staining the white Formica. "Wha—" I stammered. "WHAT?!"

Mom set down the knife and turned around. "Well, you didn't seem like you cared much last night," she said, sounding almost smug, "so I didn't think you'd mind."

Her statement felt like a punch, and the rage had now ascended to my throat. "You're lying," I said softly, barely controlling myself. Mom took a step toward me.

"What did you say to me?" she asked, ready to launch a rebuke.

I looked her in the eye, her absurd reaction making me even angrier. Unable to contain my fury, I grabbed the nearest object, a glass pitcher, and threw it as hard as I could at the wall behind her head.

"YOU'RE A LIAR!" I screamed.

The pitcher exploded against the wall, showering my mother with tiny shards of glass. Harlowe started crying. I stomped out of the kitchen and up to my room, growing more resolute with every step. Enough was enough. I was done with it. Bad behavior, good behavior, honesty, lies; none of it mattered. *Everything* got me in trouble. And I was sick of constantly trying to play by rules that were always changing for no good reason. From now on, I was going to do what *I* wanted. What did I have to fear? Nothing, that's what.

I made it to my room and slammed the door. I only had a few seconds of quiet before the door swung open and my mother burst inside. It wasn't nearly enough time to get myself back under control.

"Patric!" she screamed. "What is wrong with you?!"

"What's wrong with *me*?!" I screamed back, shaking with anger. "You took my little sister out of school so you could bury *my* pet!" I yelled. "AND YOU WANT TO KNOW WHAT'S WRONG WITH *ME*?!"

There was a smudge of blood on Mom's cheek where she'd been cut by a piece of glass. She wiped at it as she took another step forward. "I assumed you wouldn't care." Only she said this with much less confidence.

"*Bull*shit."

It was the first time I'd ever cursed in front of her, much less *at* her. But I didn't care. "You were mad because I didn't react the way *you* wanted me to. You were mad because I *never* react the way *you* want me to." Mom looked down as my words hit a nerve. "You did this to punish me," I spat. "You did this because I'm *different*."

Mom looked at me. Slivers of glass glinted in her hair like diamonds. "I thought it would teach you a lesson," she said, daring to look shocked.

"And what lesson is that?" I asked, stepping toward her. "That I should be more like everyone else? More like *you*?" I laughed sarcastically and shook my head in mock pity. "You're a liar who insists everyone *else* tell the truth," I said. "You're a cheater who demands everyone else play fair." I paused for effect, then sneered, "I'd rather be *dead* than be like you."

My words dropped like the blade of a guillotine. Mom's face went white, and she backed toward the door. Her expression had changed into the *look*.

"You," she said, barely able to breathe, "are a NIGHTMARE." She shouted, "YOU STAY IN YOUR ROOM!"

She slammed the door and ran downstairs. I waited long enough to make sure she was gone, then defiantly strode out of my room. Blood pumped fiercely through my veins as I walked down the hall. It galvanized me. I had loved the confrontation. The rest of my family avoided conflict, but not me. I found it exciting, even delectable. It made me feel powerful.

You want to take something from me? I thought, walking calmly into her room. *You want to take something precious and make sure I never see it again?* I crossed to the dresser where she kept her favorite things. "Well, I can do that, too." In the top drawer was a pair of ruby earrings she'd had since she was a child. My great-grandmother had given them to her, and they ranked among her most-prized possessions. I took them into the bathroom and flushed them down the toilet.

Back in my room, I leaned against the door and stared at the opposite wall. My rage was dissipating, as was all the frustration and tension that had been building since Baby died. I felt nothing. Only now—like inside the vacant house—I liked the feeling of nothingness. It was relaxing. I wanted to *embrace* it.

With my mother already irate, I didn't have to worry about "right" reactions or "wrong" ones. I didn't have to worry about the stress that came with trying to play normal. Alone in my room, I didn't have to offer fake reactions to display feelings I didn't have. I was *free*—from emotion, from expectation, from pressure—from everything!

"I can just be *myself*," I whispered.

A line from *Who Framed Roger Rabbit?* came to mind. "I'm not bad," Jessica Rabbit says. "I'm just drawn that way." I could relate. I, too, was just drawn that way. I wasn't trying to hurt anyone or purposely cause trouble. I just wished I could make my mother understand.

"It's not my fault I don't feel the same way everyone else does. So what am I supposed to do?" I glanced at my bed and realized I was exhausted. I collapsed on top of my comforter.

Several hours later I woke with a start. My bedroom was dark and the house was silent. *What's going on?* I thought. *What time is it?* Then I remembered. The ferret. The fight. The earrings. I sighed and rolled onto my side. In the bed next to mine, Harlowe was asleep. It was after midnight. Mom must have come in at some point to put her to bed. I rubbed my face and sat up, the enormity of the situation dawning.

The sound of whispering broke my concentration. The voices were coming from my mother's room. She was on the phone. "I was only trying to get a reaction," I heard her say, sobbing quietly into the receiver. "I know I went about it the wrong way, but I don't know what to do. She doesn't seem to *feel*. She doesn't seem to *care* . . . about anything!"

My mind raced. I stepped into the hallway and crept closer to Mom's door, hugging the wall so she couldn't see me.

"Baby *died*," she continued. "Harlowe has been beside herself with grief since it happened. But Patric? Nothing! And that's not all! This afternoon, she threw a pitcher at me. Last month, they called me from school because she locked some kids in a bathroom. I DON'T KNOW WHAT TO DO!"

I grimaced. I'd forgotten about the bathroom. The pressure at school that day had been unbearable. It had been building for weeks and for some reason, no bad acts seemed to ease the strain. In class, I had felt like I couldn't breathe. The room had felt like it was shrinking, and a familiar thought bubbled to the surface: "What if it doesn't stop?" It was a question that frequently haunted me. In the back of my mind, I wondered, *If I can't get the pressure under control, what will happen next?* I thought about the men inside the prison, then remembered the day I'd stabbed Syd—how quickly the tension had faded and how amazing it felt in the aftermath—and I tried to push the temptation of that release from my thoughts.

No, I said to myself. *No. No. No.*

My head felt like it was swelling as I fidgeted angrily in class. Hoping some air might clear my mind, I excused myself to the bathroom. A group of sixth-grade girls shuffled down the hallway ahead of me. They were headed to the bathroom, too, and when they were inside, the heavy metal door closed behind them with a thud.

I stood outside the door. Above the handle was a deadbolt that latched from the outside. I'd always found it interesting. Why would anyone want to lock a bathroom from the *outside*? But more importantly, what would happen if *I* did?

The corridor acted as a breezeway, and the air was cool as I stepped forward. I wrapped my fingers around the large deadbolt and registered how tiny my hand looked against the metal handle. Was I strong enough to twist such a lock? At first, I couldn't. Then I remembered how our patio sliders had to be pushed slightly forward for the bolt to catch. Leaning against the door, I felt the tumbler begin to turn. I twisted it slowly until I heard it click into place. Then I stepped back.

It only took a little while for the girls to realize they were trapped, but to me it was a rapturous eternity. It reminded me of jumping on the giant trampoline in gym class. My favorite part was that millisecond when I'd soared as high as I could but hadn't yet started to fall back down. It was a freedom unlike any other. In an instant all the pressure was gone. In its place I felt calm. I felt *high*. And this time, no one was bleeding.

The girls started banging on the door and screaming. I listened to them with detached interest. Why would someone be afraid of being locked inside a bathroom? I was pondering this very thing when I was surprised by a voice from down the hall.

"What *exactly* is going on here?"

I spun around to see Mrs. Genereaux, the sixth-grade teacher. She rushed past me and hurriedly unlocked the deadbolt. The girls spilled out, their faces streaked with tears.

"Did you do this?" she asked, close to shouting at me. "Did you lock this door?"

The juxtaposition between the intense peace in which I'd only just been immersed and the messy scene unraveling in the hallway rendered me uncharacteristically careless. I tried to stammer out a denial, but it was no use. My guilt was obvious. Before I could compose myself, Mrs. Genereaux grabbed my wrist and marched me to the principal's office.

Later, as I sat next to the reception desk waiting for my mother to come get me, I had a strange sense of bewilderment. I'd never been caught like that. *I wasn't thinking*, I rationalized. And the danger in allowing the pressure to rise for so long became apparent. *It made me sloppy*, I realized gravely. *It made me* dangerous.

I thought again of the men locked inside the prison and Officer Bobby's response when I'd asked if all sociopaths ended up in jail. "Probably," he'd said. "Unless they're really smart."

That's what I have to be, I decided. *Really smart.*

Inflicting pain (or distress) was a guaranteed, instantaneous method of pressure elimination. I didn't know why. All I knew was the release after stabbing Syd was the best feeling I'd ever had. It wasn't just that I didn't care. It was that I didn't care that I didn't care. I was a kite flying high in the sky, beyond the reach of pressure and stuck stress and any expectations of emotion. Yet somehow, I knew there was an inherent risk in allowing myself to do something so amoral. It was dangerous, for one thing. But worse, it was addictive.

Even as young as I was, I understood: So much of my energy was spent trying to keep the pressure at bay. Succumbing to my darkest compulsions was effortless and required no energy. God, I loved that release. It was like I could float along on a wave of submission. Was there a name for this feeling?

"Surrender."

The word appeared on my lips as if spoken by someone else, and I knew it was true. At the same time, I was confused. *Surrender to what?* I wondered. My dark side? My "bad" urges?

Standing outside Mom's bedroom, I was desperate to understand. My thoughts were interrupted as she cried into the phone. "I'm afraid," she faltered, "I might have to send her to boarding school."

My eyes widened. Boarding school? She fell quiet as the person on the other end spoke. I sighed and hung my head.

To be fair, I'd always harbored a secret desire to be sent off to boarding school. Miss Porter's School in Connecticut, for instance, seemed like an excellent place to ride out my adolescence. After all, I was about to start junior high. I hadn't exactly worked through the details, but I could imagine myself in a crisp plaid uniform with neatly plaited braids concealing dozens of lock-friendly bobby pins. *A fresh start*, I thought. A new place where I could hide in plain sight. It sounded wonderful. And yet, I hated the idea of leaving my mother. Despite what I'd yelled in anger, and the peace I'd experienced after our fight, I loved my mom. I was leery of a world without her guidance, even if I was reluctantly starting to grasp that her guidance was just an illusion. It would never adequately apply to a person like me.

Why can't she just get it? I thought, frustrated. Maybe if I didn't feel like I had to constantly pretend to be like everyone else—maybe if I didn't feel like I constantly had to *hide* from everybody else—I wouldn't have the stress. Maybe then I wouldn't feel the pressure. I wouldn't have the urge to be bad. *Why can't she understand?*

Because she's incapable of understanding, replied my dark side. And I knew at once that it was true. A person like my mother, a normal person with scruples, would never understand what it was like to be someone like me. She could never relate to feeling nothing. She could never comprehend my compulsion to harm others or do bad things. Nobody could. Despite Mom's insistence to always want the truth, she couldn't accept the truth. And deep down, I knew it was unfair to keep putting her in that position.

I realized I had to use the bathroom. Trying to be as quiet as possible, I crept to the toilet and lifted its lid. That's when I saw the earrings sitting next to each other at the bottom of the bowl. The water hadn't been strong enough to carry them away. I reached in and grabbed them. As I dried them off, I was filled with understanding for my mom.

She didn't know any better, I thought. *It isn't fair to her.*

I returned to the hallway. Mom's door was no longer open. She must have heard me in the bathroom and closed it. Pressing my ear against the wood, I could tell she was still on the phone, only now I couldn't make out what she was saying. It didn't matter. I already knew what had to be done. I stared at the earrings and remembered how good it felt when I thought I'd destroyed them. *I was so out of control*, I thought. *But then I did something mean, and I was calm.* And what's worse, I *liked* that feeling.

This, I knew, was probably a bad sign. Except I didn't feel bad. Just as when Mom told me Baby was dead, so many of my feelings seemed separate from me, like a shadow on the wall. And the emotions that *did* resonate (like happiness and anger) were often fleeting, as though I could turn them off and on like a switch.

I snapped my fingers shut. The backs of the earrings dug into my palm, and I let them. Looking back again at my mother's closed door, I felt a wave of sadness. I knew I'd miss having an emotional connection to someone, as delicate as it was. I might not be leaving her physically, but never again would I be able to tell her the truth. Not the full truth, anyway. *What*, I asked myself, *am I going to do without her?*

The thought of being psychologically severed from my mother made me extremely uneasy, but I pushed the discomfort out of my head. *No*, I thought sternly, *you can't trust her anymore. It's not her fault, but* you *will keep paying the price if things continue like this*. It was true. My mother had taken me as far as she could but, like a car that hadn't been prepared for such an arduous journey, she was starting to break down. Mom was never going to understand or accept who I was. And I could never change who I was. I would just have to hide my true self from her.

Closing my eyes, I leaned against her bedroom door and rested my head against the back of my hand. "I love you so much, Mommy," I whispered. "But I can't keep my promise."

A few minutes later, I returned to my room. Harlowe still lay sleeping. Opening our shared closet doors, I crept to the crawlspace in the back where I kept all of my favorite treasures hidden behind a broken air vent. I tugged on the grate and it came loose, revealing all sorts of knickknacks I'd collected over the years. I set the earrings between Ringo Starr's spectacles and a set of keys I'd stolen from a teacher I didn't like. The boldness of their ruby sparkle seemed to protest the injustice of their new resting place.

Tomorrow, I reasoned, *I will apologize.* I would explain to my mother that my grief over the loss of Baby had been delayed, and that I was out of my mind to have spoken to her that way. And Mom, already feeling guilty about what she had done, would accept my apology. She'd believe my tears were authentic so long as I pushed them to flow. After that, I decided, I would start acting like the girl she wanted me to be. But I would keep the darkness for myself.

This is how I would keep myself safe. I would embrace my independence rather than shrink from it. I would stop trying to change my nature. *Instead*, I decided, *I'll just figure out a way to be invisible.*

The relief of this decision was instantaneous. I smiled softly as my thoughts drifted back to the intense liberation I'd felt earlier that night. Without the stress of having to force normal reactions or the anxiety of rising pressure, I could just be. I rather liked it. I liked being . . . *me.* I liked being free. *Maybe being on my own isn't so bad*, I mused. After all, I was capable of making good choices. *And to prove it*, I thought, *I'll put the earrings back when I can get into Mom's room without her noticing.* But as I replaced the grate and crawled out of the closet, a part of me balked at this decision. Mom might have convinced herself she was only trying to help, but what she had done was downright mean, not to mention premeditated. "Actions have consequences," she was always saying. My dark side agreed. Considering what Mom had done with Baby, maybe she deserved to lose those earrings after all.

Stop it, I said to myself, pushing back against the darkness. *I'm on my own now. I have to be smarter.*

Exhausted, I got into bed. On the wall across from me was a window that faced a fence and, beyond that, the ocean. I stared through the window and watched as a cat walked along the top of the fence.

I wish I was a cat, I thought drowsily. Then, before I knew it, I was asleep.

CHAPTER 5

Mrs. Rabbit

We moved a few months later. The townhouse, Mom had decided, was "too stifling." She wanted something different. So, after an exhaustive search, she settled on a bigger and better house. "This," she said, would be "our forever home."

I liked the new house. It had a pool, three bedrooms on the same floor—so I no longer had to share one with my sister—and it was close enough to the beach that I could still count the waves every night as I went to sleep. My room, with its giant front-facing window, was like its own little world. The night we moved in, I sat on my bed and stared outside for hours. It reminded me of Lucy's secret passageway to Narnia in *The Lion, the Witch and the Wardrobe. It's like my own private entrance*, I thought. *I could walk right through it if I wanted to*. And I *did* want to.

Like my limited grasp of emotion, the concept of boundaries was muddled for me. What's more, it solidified my understanding that I was very different from other people my age. Most kids seemed to inherently get the idea of limits. They understood when to stop and when to go. They had an emotional connection to right vs. wrong. But that was never the case with me, particularly when it came to rules that I felt were open to interpretation. Like stealing. And lying. And breaking into our old house so I could get something I needed.

It was a week after we'd moved. I was sitting in my room unpacking boxes when it occurred to me that I couldn't find my locket. Determined to locate it, I tore the bedroom apart. But after thoroughly searching, the reality became clear: I'd left it behind the grate inside my old closet.

Horrified, I rushed to the kitchen, where my mother was putting away breakfast dishes. "Mom," I said, "I have to go back to the townhouse. I left something in the closet."

"You can't, honey," she said somberly. "Once you move out, anything you leave behind belongs to the new owners. There's a law." She shook her head sympathetically. "I'm sorry, sweetheart."

I stomped back to my room, stifling the urge to scream. Fuck *the law*, I thought. And fuck my mom for not being more proactive, more *creative*. That locket was mine. I wasn't just going to leave it behind. I knew it would never be found. Unlike everything else behind the grate, I'd placed it underneath a loose brick as an extra layer of security. I'd hidden it so well that even *I* had forgotten it was there when I retrieved all my treasures the night before we left.

"Mother*fucker*," I hissed quietly. Normally I was meticulous. I didn't make mistakes like this. I didn't misplace things or lose track of time or FORGET TO GRAB THE ONLY THING I REALLY CARE ABOUT FROM ITS FUCKING HIDING PLACE IN MY ROOM BEFORE MOVING AWAY. I mumbled this last part to myself as I kicked over a box of junk from the garage. A bicycle bell rolled onto the floor and, when I saw it, a solution came to mind.

The townhouse was only a few blocks away. Looking out my window, I could see the main road that connected our new neighborhood to the entrance of our old housing community. *It's not that far*, I thought. *I can handle this myself.* So that's what I did.

A short time later, I stood beneath a bathroom window at the back of the townhouse. I knew its lock was broken. My sister had snapped the bolt years before, and Mom had never bothered to fix it. "That window is so small," she'd said. "I'm not worried about any bad guys getting in."

The pane opened with ease, and I smiled as I pushed it open and hoisted myself inside. Mom was right. A bad "guy" couldn't have squeezed through the tiny windowpane. But a bad *girl* certainly could. I slid down the wall until I could find my footing and then waited, listening. It didn't sound like anyone was home. *Perfect*, I thought.

I looked at my watch. I'd promised Mom I'd only be gone for thirty minutes. So far it had been ten. *That gives me ten minutes to get the locket and ten to get back home*, I thought, practicing some new algebra. Plenty of time.

I peeked out the door to scan the kitchen and living room. There were lots of boxes and misplaced furniture, but no people. I exited the bathroom and made my way down the hall, through the dining room, and up the stairs.

The door to my old bedroom was closed, and for a second I was lost in nostalgia, remembering the way it looked before we moved. I was so caught up in my reverie that it didn't occur to me to check the room before I entered. I pushed open the door and was startled to see a girl sitting on the floor. In her lap was a green Trapper Keeper with a horse on the cover. She was coloring its white hooves a bright shade of pink.

I gasped, and the equally stunned girl locked eyes with me. She looked to be about my age. "Who are you?" she asked.

"I'm Patric," I said, quickly regrouping. "I used to live here."

The girl blinked several times. "I'm Rebecca," she said tentatively. I smiled, putting both of us at ease.

"I'm so sorry if I scared you!" I laughed and rested my hand on my heart, leaning slightly forward. It was a mannerism I'd picked up from Harlowe that people seemed to like. "I called out, but nobody answered."

Rebecca gave me a timid smile. "Oh," she said. "That's . . . okay. My parents must have left the door open. They just ran to the store . . . but they'll be right back." She added that last part quickly, and I could tell she was nervous. But I wasn't.

"Great." I took a few cautious steps toward the closet, saying,

"You know, this used to be my room." I put my hand on the sliding door. "I thought I'd gotten everything out of it before we moved." As I spoke, I pushed the door open. "But this morning I remembered that I left something." I stepped into the closet. "So, I figured I'd come get it." I turned around, knelt down in front of the grate, and yanked it open. "Hey, Rebecca!" I called. I wanted to keep an eye on her to make sure she didn't do anything stupid. "Take a look at this."

She appeared in the doorway next to me. "What is *that*?" she asked, eyeing the hole in the wall.

"I used this as a secret hiding place," I said. "You can, too, if you want." Rebecca stood behind me as I removed the loose brick and carefully recovered the necklace. I wrapped my hand around the locket and squeezed. My relief was overwhelming.

"Oh, wow," she said. "That's so cool."

I carefully replaced the grate and stood up. "Yeah," I said. "It's an awesome secret." I waited for Rebecca to say something, but she only nodded. After a few impatient seconds, I smiled politely and then maneuvered past her back into the bedroom. I paused at the door. "Well," I said. "See you around."

Rebecca smiled. "See ya."

I waved and walked backward out of the room. Then I raced down the stairs, out the front door, and made it home to my unsuspecting mother with seconds to spare.

That night, with the locket safe in a new hiding place, I lay in bed and thought about my adventure. *That was awesome*, I thought. And the reason, I theorized, was because my errand hadn't been set in motion by the feelings of pressure. This "bad" thing I did wasn't something I'd *had* to do. Quite the contrary. It was something I'd *wanted* to do. I knew what I'd done was technically wrong, but I didn't care. I didn't feel bad about it at all. In fact, I wanted to do it again.

I was starting to understand why doing bad things made me feel . . . *something*. However brief, it connected me to the way I imagined everyone else felt all the time. Lurking beneath my surface I always had an urge to prowl or steal or stalk, sometimes even to hurt. This wasn't because I *wanted* to, but because some part of me understood that it made me feel better. It made me feel, period.

My moderated bad behavior was a form of self-preservation— a clunky attempt to keep myself from doing something really bad. Most of the time such behavior had occurred at random. Because I was always trying to maintain the tether with my mother, I'd always been careful never to engage in it unless I *had* to. But now things were different. Without the burden of needing to be "good" for my mom, the idea of freedom was exciting. The problem was I wasn't quite sure how to modulate my actions. Alone and with nothing and no one to stop me, I was aware my dark side might take things too far. But what if, instead of working so hard to try to beat my dark side, I opted for a treaty?

My mind drifted to my grandfather's farm in Mississippi and the wild horses there he would train to be ridden. "They're mad at first," Granddaddy once explained.

We were standing in a grassy paddock near the barn. A young horse was standing next to the fence, and I watched as my grandfather approached him and carefully slipped a halter around his neck. The horse objected, but then settled. "They kick," Granddaddy continued softly. "They buck. They try to throw you off. But if you're consistent, you can gain their trust."

He tugged slowly on the halter, causing the animal to gently lower his head. "You introduce pressure so they learn to release their will," he demonstrated. "And most importantly"—Grandaddy reached into his pocket and pulled out a handful of sugar cubes—"you reward their progress to encourage obedience." The horse munched eagerly on his treat, and I giggled. "And that," he said, winking, "is how you break a horse."

Sitting in my room, I decided I would use these steps to deal with my dark side. Except I didn't want to break her. I wanted to *tame* her. I decided to start that night.

I got out of bed and opened the giant window. The sound of the ocean filled my ears as the wind rushed in, planting salt-air kisses on my face. As expected, the urge to crawl through and disappear into the night was nearly impossible to resist. But I held steady. For a few seconds all I did was stand there, basking in the satisfaction of my discipline. Then I forced myself back to bed.

Things continued like this for weeks. Once the sun went down, I would close the door to my bedroom, turn off the lights, open the window, and look outside. For a while, that was enough. But then one night, I decided to loosen the reins.

It was a weeknight, and the house was still. The Cowboy Junkies' cover of Lou Reed's "Sweet Jane" played softly from the silver boom box sitting on my dresser. I crossed the room and quietly opened the window, singing to myself. "Heavenly widened windows, seem to whisper to me . . ." It was one of my favorite activities—rewriting lyrics to melodies that I liked. With so many songs written about emotion, it was often hard for me to relate. But with a switch of a few words now and then, I found that I had a much better time singing along. "Heavenly widened windows, seem to whisper to me," I sang again, "and I smile."

Crawling up the wall onto the ledge, I pushed away the screen and pulled myself sideways onto the windowsill. I stared at the street. Moonlight drew a line down the center of my body and illuminated my left side with a bright glow. "Half light, half dark," I said with a grin. The equilibrium was invigorating.

I leaned back and gazed across the yard to the sidewalk, spying on all the people out walking at night. Our street, so close to the beach, saw a great deal of foot traffic. There must have been a dozen pedestrians passing by that evening. But they couldn't see me. Hidden in the shadows of our front yard's large oak tree, I was invisible even to someone looking right in my direction. Yet there I was, watching.

Who are these people? I always wondered. What were they doing? Where were they going? I wished I could find out. Then it dawned on me: *Maybe I* can.

It was the man with the German shepherd. I'd seen him several times and had found him so interesting. Was he married? Did he have kids? Where did he live? It couldn't be far; he walked by almost every day. I watched him as he crossed in front of our house. And then—without really thinking about it—I inched my foot from where it rested against the outside of the window and dropped it to the ground. The action was much simpler than I'd anticipated. I paused and waited for something to follow it, like a rush of excitement or my mother's voice screaming at me to get back inside. Except there was nothing. I was on my own.

I turned my body and dropped the other foot. The gardeners had sprinkled mulch around the bushes in front of my bedroom window, and the pieces felt wet beneath my bare feet. It occurred to me that I needed shoes. *I should grab a pair*, I thought. But the man and his dog were moving quickly, and I didn't have much time. So I left.

A calm sensation pulsed slowly through me as I followed him. *It feels so good to* feel, I thought. I quickened my pace.

He was standing at an intersection a few houses down the street, and I didn't want to lose him. When he turned and I could no longer see him, I began to run. The hem of my nightgown got wet as I raced across lawns, taking a shortcut through neighbors' yards until I saw him again. He was walking up the driveway to a house on the street behind mine. I'd never seen it before. The garage door was open. It stayed that way even after the man walked inside and into the kitchen, where a woman was waiting. From where I stood, I could see it all through their living room window. I shook my head. *Why do people leave their curtains open with the lights on after dark?* I thought. It was like an invitation. The man kissed the woman, who was putting a baby into a high chair. *They're a family*, I observed.

I moved closer to get a better look. Was the baby a boy or a girl? I couldn't tell. I took a few more steps until I was only inches away. The woman was opening a bottle of wine and the man was smiling at her. It all looked so normal and wonderful. *One day I'm going to be just like them*, I thought.

"HEY!" someone shouted. "What are you doing?"

I whirled around to see an elderly couple down the street. They walked by my window several times each week with a younger man I assumed was their son. I stepped away from the window. The full moon turned my light blue nightgown a brilliant white, making the man uncomfortable. He hadn't expected to see a young girl. I winked and brought my index finger to my lips.

"Shhhhhhh!" I whispered playfully. "We're playing hide and seek." Then I shot him a wicked smile and took off running. The side yard opened onto a park I knew was only a short distance from my house. The moon lit my path, and in no time I was crawling back through my bedroom window.

In bed that night, I was pleased with myself. I had allowed my dark side to have some fun, but I'd maintained control the whole time. I imposed boundaries—*my* boundaries. My dark and light sides were no longer conflicting but coexisting. And yet, I still had some things to figure out.

Breaking into our old townhouse and following strangers after bedtime weren't the "right" things to be doing. This I knew for sure. But who got to decide? *Who is it hurting?* I wondered. If discipline and boundaries were things that kept my dark side in check, then it would seem that outright harmful actions were the only ones that were truly "bad."

"Everything else," I said to myself, "is fair game." I found a notebook and pen in my nightstand and began a list.

Patric's Rules

I wrote.

#1 NO HURTING ANYBODY

I stared at the page for a few seconds and then leaned back in my bed, satisfied. It might have been just one rule, but to me it was the start of a very important code of conduct. Despite the fact I'd some-how managed to keep most of my worst impulses in check, I under-stood all too well that physical altercations with other people had the clearest impact on the pressure in my head. Whether it was stabbing Syd with the pencil or locking the girls in the bathroom, I knew that doing bad things to other people made me feel *alive*.

All the same, I knew that hurting others couldn't be a long-term solution. This, too, was a decision based on self-preservation. Acts of violence, however effective at reducing the pressure, attracted a great deal of attention and increased my odds of getting caught. *I need to find something less extreme*, I thought.

Indeed, my options until middle school had been limited. As a child, stealing and the occasional breaking and entering had been my only outlets for tension-reduction. But now that I was older—and without the tether of my mother's conscience—I could experiment with other methods.

In the months that followed, I continued to sneak out and follow various strangers around my neighborhood. Because this method of rule-breaking was boundaried, I took it to mean that I was finally learning how to maintain discipline, and I was doing it all on my own. (That I was essentially stalking people like a lo-fi lunatic never fac-tored into my decision-making.)

"What people don't know can't hurt them" had become my man-tra. In keeping with this belief system, I turned to deceit as a natural layer of protection. Lying had always been easy for me, and not just because of my fundamental temperament. Dishonesty, in my eyes, was a logical choice for someone like me. "When in doubt, tell the truth. The truth helps people understand." But the more I thought about it, the less I believed it. As a child who never felt remorse and rarely felt fear, the truth almost never helped people understand me. Usually, it was the one thing I could count on to make people *more* confused and to cause *more* trouble. People tended to get angry when I told them the truth. Lying, on the other hand, always kept me safe.

This life strategy reminded me of Capture the Flag, a game we played in school. Groups were divided into teams on opposite sides of the field and each team had a flag to hide inside their "base." Identifying the opposing team's base was the only way to find their flag. And the most obvious way to discover the location of their base, I quickly surmised, was to lie.

"Hey," I said to a kid named Everett, as I was casually strolling toward the opposing team. "Where's the flag? It's my turn to guard it."

Everett stared at me. "What are you talking about?" he asked. "You're not on my team."

"What are *you* talking about?" I shot back, planting my hands firmly on my hips. "You think I'd just be standing here if I wasn't on your team?" I rolled my eyes at Everett, who had started to scoff.

"Whatever," he said. "You're a *girl*."

"That's the whole point, dummy." I turned to look over my shoulder, nodding at what were, in reality, my teammates. "They'd never think we'd let a girl guard the base."

Everett shot me a snide smile and then led me to the flag. I waited until he was a safe distance away before shoving it into my pocket and then calmly walking back to the other side of the field.

"Wait five minutes, and then say you found this behind the bushes," I said, as I handed the flag to my team captain.

He looked at me incredulously. "Don't you want the credit?"

"Nah," I said, shaking my head. "I just want the win."

That's how I felt about life. I didn't crave attention or acknowledgment. I merely wanted to achieve my objective, to live life on *my* terms. Lying was clearly the best way to do it. It was like having a superpower that I had only recently let myself use. Being dishonest didn't just make me invisible. It made me *invinc*ible. It meant that all the things I knew about myself but couldn't change—things like not being sorry or not feeling afraid—couldn't be used against me.

I found that I loved being alone with my secrets almost more than anything. I loved being alone, period. Being alone was the only time I could truly be myself—and truly be *free*.

In junior high we had three classes after lunch, all of them led by instructors who were overworked and overwhelmed long before noon. *I'll bet nobody would even know if I wasn't there*, I thought one day. *I should just skip them.* So, later that afternoon, I did.

Instead of going to the cafeteria for lunch with my classmates, I disappeared, nonchalantly cutting through the parking lot and out onto the street, where I marveled at just how easy it had been. I kept a close eye on the phone when I got home. I assumed someone from school would alert my mom. Certainly someone was aware I was gone and would call the house. But nobody ever did.

Even after weeks of doing this every few days, the phone never rang. With nothing to stop me, I decided to make my half-days a regular occurrence. I made it to class exactly enough times to turn in my assignments and take my tests. But most days I left campus in search of something more interesting to do. The first few times I just walked home. It was nice to have the place to myself. But after a while, it became obvious I needed to come up with a better long-term plan. *I need a base*, I thought.

I was hiding under my bed, waiting for Mom to leave after she unexpectedly turned up during one of my half-day afternoons. She was by then a successful real estate agent and spent most weekdays showing houses to potential clients. My bedroom door was partially open, and I could see her feet moving back and forth down the hallway until, at last, I heard the garage door close, and I knew the coast was clear.

I watched through the window as her car drove away, and then I wandered into the home office, where I knew she kept a list of all the houses she had for sale. I'd spent a huge chunk of my childhood visiting empty homes with my mother. Bored out of my mind, I didn't pay attention to much. But I never forgot how we got inside. On every front door my mother would hang a little combination lockbox that held the keys to that house. Every so often she let me or Harlowe enter the code.

"09127," I remembered. From then on, I continued to leave school early. Only instead of going home, I would walk to an empty property on my mother's list and let myself in using the code and the key. Those afternoons were among the happiest of my life.

Sometimes the homes were massive, with sleek hardwood floors, deep marble bathtubs, and warm running water. Other times they were tiny, with musty carpeting, moldy wallpaper, and no electricity. The amenities were irrelevant. All that mattered was that I was relaxed and unfindable, and no one knew the truth except for me.

"Why are people so afraid of being alone?" I wondered aloud one day. I was lounging on the floor of a beachfront property. Ocean air poured through an open window, and I couldn't imagine anything more wonderful. I was almost drunk with happiness. And yet, a nagging truth kept tugging at my thoughts. I knew what I was doing was against the rules, yet I couldn't bring myself to care.

Being in this house isn't hurting anyone. And it doesn't feel *bad*, I thought. *So who's to say that it is?*

It was the same as skipping school. My junior high was a notorious cesspool. Fights, sex, drugs, you name it. The place was terrible, and everyone knew it. *So why is it "bad" that I leave?* I wondered. I chose to remove myself from a shitty environment, and I wasn't hurting anyone in the process. How was that wrong? It didn't make sense. I thought, once again, of Jessica Rabbit. "I'm not bad," I whispered. "I'm just drawn that way."

Was there anyone else who was "drawn" the way I was? Or, perhaps more importantly, was there anyone in the world who would like a person like me? It wasn't the first time I'd wondered this. Despite my comfort with solitude, I couldn't help but think that life might be more fun if I had someone in whom I could truly confide. Many of the girls at school had boyfriends. Would I ever get to have one? Was romantic love even possible for a person like me? And if so, did I care?

I would soon find out.

CHAPTER 6

Estate Planning

I met David at summer camp when I was fourteen.

My mother had enrolled me in a creative arts program after I refused to join Harlowe at church camp. "You're not going to spend the summer sitting alone at home all day," she'd said. "So either you go to camp or you start coming to work with me."

Surprisingly, I loved it. The program was held in what had been one of oil magnate John D. Rockefeller's winter homes. A few weeks after arriving, I'd heard a rumor that Rockefeller himself had overseen construction of a series of secret tunnels beneath the house that extended to various buildings around town. I became obsessed with that rumor and had to know if it was true.

In the administration office was a drawer full of documents related to the house. Determined to get my hands on them, I started spending all my spare time hanging out there. I was loitering inside one day, hoping for a chance to snoop, when an achingly handsome boy walked through the door.

"How's it going?" he said.

I was momentarily speechless. David was slightly taller than me, with hair that matched his dark brown eyes and a deep suntan complemented by a plain white T-shirt. He was wearing faded peach board shorts and had a big ACA Joe duffel bag slung over his shoulder. I wondered if I was small enough to squeeze inside it so he could take me wherever he went.

"Patric," the camp director said, as she entered the office and interrupted my bizarre daydream. "This is David. Today's his first day."

"Cool," I replied, as casually as I could.

The camp director stepped into an interior office, leaving us alone. David grinned at me. I turned my attention to the drawer where the historical documents were kept. Seizing the opportunity, I quickly pulled it open and removed a set of blueprints. Then I turned back to David, giving him a broad smile as I shoved the ancient paperwork into my knapsack.

"First time here?" I asked.

"Yeah . . ." he replied, eyeing me suspiciously.

The camp director walked back in. She handed him a welcome kit and a map of the property. "Patric," she said, "would you mind showing David around?"

"Of course," I replied.

"You're in good hands, young man," said the director, smiling. "Patric probably knows her way around here better than I do!"

She was right. Obsessed with the tunnel rumor, I'd covered every inch of the estate over the past few weeks. Usually, I made my forays during lunch breaks or after hours when nobody else was paying attention. But, thanks to David's unexpected arrival, I now had an excuse to wander the grounds without raising any questions.

Together, the two of us roamed the property. Notebook in hand, I diligently detailed all three floors of the house, making notes of the rooms and structures that I matched to the blueprints.

"You sure are thorough," David observed. It was an hour into his "tour" and I had yet to show him any actual camp-related aspect of the estate.

"Well, it's a complex layout," I explained, as I guided him down yet another hallway of closed doors. "It's important to know how to get around."

"Still, I'm not sure I need to see every one of these rooms." Then he added, "Not that I mind. It's not every day I get to take a walk with such a beautiful girl."

His comment caught me off guard. Nobody outside my family had ever called me beautiful. I looked at David curiously. It was such a bold statement for him to make and one, I reasoned, that revealed more of him than it did of me.

I raised my eyebrows with a smile and folded my arms across my chest. "Can you keep a secret?" I asked. I headed for a nearby conference room and gestured for him to follow. Inside, I laid the blueprints on the table and told him all about the hidden tunnels and my mission to discover whether the rumors were true. Involving someone else in my plan was risky and highly uncharacteristic of me. Yet something about David made me want to tell him . . . everything.

He listened intently as I spoke, thoughtfully looking at my notes and the blueprints. "So this," he said when I was done, pointing to a section of the outline, "is where we are."

"Yeah," I said, nodding. I began to make a note on the map. He grabbed my hand to stop me.

"Don't write on these," he whispered. "Pencil lead could damage the paper." He grinned. "You know, if we had our own copy, we could mark it up however we want." He gently let go of my hand, thought for a moment, and then combed his fingers through his thick brown hair. "I saw a copier in one of the offices," he said, carefully rolling up the delicate paperwork. "You keep watch. I'll be right back."

After that, we were inseparable. David was heading into his senior year, several grades ahead of me. He worked two jobs to help support his mom and sister. He smoked cigarettes, had a fake ID, and drove his own car that he bought with his own money. And, like me, he was quick to break the rules if he thought they didn't make sense. But beneath his rebellious surface, he was a straight-A student, a kind and thoughtful soul unlike anyone I'd ever met. Whereas I was objective and cool, David was emotional and passionate.

My feelings for David, albeit strong, were hard for me to understand at first. Granted, most of the knowledge I had of young love was what I'd gleaned from V.C. Andrews novels. And though I was pleasantly surprised to find that my emotions were neither incestuous nor tumultuous, I also found them difficult to fully internalize.

My emotional constitution, it seemed, was a lot like a cheap set of crayons. I had access to primary colors—joy and sadness. But more nuanced hues—complex feelings like romantic love and passion— had always been outside my reach. I knew such things existed, because I'd read about them in books and seen examples on TV, but I'd never been able to relate to them.

In school we'd read *Wuthering Heights*. The girls in class swooned over Heathcliff and professed a deep connection to Catherine "Cathy" Earnshaw, the female protagonist who falls (and ultimately goes mad) for him. To them the book was a compelling star-crossed-lovers trag- edy. But I didn't get it.

The night I finished, I breathed a sigh of relief and tossed the book behind the couch, making a face at my mother. "You didn't like it?" she asked. "Why not?"

"Because Cathy's an idiot," I replied. "She's a Heather," I said, referring to the classic eighties film. "She acts all 'unruly' and 'wild,' but it's clearly for show because all she really wants is status and some boring husband. Meanwhile, she's fainting and crying over Heathcliff. She doesn't even understand Heathcliff." I rolled my eyes. "He's no prize, either, by the way." I shook my head and said, "I can't believe *that* book is supposed to be the be-all-end-all of love stories. I would kill myself if I acted like that."

"Just wait 'til you meet someone you really like," Mom had replied.

Then suddenly, I did. But it was nothing like *Wuthering Heights*.

My feelings for David weren't obsessive or possessive; they were effortless. I wasn't out of control or delirious, like Cathy was for Heathcliff. He didn't "sweep me off my feet," either. My feet were very much rooted in place. Maybe for the first time in my life. But the best part was that I had a really cool person whose feet were planted right next to mine—the coolest person in the world, as far as I was concerned. Meeting David was like finally solving a complex riddle. *Oh*, I thought, *so this is how this works for me.*

Romantically speaking, David didn't just represent everything I wanted to have. He represented everything I wanted to *be*. He had the ability to access and express a full range of feeling, but never made me feel bad that I didn't. Being with David made me feel whole. I no longer felt like I had to keep my "dark" secrets to myself. His acceptance made me feel safe, like I could talk to him about anything.

"So," David said, "tell me about this pressure again."

It was a couple of weeks after our encounter in the director's office, and we were sitting on the grass overlooking the river. The Rockefeller estate encompassed a large swath of waterfront property, including a park that backed up to the riverbank. With a vast assortment of willow trees and a giant waterwheel driven by a winding creek, the park offered plenty of natural hiding places that David and I used to our frequent advantage as we got to know each other.

That day he'd brought a portable CD player and we were listening to the Smiths. I raised my eyebrows and reached for the cigarette dangling from his lips. Taking a long drag, I dipped my foot in the stream and wiggled my toes in the water to the beat of the music. It was the first time I'd ever told anyone about the stuff that went on inside my head, and I was surprised to find that I liked talking to him about it. It made me feel grown-up.

"There's not much to it," I replied, doing my best not to cough on the smoke I tried to casually exhale. "I've been feeling it for as long as I can remember."

David frowned. "Okay," he pressed. "But what's it *feel* like?"

I looked down and tugged at the grass as I thought about how to respond. The blades felt like tiny satin swords between my fingertips.

"It feels like a full pot of water on a hot stove," I cautiously began. "At first it's flat. But then tiny bubbles start to form." I grimaced slightly as I forced myself to explain things in detail. "By the time it's simmering, I start to get really antsy," I continued, "because I know I have to do something to keep it from boiling over."

"Why?" David asked. "What happens if the water boils over?"

"I get violent," I answered. I'd never admitted to something so unfiltered. It was liberating and terrifying to do so. For a second, I thought I might have revealed too much. But David simply nodded.

"So you do little things to keep the water from boiling over," he replied. "Like when you went to what's-her-name's house and stole her statue." David snapped his fingers as he tried to recall the story I'd told him.

"Amanda," I reminded him. "And it was a trophy, not a statue."

She was the star cheerleader at my school. I'd earlier recounted to David that I'd hated her ever since she spotted me leaving campus one time and ratted me out to the principal. I'd managed to get out of trouble, but I'd never forgiven her for poking her nose where it didn't belong.

Amanda lived in a giant house not too far from mine, and her parents always left the garage door open. One night on one of my excursions, I'd snuck into the garage, crept into her house, and stolen her cheerleading trophy—her most-prized possession—from the living room mantel.

David shot me a mischievous grin. "After camp is over, you have to take me on one of your expeditions," he said.

"Why don't you come with me to Amanda's?" I taunted, mimicking a provocative tone I'd heard on a rerun of *Moonlighting*, a show my grandmother liked to watch. David snickered.

"You can help me put the trophy back," I told him. "That'll *really* twist her up."

"Jesus." He laughed. "You are dark!"

The speakers erupted with "How Soon Is Now?" I jumped up to sing along, interjecting my own lyrical interpretations. "I am the queen / And the heir / Of a numbness that is criminally vulgar. / I am the queen and heir . . . / Of nothing in particular."

I increased the volume and belted out: "You shut your mouth / How can you say / I go about things the wrong way? / I am human with no need to be loved. / Not like everybody else does!"

David grabbed me by the waist, pulling me into his lap. He gazed at me intently. "Is that how you really feel? About love?"

I looked at him, perplexed. The truth was I didn't know. I knew that girls in school and characters in movies talked about love as if it was a type of life force, something they needed to be happy. But I'd never felt that way. Love, to me, was like a beautiful assortment of lifeless couture behind a thick pane of department-store glass. Certainly I could appreciate it. I acknowledged that my mother always seemed happier whenever her boyfriend was in town. And movies that ended with romantic resolution always seemed to be the most popular. I, though, had never had much use for it. The idea of love sounded great in theory. But in practice the concept seemed dangerously transactional and—where I was concerned—heavily reliant on a willingness to adhere to some "normal" type of strict social contract.

David nudged me, looking for a response. "I don't know," I admitted. "I've never had that . . . that *drive*," I said. "That need for love."

I braced for what I assumed would be a disappointed reaction, but David instead seemed impressed. "That's so interesting," he said.

"Interesting?" I was surprised. "How do you figure?"

"Because you're different," he offered. "You can be objective about things most of us have no control over. Like you said, you appreciate love. You can enjoy it, but—since you aren't *craving* it—it doesn't control your life." Then he sang, "Not like everybody else does."

I pondered his observations. It was my Jessica Rabbit argument again: What if the bad parts of my personality weren't bad at all. What if they were simply different? The idea kept occurring to me, and with good reason.

My entire life, I'd always tried to conceal the type of person I truly was. Not to investigate it or understand it, but to hide it. Deny it. Eliminate it. Only now—suddenly—I was confronted by someone doing the exact opposite. I showed David who I really was, and he didn't want to change me. He accepted me. David, unlike anyone else I'd ever met, actually seemed to *see* me. Better yet, he *liked* what he saw. That, too, was a new experience. Though I'd never

particularly disliked myself—it had never occurred to me to formu-
late an opinion—I'd come to accept that the attributes separating me
from everyone else were not deserving of praise. But now I started to
rethink that.

As our weeks at camp progressed, I found myself coming around
to the idea that, despite my differences, I could be a valued person, a
good person. After all, David seemed to think so. And he was the best
person I'd ever met. He was the coolest person I'd ever met. Best of
all, he didn't discourage me from indulging my mischievous side. In
fact, he volunteered to help.

"This is bullshit," I said, frustrated.

It was late in the afternoon and we'd snuck out of an art class in
search of a door on the blueprints. We hadn't been able to find it, but
now we understood why. The spot where the door was supposed to
be was in the middle of what had become a commercial kitchen and
was covered by an imposing china cabinet that took up half the wall.

"There's no way we're gonna be able to move this," I complained.
Dropping to the floor, I shined my flashlight underneath the hutch.
Though my vantage point was limited, I could clearly see the base of
what appeared to be a narrow wooden door. "David!" I whispered
excitedly, twisting my head for a better look. "It's here!"

He didn't respond. He was sitting in a corner of the room focused
on something in his lap. I shined my flashlight at him. "David!" I
whispered again, this time louder. "Did you hear what I said? I can
see the door!"

"Shhhhhh," he responded. He had his trusty Swiss Army knife in
hand. "I'm cutting felt," he said calmly.

"What does that even mean?" I asked with an exasperated sigh.
"We don't have time for this!"

David pushed himself off the floor and approached the cabinet.
Then, sizing up the enormous cupboard, he tilted it gently backward.
"Make yourself useful," he instructed. "Hold this for me."

I scrambled to my feet to keep the cabinet in place. "It's easy really," he explained as he knelt down. "The fabric reduces friction."

My jaw dropped as I watched him attach the soft material to the cabinet's feet. God, he was smart. And resourceful! David spent a few weeks every summer loading freight for his father's trucking company in Boston, so he knew everything there was to know about moving things. He seemed to know everything about everything.

Our skill sets were a lovely match. Whereas I could tell a lie or lift a wallet, David knew all about history and science and had an astounding ability to solve practical problems.

He's the yang to my yin, I thought, watching him attach the last piece of felt. He'd cut the fabric into tiny squares, making them nearly invisible. Unless you were staring directly at the feet of the cabinet, you wouldn't know they were there. He moved to the side and pushed. With its new felt feet, the cabinet slid from the wall with hardly any effort. And there, just as the blueprints said it would be, stood a narrow wooden door.

Giving David an excited glance, I carefully twisted the knob until it clicked. The hinges creaked loudly as the door opened. We stood there frozen, waiting to see if anyone heard. Then, when we were sure the coast was clear, we squeezed through the frame and slipped into darkness. I adjusted my flashlight.

As we'd suspected, the door opened directly onto a set of crumbling stairs leading steeply down. The darkened stairwell led to another doorway, the frame of which was gruesomely bent as if a giant had yanked it from its hinges and thrown it to the side.

"Creepy," David said. I smiled. Carefully, we descended the stairs and ducked under the bent frame into what appeared to be a huge unfinished space roughly the size of the entire first floor of the house. I scanned the room with my flashlight, and we both gasped when it illuminated an archway in the corner, sealed off by a thick layer of bricks. There was a heavy iron chain stretched across it. I rushed over and ran my hand along the reddish blocks. They looked newer than the ones that framed the rest of the basement. *This has to be it*, I thought, taking a step back. "And even if it's not," I muttered, "I'm gonna say that it is."

David was right behind me. He wrapped me in a bear hug and exclaimed, "Holy shit! You did it!" He spun me around to face him and said, "You found the tunnel!"

And then he kissed me.

Caught by surprise, I took in a quick breath, which amplified the flavor. He tasted like smoky dark chocolate with a hint of tobacco. "Hungry" was the word to describe it. I was famished, ravenous for . . . what? I didn't know. I moved one hand to the small of his back. The flesh was warm. He squeezed me close to his chest, and I found myself wishing I could crawl inside his T-shirt. Then I dropped the flashlight, and we plunged into darkness.

That trip to the basement was the first of many. Over the next few weeks, I went downstairs any chance I could to explore the huge space and map out every square inch as my own. I spent entire afternoons there, basking in the solitude. David accompanied me sometimes, but for the most part I had the place to myself. My favorite area was the antechamber in front of the tunnel. On one trip I even smuggled down a chair and small table to create my own private parlor. There I would play my Sony Walkman and listen to jazz by flashlight.

I'd discovered jazz during family trips in grade school. My father kept an apartment in New Orleans, a pied-à-terre on the second floor of a building in the French Quarter. Anytime we visited my grandparents in Mississippi, we'd make a side trip to that sultry Southern city, and I savored our time there. Nights were my favorite. Harlowe and I shared a bedroom with a balcony that overlooked Decatur Street. After everyone was asleep I would step outside, with blues from the bars below putting me in a trance.

Jazz, I'd decided, was my favorite thing in life. In a universe where everything seemed to be associated with everything else, jazz was in a world all its own. The untethered notes didn't propel me backward in time or force me into imaginations of the future. Rather, they kept me in place, bounced around by tempos that didn't seem to be bothered by rules any more than I was.

Like jazz, the hidden basement had no rules or discernible structure. After a few visits, I found I was more comfortable below ground than I was above it. I was particularly fascinated by the time around lunch, when I could sit beneath the floorboards of the living room and eavesdrop on people chatting above me. *I'm like a ghost*, I thought. My new boyfriend seemed to agree.

"You *are* like a ghost!" David teased. "Here one minute. Gone the next." We were hanging out in the park a few weeks after we'd discovered the tunnel. "Why do you like it down there so much anyway?"

"It's relaxing," I told him. "I like being invisible." We were lying on a blanket and I was flipping through some books I'd found in the library. I wanted to see if I could find anything more about the tunnel.

"You say that a lot," David observed. "Why do you want to be invisible so much?"

"Because when I'm invisible, I don't have to worry about people noticing I'm different," I replied candidly. "I feel safest when people can't see me because that's when I can just be myself."

David frowned. "But you're not invisible with me," he said. "I see you." He cocked his head quizzically. "Are you stressed around me?"

"No." I smiled. "But you're unique."

David didn't reply, and I wondered, once again, if I'd said too much. "You should come look at these books," I said brightly, switching topics. "You'd love this stuff. It's right up your alley."

David loved anything having to do with history. And literature. And art. He was like my own personal encyclopedia. I loved getting his take on things, especially music. We'd sneak away for hours in his car, listening to everything from Coltrane to the Cure, dissecting lyrics and talking about who we wanted to see in concert.

David gestured to the books strewn about. "I swear, Patric," he said, doing his best to sound stern. "You better not keep any of these. I draw the line at stealing from libraries."

"Then you probably shouldn't look at my bookshelves at home," I muttered.

"You're such a paradox," he said.

I shrugged. "I don't know what that means."

He grinned widely, then leapt up and started singing. "A paradox! A paradox! A most ingenious paradox!"

I laughed. I knew it was from *The Pirates of Penzance*, his grandfather's favorite movie. They'd watched it many times, and David could recite every lyric, a quirky trait that was as adorable as it was annoying.

"You're not helping!" I shouted above his outburst.

"No, I am," he explained when I pulled him down next to me. "A paradox is when two conflicting ideas are both true. Frederick the pirate was twenty-one but he'd only had *five* birthdays."

"Huh?"

"He was born on February 29th. So, although he was *technically* old enough to leave his pirate indentures, he couldn't. Because the pirates only counted birthdays. And going by birthdays, he was only five . . . and a quarter."

I raised my eyebrows. "So I'm a five-year-old pirate?"

"Sort of!" David laughed. "Think about it. Everything about you is contradictory. You're warm and generous, but sometimes sharp and vicious."

I shrugged. "That's anyone."

"Maybe," he said. "But with you it's more extreme."

I heard a slight edge in his voice that made me uncomfortable. It reminded me of the tone my mother used to take when we lived in San Francisco, when I'd tell her the truth and she'd get mad. I studied David's face from the corner of my eye and shifted slightly on the blanket. "Oh," I said finally, as I struggled to work out a response. "Well, I can try to work on that."

As soon as the words left my mouth, I got annoyed. It was the same reaction I'd have as a child, when I thought I needed my mother's guidance to keep me in line. Back when I'd have done anything to keep the tether intact, even if it meant pretending to be something I wasn't.

What, exactly, am I supposed to "work" on? I raged inside. *Acting like everyone else?*

I shuddered just thinking about it. For the first time in my life, I *liked* being me—and not just on my own but around somebody else! I didn't want to change. And I certainly didn't want to have to pretend. Fortunately, David seemed to agree.

"Don't be silly," he said. "It's not a character flaw." He grinned. "You just gotta be careful with that pressure cooker of yours." He gently tapped my forehead. "Make sure you're the one who's in control."

I nodded, but found myself wondering, Am *I in control?* It was a question I'd had for years. Nobody was forcing me to do the things I did. Yet there were times I felt I couldn't resist. The pressure always seemed to find a way to build, and the only way to stop it was to . . . what? *Do the wrong thing*, I admitted silently. I recalled a magazine article I'd read about a kid with obsessive-compulsive disorder. People with OCD had uncontrollable thoughts and behaviors they felt compelled to do over and over. "Compelled" was the perfect word for how I felt. Only instead of washing my hands or counting sidewalk squares, I liked to follow strangers and break into houses. But so what? I reasoned. Wasn't it harmless? Wasn't my behavior, on some level, more or less the same as theirs? It certainly seemed so.

"OCD is a disorder over which the afflicted have very little control," the article had said. And I could relate. Even though I could theoretically prevent myself from doing bad things, I wasn't able to hold out for long. I, too, usually lost the battle. Just like I had one summer in Virginia.

We'd gone to visit my great-grandmother near Richmond shortly after Mom moved us to Florida. I'd been on my best behavior, still trying to toe the line with her. But nothing in our new surroundings ever felt quite right, and after we got to Virginia things didn't seem any better. My great-grandmother lived close to the beach where my mother had spent many months as a child. Her cottage was like a second home to Mom, and she was so relaxed and happy to be there. Everyone was relaxed and happy except me. I felt a growing tension, like a bomb waiting to explode.

There was nothing to do there, no adventures to take, no boundaries to push. The only activities were playing cards and walking to and from to the beach. There wasn't even a television to distract me from my growing restlessness. So when I took a walk one day and saw a cat lying in the sun by a deserted country road, I didn't think. I just grabbed it and pulled it into my chest like a mouse in a trap.

The cat struggled. It dug its claws into my arm and tried to bite my hand, but I wouldn't stop. I held its body in place with my knees, wrapping my hands around its throat. I tightened my grip. Watching as it squirmed and tried to cry for release, I slowed my breathing, just like the cat. Seconds passed. Time seemed to stop as I squeezed tighter and tighter. Then, abruptly, I let go. The cat pushed away from me, gasped for air, and took off running for the reeds that lined the road. I watched it leave, feeling euphoric. Then I sat there for a minute or two, basking in the glow of feeling, before finally acknowledging what I knew to be true.

"That," I said, "was not good." I stood up and stared at the tracks the cat had left as it ran, my thoughts drifting to the list I'd made. "No hurting anybody," I recalled. That rule had been intended for people, but I knew hurting the cat counted. A few years before, Mom had forced me and Harlowe to watch *Not My Kid*, a tragic movie about a kid who gets addicted to drugs. It starred Stockard Channing, my favorite actress, so I paid attention. At the time I didn't understand why Mom was so worried about us smoking pot or what a "gateway drug" was. But now it made sense. Violence of any kind was a slippery slope for me, and one that could potentially lead to real trouble. Not to mention I didn't particularly *want* to hurt animals. I knew I'd never do anything like it again.

I looked at my boyfriend now. *How would he react*, I wondered, *if I told him about the cat?* I decided I should find out. But just before I opened my mouth, David squeezed my hand.

"Can I tell you something?" he asked, his big brown eyes settling deeply into mine. I found myself nodding again.

"I love you," he said softly.

Those three little words took me by surprise. A tune from *Cinderella* sprang to mind. *So* this *is love*, I thought. Except it didn't feel transactional. Or conditional. Or dangerous or useless. This feeling was perfect—perfectly symbiotic in that I was simultaneously experiencing what it was like to care about someone not related to me and, by the grace of that connection, what it was like to care about myself. For the very first time.

"I love you, too," I heard myself saying. And I meant it. I *did* love him. David, a bastion of kindness and responsibility, was the perfect guy for me. He was the living embodiment of the conscience I imagined I was lacking. Better yet, he represented what I now realized I'd always wanted: a partnership with someone who accepted the person I was and encouraged me to be myself.

Understanding. Acceptance. Safety in honesty. I'd long yearned for these things, and now I had them. David filled in all of my blanks. He never gave me the *look*, and after a while I realized there was no pressure when we were together. I loved him more than I ever thought I was capable. The fact that he made me feel like I, too, could be worthy of love was really just a bonus.

I kissed him, a potent mixture of Trident and tobacco filled my mouth, and it struck me that I didn't need blueprints or darkness or the basement or anything else for that matter. In David's arms the only thing I felt compelled to do was . . . stay there.

And so I did. For the rest of that summer. I flourished in the shared experience of a relationship—and friendship! For the first time in my life, I didn't feel consistently devoid of emotion. Quite the contrary. I felt love! Without even knowing, David taught me how to adapt to things like communication and affection, concepts I imagined came easily to most people but not me.

David was very patient with my learning curve. Though he was several years older than me, he never once appeared to perceive it as any sort of impediment. He seemed to *like* being my boyfriend. Or so I thought.

On the last day of camp, I made my way into the kitchen. I'd stashed the blueprints I'd swiped from the director's office underneath the china cabinet. As I pulled them from their hiding place, I grinned, remembering the first time I'd seen them.

"You gonna put those back?" David called out unexpectedly from the doorway.

I smiled. "Yes," I replied dutifully. "I was going to on my way out."

He nodded and asked, "Is your mom almost here?"

I shrugged and rolled my eyes. He'd offered to drive me home but—to our chagrin—Mom wouldn't hear of it.

"You are a fourteen-year-old *girl*," she'd said, when I'd called to ask. "And he's what? Almost eighteen? Absolutely not."

I was disappointed. We'd spent nearly every day of the summer together. What was a measly car ride? But David understood, and—ever the gentleman—insisted on sticking around while I waited for her.

"Yeah, she'll be here soon," I said.

He looked down at the floor. I could tell he was sad.

"Hey," I said. "What's up with you?"

"What do you think?" he replied, a little too sharply. "I'm gonna miss you."

I gave him an exaggerated pout and crossed the room, wrapping my arms around his waist. "Awww," I purred. "But you don't live too far away. We'll still see each other all the time."

"Not really," he said.

"What are you talking about?" I asked. "You have a car."

"Yeah, a car your mom says you're never allowed to get in." He was quiet as we held the embrace. When I looked up at him I saw an expression that was somehow both sad and angry. "What's it matter anyway?" he asked. "We go to different schools. And next year I'll be in college." He shifted his weight and shook his head, as if trying to steady himself. "I mean, you're only in *junior* high . . ."

A familiar sense of unease crept into my chest. I pushed away from him. "Wrong," I snapped. "I'm about to start high school. And since when do you care about *that?*"

I was getting angry. We'd been together for weeks and David had never mentioned my age or the fact that we went to different schools. Now he was using it as justification for . . . what? Dumping me? It didn't make sense. Not knowing what else to do, I decided to switch tactics.

"Besides," I said, using my sexy *Moonlighting* voice, "you said you wanted to come explore my neighborhood."

It was a last-ditch effort to snap him out of whatever was bringing him down. For a moment it seemed to work. He started to smile and shifted his giant brown eyes up to look into mine.

"That does sound fun," he relented.

"See?" I replied, wrapping my arms once more around his waist. I kissed him softly on the cheek. "How am I supposed to stay safe without you around?"

One of the administrators poked her head into the room. "Hey!" she said sharply. "You lovebirds aren't supposed to be in here." She scowled at David. "Besides, Patric, your mom's here."

"I gotta go," he said quietly, and I knew my spell was broken.

"Wait," I said. I looked pleadingly to the administrator. "Can you give us, like, two seconds please?"

"You can have all the time you want in the lobby."

"No, it's okay," David interjected. He gave me a kiss on the cheek and whispered, "I'll see ya."

Then he walked out the door.

PART II

CHAPTER 7

Pops of Color

Streetlights reflected off black asphalt as I sped down Sunset Boulevard. Without the sun, the temperature had plummeted, and I was only wearing shorts and a T-shirt. But as I reached to turn up the heat, I realized I had no idea how to do it. The car wasn't mine.

I pulled over and scanned the dash until I found the temperature controls. I'd stolen the car several hours earlier and had been so busy zipping around the late-night streets of Los Angeles that I hadn't yet figured out the buttons. But now that the thrill of what I'd done was gone, I just felt cold—cold and detached and impatient.

The vents whirred when I found the right button. Hot air rushed through the slats, and I leaned back, grateful to be warm. The dashboard clock clicked to midnight and reminded me I was once again breaking dormitory curfew. I sighed and looked at the ceiling, wondering if I would ever care about the curfew, wondering if I would ever care about anything. The possibility, at least, was entertaining.

My mood began to rise along with the temperature. For a few minutes I simply sat there, parked in front of a CVS. On the passenger seat was the car owner's wallet. I grabbed it and chose one of the credit cards inside. Then I got out of the car and walked into the store, warming up again as my next adventure unfolded.

It had been six months since I'd left home for college, and nothing was going according to plan.

I'd decided to apply to UCLA during my junior year of high school.

"It's a bit late to apply to an out-of-state school," my guidance counselor, Mrs. Rodriguez, had snipped.

I was sitting across from the woman at her desk. Behind her was a framed poster of a man standing in front of several Lamborghinis. It was captioned "Justification for Higher Education," and I wanted to throw it out the window.

She looked at my grades and commented, "Out-of-state applicants are advised to start the process *early*."

I already hated Mrs. Rodriguez. Her preference for Easter-hued ill-fitting pantsuits notwithstanding, I could tell she was an aggressive rule follower. She was also deeply pessimistic, the worst possible combination.

"Actually," I said excitedly, "my dad lives in California. So I'll be considered in-state." I hadn't said this to be argumentative, but Mrs. Rodriguez looked like she wanted to slap me. She shifted in her seat and began to toy with a caterpillar-shaped rhinestone pin that gleamed hideously from her purple lapel.

"Well, I don't know about any of *that*," she remarked. "But I don't think there's any sense in applying to UCLA this late in the game, and certainly not when you've got so many excellent schools right in your backyard! After all, how would *you* feel if you found out a California student was applying to the University of Florida as an in-state candidate?" she asked.

I was one hundred percent certain I wouldn't care at all. Nor was I about to take life advice from a woman whose idea of "success" was serial purchases of outdated sports cars. But I wasn't going to get into that with Mrs. Rodriguez.

My choice to attend UCLA had nothing to do with academics and everything to do with distance. As a teenager approaching adulthood, I wasn't any closer to figuring out what made me so different. But worse, I hadn't been able to figure out less destructive ways of dealing with it. I knew I'd been lucky so far. Between late-night stalkings and empty-house explorations, I'd managed to find secretive outlets for my darkness throughout most of middle and high school. But the balancing act was difficult. In the small, conservative town where I lived, it was only a matter of time before my luck ran out.

What I need is a big city, I thought, imagining a place where invisibility wouldn't require constant effort, somewhere I could hide in plain sight. Then one night it occurred to me. *Los Angeles!* The city where my father now lived afforded me a luxury I'd only ever dreamed of: automatic obscurity. With its vast geography and millions of residents, I could be anyone I wanted in LA. I could blend in. I could disappear.

My mother wasn't thrilled with the idea of me moving all the way across the country for school. But, for multiple reasons, I was insistent. Although I loved my family, I knew I had to get away from them—for their sake as much as mine. This was particularly the case with my sister, whose ability to see through my "good girl" veneer had become a cause for concern.

"Look at this," she'd said to me one afternoon.

It was a Saturday, and we were in the den. Harlowe was on the couch drawing in her sketchbook while I played a video game. My sister loved to draw and had blossomed into an exceptional cartoonist. She slid her latest work in front of me, a character she'd created. In the center of the page, she'd drawn a large "A" and a masked female superhero wearing a cape. "CAPTAIN APATHY," it was captioned. "For Untruth, Injustice, and the Anarchist's Way."

I studied the image of the caped crusader and the words she'd added to the speech bubble above her head. "Never fear!" she said. "Captain Apathy doesn't care!"

"Whoa," I said quietly. I was uncharacteristically speechless. Harlowe grinned.

"It's you," she said proudly. "My favorite superhero, Kaat!" Then she skipped off happily into the kitchen to prepare her favorite snack, delicately microwaved Chips Ahoy! cookies. I sat there and stared darkly at the cartoon. I may not have known what made me so different from everyone else, but I *did* know that I was no superhero.

If anything, Harlowe was *my* superhero—a naturally good person. She didn't have any demons to slay or secrets to keep or destructive urges to navigate. It was almost as if, when we were born, I was accidentally given an extra dose of darkness. *Her* dose. Whereas I was gifted with a predilection for mischief, Harlowe was gifted with pure lightness. I'd always known the differences between us were stark, but Captain Apathy made it obvious I wasn't the only one who did.

Fortunately, college provided an ideal solution. If I moved away, I knew I would no longer have to worry about hiding from my mother or rubbing off on my sister. I could live life on my own terms. Without anything to rebel against, I wondered, would my destructive urges go away? I suspected they would.

Maybe then I could just be normal.

The words entered my consciousness one night like a lightning bolt and I couldn't chase them away. The idea of such a life—one not bogged down by dark urges or rising tensions—was never far from my thoughts. It was something I'd been cautiously wondering for as long as I could remember, but I'd always known better than to get my hopes up. Until then.

Maybe once I get to college, things will be different.

Initially that was the case. Life in Los Angeles was blissful, normal even. Dad picked me up at the airport the day I arrived, and we spent the following weeks exploring UCLA and getting me settled into my dorm. My room was on the second floor of a converted sorority house overlooking Hilgard Avenue. It had floor-to-ceiling French doors and a tiny decorative balcony, the only one in the house. I loved it.

I had the place to myself for the first few days. I'd been assigned a suitemate—her name was written in chalk next to mine on the door—but I had no idea who she was or when she was planning to arrive. As the days crept by, I held out hope she might never actually appear. But my dreams of solitary living were dashed when, the day before classes started, the door flew open and a stunning Chinese girl lugging several large suitcases stepped across the threshold.

"Hi, I'm Patric," I said carefully.

The girl stared at me with beautiful wide almond eyes. Then she reached into her enormous purse. After digging for several seconds, she found a small silver box roughly the size of a graphing calculator. It had a speaker on one end and a microphone on the other. She spoke quickly into the box, her Mandarin message converted to English by a monotone male voice that erupted forcefully from its speaker: "Nice to meet you I am Kimi."

"A translator!" I stared at the magic box. "You take this every-where you go?" The box communicated my message to Kimi, who nodded enthusiastically. Kimi was an international student. She'd never been to the United States and didn't speak English.

"Translator, yes," Kimi said. "Machine." She patted the box.

"Well, it's nice to meet you, Kimi," I said. Then I addressed the box, "And you as well, Machine."

A room with a view and a roommate who can't talk to me, I thought. Life couldn't have been more perfect. At first, I was happily over-whelmed with classes and coursework. I enjoyed being busy. When I wasn't studying or sitting in class, I was exploring the campus. My heavy course load, combined with the novelty of my environment, drained every ounce of my brainpower. Each night I collapsed into bed and fell into a deep sleep, only to wake the next morning refreshed and relaxed. It was wonderful. It was powerful. It was *normal*. But it didn't last very long.

After the first semester, things slowed down. No longer consumed by the busyness of acclimation, I found myself drawn into familiar feelings of restlessness and apathy. I could sense the mounting pres-sure and the acute stress that always seemed to accompany it. I still had my newfound freedom, but the peace was gone. Without enough to distract me, I realized that my destructive urges were still very

much present. And without the convenience of my childhood bedroom window, I again had to come up with creative outlets.

"Captain Apathy," I said.

I was leaning against the wall overlooking the quad outside my
dorm, waiting for the sun to set. Beneath me the hillside descended
along with most of the campus. I'd come to love this view, especially
in the late afternoon when the California sky turned everything blood
orange. Some guys were skateboarding on the landing below. I saw
one take a nasty fall and rip open his knee. Several bystanders rushed
to his aid and helped him to his feet. But I just stared.

"Never fear. Captain Apathy doesn't care," I whispered.

I sighed and tilted my face toward the disappearing light. *I'm a
paradox*, was all I could think. I didn't care about anything except the
fact that I didn't care. And *that* made me feel like finding someone to
stab. But at least now I had a better understanding as to why.

Intro to Psychology was my favorite class that first year. I'd always
struggled to understand my own antisocial behavior and thought taking the class might give me some insight. But just how *much* insight I
never could have imagined. Our professor was Dr. Slack, a psychologist I liked from the start. The class was a survey that started with
an introduction to the "normal" psyche. Most people, she taught us,
are born with a wide range of emotions, and an individual's mental
health and propensity for abnormal behavior are largely based on the
appropriateness of their emotional responses.

People who demonstrate extreme reactions and behaviors are
sometimes diagnosed as having a mental illness or personality disorder. But what's important is that these extremes extend in both directions. We learned that in addition to those who experience too *much*
emotion, there are others who experience too little. Their personality
types are not categorized by the presence of feeling but by its *absence*.
Not surprisingly, these were the personality types that interested me
the most.

"'Apathy' is another term for this lack of feeling," Dr. Slack told us. It was a month or so into class and we had ventured into the subject of antisocial psychology. "Apathy is the hallmark trait of many of the antisocial disorders," she said. "Take sociopaths, for instance." Dr. Slack paused and wrote the word on the chalkboard. "Sociopathy is a disorder characterized by a disinclination to empathize with others," she continued. "Psychologically speaking, sociopaths aren't well-versed in compassion. They don't experience guilt like everyone else. They don't process emotion like everyone else. They don't *feel* like everyone else. And it is this lack of feeling, many researchers believe, that causes them to behave aggressively and destructively. The sociopath's subconscious *desire* to feel is what forces him to act out."

I was spellbound. It was the first time I'd ever heard someone actually explain the term. Officer Bobby had used it to describe the men in his prison, and for nearly a decade I'd tried to find the definition. Over the years it had become a game. Whenever I came across a dictionary, I'd search for "sociopath." But every time I was disappointed. Either the word wasn't there or the definition offered no meaningful insight. It was like it didn't exist. But I always knew it was real. And, now, here it was.

Dr. Slack's lecture may as well have been about *me* as far as I was concerned, and I couldn't soak up the information quickly enough. Granted, I knew this was not a "normal" reaction. Most non-sociopaths, I understand now, would not be flooded with relief to find themselves identifying as one. But I was thrilled.

I'd always longed for some sort of evidence that I wasn't alone, validation that I wasn't the only person in the world who *didn't* feel things like everyone else. I'd always suspected, but now I knew for sure. There were enough people like me to justify an entire psychological category. And we weren't "bad" or "evil" or "crazy," we just had a harder time with feelings. We acted out to fill a void.

Suddenly it was all so simple. The *pressure* I'd experienced my entire life was most likely caused by my own subconscious drive for feeling. It wasn't some insurgent that needed to be eradicated.

It was more like a psychological software patch my brain applied to counteract my lack of emotion. My bad acts *were*, in fact, a type of self-preservation. They counteracted my apathy. My internal emotional world, like Harlowe's *Captain Apathy* sketch, was in black and white. Doing something I knew was morally unacceptable was a way to force a pop of color. I craved it. Which is why, on that night during my first year at UCLA, I found myself cruising the streets of Los Angeles in a stolen car.

The owner was a sloppy-drunk frat boy named Mike, heir to a potato chip dynasty. He was not my first victim. In the second half of that first year, going to fraternity parties and "borrowing" cars had become something of a go-to feeling-finder. Though the first time it happened had been entirely serendipitous.

I'd gone to a Saturday night mixer at the Sigma Phi Epsilon house a few weeks before Christmas break. I'd been feeling punchy. By then I understood the consequences of letting the pressure build unabated, and I was annoyed with myself for having let it fester for so long. So when I'd heard about the party from classmates, I agreed to meet them there. I rarely passed up an opportunity to attend a party, but not for reasons most would understand. College parties offered some of the best people-watching in town. These gatherings were a virtual master class in social interaction and featured every type of behavioral observation imaginable. Attending them was like getting a jolt of feeling by osmosis.

The bigger the party, the easier it was for me. I'd arrive and then disappear into a flood of strangers, reveling in my invisibility. Sometimes I'd find a chair in the corner and just sit. Other times I'd wander around. The partygoers, with their animated responses and emotional reactions, were wildly different from me—but so interesting. Watching them helped me identify the right facial expressions to use and the proper way to react to others, and all with minimal personal interaction. It was like being an emotional anthropologist.

After weeks of "partying" like this, I discovered something important: An internal emotion wasn't a requisite to produce an external reaction. I didn't need to *feel* something to react as if I did. As long as I could match the proper physical response to the proper circumstance, I could act like everyone else. I could *mimic* the correct behavior. It wasn't the first time I'd realized this. Growing up, I'd often looked to my younger sister for emotional cues. It's how I was able to (mostly) fly under the radar thus far, by playing the "good girl." By playing my sister. The problem was that this disguise never seemed to fit.

Harlowe, with her vast emotional depths and limitless empathy, was nothing like me. Adopting her personality was like wearing a dress that was two sizes too small. It was manageable for a little while, but not for long. What I needed was diversity, personality traits I could stitch together to create a bespoke psychological disguise. And now, finally, I had the material.

Going to college parties was like gaining access to an unlimited amount of fabric with which I could craft my disguise. I experimented with as many emotions as I could, then altered the most suitable ones to fit. Alone in my dorm, I practiced mannerisms I'd picked up from people I saw at parties. Once I had them perfected, I tested them on live subjects. The results were astonishing.

I learned that touching someone on the arm during a conversation quickly rendered them more comfortable. I also learned that starting any conversation with a compliment or an unexpected question was the easiest way to disarm a stranger. I began to implement these practices in my daily life and was astounded by the immediate difference. For the first time, people seemed to warm to me—*authentically*. That there was nothing authentic about *my* interactions didn't matter. Classmates were suddenly eager to chat me up around campus. Dormmates were stopping by my room to socialize. These changes, hardly noticeable to anyone else, were extremely powerful to me. They were like breadcrumbs, leading me down a path toward social inclusion.

To be clear, it wasn't approval that I craved. It was integration.

I didn't *want* to stand out in a crowd. My entire life, I'd wanted to disappear. But once I got to college, I realized I'd been going about it all wrong. The trick to going unnoticed was not to isolate but to infiltrate, to *assimilate*. By assuming the personalities of other people, I was no longer getting the *look*. Dishonesty, once again, had proven to be the safe choice. Hidden behind my personality fabrics, I was, for all intents and purposes, invisible.

This was a huge breakthrough. I hated that people always sensed I was somehow different. It made me more conspicuous. It made me easier to spot. But now I had the tools. Whatever it was about me that made others uncomfortable no longer mattered. I could simply distract them by impersonating them. It was like casting a spell. The second I'd meet someone new, I'd adopt their stance. Imitate their mannerisms. Copy their cadence. Find out their likes and dislikes, then project them as my own. The effect was like holding up a giant mirror. Men, women, old, young—it didn't matter. People were always charmed—not with *me*, but by my reflection of *them*. All I had to do was mimic behavior. Behavior I was observing—and also practicing—at various social gatherings.

Granted, my approach to the learning process had to be adjusted from time to time. At fraternity parties, for example, I learned that sitting in the corner, staring at people, and scribbling observations on a legal pad didn't exactly help my cause. Usually, the only reactions I'd observe from that viewpoint were ones of extreme discomfort. So instead of watching people where I could be seen, I sought out empty rooms where I could eavesdrop and/or observe unnoticed through a window or door. Eventually I began to rate frat parties based on the venue's layout. Rather than considering the physical attributes of their pledges, I ranked them on the sneak-factors of their common rooms. I knew that the Delta Tau Delta house, for instance, was older, larger, and set back from the road. This offered far more hiding opportunities than, say, the Pi Kappa Phi house, which was smaller and didn't have any ground-level exterior front windows. I even kept a list, noting the best places to hide next to the names of nearly every Greek house at UCLA.

My favorite spot was the dining room at Sigma Phi Epsilon. It had interior pocket doors with windows that allowed for mostly unrestricted views into the other common areas, as well as floor-to-ceiling glass sliders that looked out onto the backyard. As long as the doors were closed and the lights were off, I had two perspectives from which to watch people—for *hours*. The main reason I was so excited to attend the party that Saturday was because it was at the Sigma house. To me, people-watching from my hiding place sounded like a delightful way to spend an evening. As soon as I arrived, I made a beeline for the dining room to stake out my spot. But on the way there, I was knocked to the ground by a very drunk fraternity brother.

"Oh, no!" he stammered, regaining his balance and awkwardly trying to help me up. "I'm so sorry! Are you okay?"

"Yeah, it's no problem," I said, picking up my purse.

"I'm Steve," he said, his bleary eyes blinking slowly. Unlike most sober partygoers, I *did* enjoy interacting with drunk people. Their recollection of me the next morning would be hazy, at best. It was sort of like being a ghost.

Steve grinned and pointed an unsteady finger at my chest. "Hey." He paused. "Don't I know you?"

"No," I said, laughing.

"Yeah," he continued, as if I hadn't answered. "You're Sarah."

I said nothing and was momentarily stunned when he pressed his body to mine and my back against the wall of the hallway. Steve's lips grazed my ear. "Guess what?" he whispered. "I'm out of cigarettes. Go get us some," he mumbled, "and I'll owe you forever."

He took a clumsy step backward and pressed a set of keys into my palm. I stood there, unsure of what to do. Mistaking my confusion for reluctance, Steve nodded and waved a finger at me again in some unspoken understanding I had no part of.

"Right," he slurred, reaching into his pocket and handing me a thick wallet. "Gotcha. Get whatever you want," Steve said. He grinned and turned to stumble back down the hall toward the living room. There he collapsed onto a couch in a fit of semiconsciousness.

I looked at the keys and wallet in my hand. Only moments before I'd planned on spending the evening sitting alone in a dark room watching other people interact. And that was fine. But this was so much better!

It was easy enough to find the car. I raised the keys above my head and wandered the parking lot pressing unlock on the fob. Eventually the lights of Steve's Acura blinked from a corner parking space. I opened the door and tossed my purse and Steve's wallet inside. Easing myself into the driver's seat, I slipped the key into the ignition. I sat for a moment basking in my unexpected good fortune. Then I started to drive.

I took Sunset toward the beach and turned north along the Pacific Coast Highway, where I cruised next to the ocean for miles and miles. When I reached the mountains hugging the Malibu coastline, I took a right and crossed through Calabasas into the suburbs of the San Fernando Valley. I cruised along Ventura Boulevard for nearly an hour, then cut through the Hollywood Hills before making my way into the flats of Beverly Hills and back to the UCLA campus.

It was almost two in the morning when I finally stopped at a store. I figured it was the smart thing to do. I grabbed a sleeve of Starbursts and headed for the counter. The cigarettes were locked inside a glass cabinet behind the cash register. I asked the cashier for the brand that matched the empty packs I'd seen crumpled on the floor of the car and handed him Steve's credit card. I didn't think he would ask to see my ID, but to be safe I distracted him with some charm. I leaned forward and nonchalantly tapped the back of my hand against his wrist, staring him directly in the eye.

"What's the craziest thing you've seen, working here this late?" I asked, genuinely curious.

The clerk was caught off guard. "The craziest thing?" He ran the card through the scanner and handed it back to me, deep in thought. Then his face lit up. "One time I helped a lady get away from a guy chasing her," he said.

"Holy shit!" I said, truly surprised. "Good for you!" I grabbed the cigarettes and called, "Have a good night!" over my shoulder as I left.

A short time later, I carefully pulled the Acura back into its spot on fraternity row. I knew my adventure was over but couldn't bring myself to open the door. The vehicle felt like a decompression chamber. Driving around town in Steve's car was exhilarating—just the pop of emotional color I craved. I sat still in the darkness and noticed as all the feeling gradually dissipated. The effect relaxed me almost to the point of drowsiness. I settled into the seat. U2's *The Joshua Tree* played from Steve's CD player. I closed my eyes and quietly constructed my version of one of the verses.

"She will suffer the feeling thrill / She's running to stand still."

That's exactly what it felt like, as though my yearning to force a pop of color wasn't about emotion at all. Rather, it was designed to exhaust my experience of emotion so I could stand still—to experience apathy *without* pressure or stuck stress.

"So if right now I feel comfortably apathetic," I mused, "then what tips the scale? What causes it to become *un*comfortable?" I thought of how stuck stress always accompanied the pressure, and the claustrophobic type of anxiety it so closely resembled. Then I shook my head in mounting frustration. "How could someone feel anxiety and apathy at the same time?"

I was in too good a mood to think about it. Forcing these questions from my mind, I gazed drowsily out the window. I rested there contentedly for a few more minutes before finally pulling the keys from the ignition. I tossed them, along with the cigarettes and wallet, onto the passenger seat. Then I got out and walked back to my dorm, already thinking about how I could do it again. It didn't take long for me to concoct a plan.

That spontaneous joyride was the first of many. In the months that followed, I went on dozens of nocturnal trips—although after that they were decidedly more deliberate. I found that I wasn't as listless on days when I knew I'd soon be cruising the city in a car that wasn't mine. It wasn't so much the act itself but the anticipation of the thrill that made my pressure decrease.

Once I understood the driving force behind my compulsions—that, like Dr. Slack said, I was subconsciously motivated to do something, anything, to elevate my apathetic baseline—I was less concerned about them. They had become normalized. "Normalization is a therapeutic tool through which a state of mind or belief system previously thought of as anomalous or irregular is redefined as '<u>normal</u>,'" Dr. Slack explained, as she underlined the word on her chalkboard. "Normalizing mental disorders—specifically the various *symptoms* of mental disorders—is essential to counteracting the stigma associated with those symptoms and replacing it with knowledge, understanding and, eventually, acceptance."

This explanation resonated with me deeply and resulted in a critical shift in my own psychological awareness. Although I recognized that my destructive urges were not "normal" in the general sense, I learned they *were* typical for people like me.

So I'm not crazy, I thought.

The relief was both unexpected and overwhelming. Although I never let it dominate my consciousness, some part of me had always been uneasy with the differences of my personality type. The worst part was not understanding any of it, especially my destructive urges. Now that I had some idea of what provoked them, my reactions to them became much easier to manage. All I had to do was hold out for the weekend.

On Friday and Saturday nights, almost all of the UCLA Greek organizations would host massive parties along frat row. I'd wander the narrow street in search of the house with the loudest and most disorganized party. Then I would go inside, zero in on the drunkest resident, and find a way to deftly separate him from his car keys. Sometimes I'd drive fast, other times I'd drive slow. Some nights I'd travel far, other nights I'd only go a few blocks. The only consistent things about those trips were the relief that came from easing the stress of apathy and the comfort that came from the knowledge that I'd found a reliable, albeit temporary, solution.

I understood the potential consequences of my behavior. If caught in a purloined automobile, arrest and even jail time were very plausible outcomes. But I wasn't bothered. *That's the problem with people like me*, I thought, as I pulled a sleek BMW through the take-out lane of the Westwood In-N-Out Burger. *We don't care.* Incarceration wasn't something I feared; it was almost an incentive. I remembered how safe from themselves Officer Bobby's prisoners were. A short stint in lockup sounded interesting.

Without anything to stimulate me and no way to leave, I wondered, would I still crave emotional pops of color? Or would my black-and-white internal world become easier to manage? Part of me wanted to find out. However, I knew it wasn't likely I'd be caught. None of the guys would ever report their cars as stolen. In most cases the keys were given willingly, if not soberly. They were always too drunk at the time to even remember owning a car, much less notice it was gone. Even if one of them *had* realized their car was gone and that I had taken it, I already knew how I'd explain things.

"Here are your chips, handsome." I threw a bag of Doritos at my most recent victim, who was sprawled on top of a beanbag in the living room of his frat house. He opened his eyes and rubbed his forehead, trying desperately to focus.

"Hey, pretty," he mumbled, smiling. "Where'd you go?"

"To get you some chips, like you asked," I replied sweetly, and bent down to peck him on the cheek. "Here are your keys." I tossed them at him. "See ya later." As with every other unwitting victim, I had no interest in chatting with the boy. I was tired and relaxed from my night of joyriding. All I wanted was to head back to my dorm and go to bed. I managed to get out the door before he had a chance to catch me.

The night air was chilly but I didn't care. It reminded me of the time I walked home from the San Francisco slumber party. The streets were empty and the houses were sleepy. The night was full of possibilities.

When I got to my dorm, I bypassed the front door. I'd missed curfew, and after midnight all the exterior doors were locked. The only way to get in was to call the resident advisor. Naturally, I had no intention of alerting anyone to my nocturnal schedule. Before I'd left that night, I'd made other arrangements.

I always made sure the window in the maintenance closet at the back of the building was unlocked. I placed my hand on the glass and gave it a gentle push. Then I lifted the sash, hoisted myself onto the ledge, and crawled inside. The first floor was dark as I made my way to the stairs. Climbing quickly to the second level, I tiptoed across the landing to my room. Fluorescent panels flooded the hallway in harsh light and I opened the door as carefully as I could, not wanting to wake my roommate.

Kimi hated my late-night excursions. She had let me know on numerous occasions. She was a light sleeper, she'd explained through her translator. The slightest noise would wake her. Unfortunately, that was the least of my concerns that night. The hallway lights were stadium-grade compared to the darkness of our room. I didn't make a sound when I entered, but the aggressive overhead beams stormed in ahead of me, illuminating the room and jolting Kimi awake.

Her hands flew to her eyes as if they'd been burned. "Jesus," I said, making no secret of my disdain. "The drama."

I pulled the door shut and whispered several apologies as I climbed into my top bunk, but they fell on foreign ears. In the bed below, I could hear my roommate grumbling furiously in Mandarin as she tossed and turned. It made me smile.

Kimi, I knew, was going to request a meeting.

CHAPTER 8

Little Earthquakes

"You broke curfew you woke me up again this is inconsiderate," Machine said without inflection.

It was the day after my most recent joyride. Kimi and I were sitting across from each other at our desks. Machine occupied a neutral position on a chair between us. My roommate didn't like living with me, and I understood why. We were polar opposites. Kimi hated that I didn't seem to adhere to any moral code and that I repeatedly broke our dorm's many rules. Even minor infractions would send her into a fury. These tantrums would usually take place during "roommate chats" she insisted on having at least monthly. When Kimi wanted to have one of her meetings, she'd let me know by writing "TALK"— along with some options for dates and times—on a Post-it. Then she'd affix the note to my remote. This was almost always done while I was asleep.

Waking up to one of Kimi's Post-its was not unlike being visited by the Tooth Fairy. I positively lived for these talks, and not just because I was entertained by confrontation (although this was certainly the case). The main reason I loved our meetings was interacting with Machine. Because Kimi couldn't speak English (nor I Mandarin), the device became an unwitting mediator to our talks—and one that I'd decided was secretly on my side.

"I know," I replied earnestly, as I shifted slightly in my chair. "But it was unavoidable. I had to return the car I stole."

Kimi appeared confused by what the translator was reporting. She looked at Machine and then at me and then back at Machine. She shook her head and pointed to the list of dorm rules and regulations she kept taped above her desk, practically screaming in Chinese as she tried to get the conversation back on track.

"Midnight," said Machine evenly. "You arrived in dorm at three fifty-one you woke me up again I could not sleep you must do Greenpeace."

I rolled my eyes. It wasn't the accusation but her mention of the charity that irritated me. For some reason Kimi's chats often included a demand that I donate to one of the environmental organizations where she worked as a volunteer. It was her way of suggesting I needed to atone for my indiscretions.

"Fuck Greenpeace," I said quietly. Machine reported my sentiments back to Kimi, who reacted like I'd slapped her in the face. "Wait, no," I interjected, glaring at Machine. "I'm sorry, Kimi. I wasn't serious." The translator began to chirp my apologies, but Kimi wouldn't hear it. She covered her face with her hands and shook her head back and forth.

"WHY DON'T YOU CARE?" she exclaimed.

I was taken aback. Not only had she uttered the sentence in English, but she'd said it directly to me. I was momentarily speechless as Machine shouted Kimi's own words back to her in Mandarin.

"It's okay, Machine," I interrupted. "Take it easy."

Machine began to chirp again and I tried not to laugh. I loved making Machine speak in the third person, even if I couldn't understand it.

"Look, I'm really sorry," I said, once Machine was finished. "I didn't mean to wake you up. I won't come in late anymore. At least, not on weekdays. I promise. I mean it."

Kimi seemed pacified by what I was certain was a markedly softer tone exhibited by Machine as it translated my attempt at sincerity. She exhaled dramatically.

"Do you believe me?" I asked.

Kimi nodded upon hearing Machine's translation. Confident the meeting was over, I stood to shake her hand. But Kimi gently grabbed my arm. She stared at me, eyes wide and imploring.

"Why don't you care?" she asked again.

To hear it spoken aloud—now twice—the question I'd asked myself a thousand times was strangely ominous. The room seemed to shrink, and I slowly shook my head. I wanted the answer more than she did.

"I—I don't know," I stammered. It was the truth.

Kimi nodded in an unexpected display of compassion. She squeezed my arm affectionately, then stood and gestured to the clock. "It's dinnertime," Machine translated for her. "Will you join me?"

I nodded, grateful for the change in subject. "Sure," I said. "Just let me get changed."

Kimi pointed down, indicating she would meet me in the lobby. Then she picked up Machine and left.

Engulfed by the silence, I felt grateful to be in sync once again with my environment. The balcony doors were open, and a beam of sunlight bathed the room. I watched as dust motes passed through the light and sparkled like diamonds. Apathy, too, washed over me and I allowed it. The effect was hypnotizing.

"Why?" I wondered aloud. "Why don't you care?"

It was time to find out.

The next day I paid a visit to the psychology section of the UCLA library. "I'd like to see everything you have on sociopathy, please," I told the librarian.

The woman looked disappointed after typing the word into her computer terminal. She had shocking red hair and wore a wrap dress that matched a pair of long, dangly earrings. A name tag on her lapel read "Shelly."

"I don't think we have much on sociopathy," she said. "It's sort of an outdated term." She stood and motioned me to follow as she walked back to a large stack of books on the far wall. "In fact," she said, "I'm not even sure it's in the DSM."

"What's the DSM?" I asked, trotting alongside.

Shelly stopped to pick up a large tome from one of the shelves. She leafed through its pages. "The *Diagnostic and Statistical Manual of Mental Disorders*," she told me. "It's basically the bible of psychology. Doctors use it for assessments. Insurance companies use it to bill for treatment. Every mental disorder you can think of is in this book, along with descriptions and diagnostics." Shelly frowned after scanning the book's index. "But not sociopathy."

I stared at the tiny print. Once again, I saw where the word *should* have been—right between "social phobia" and "somatization disorder"—but it was missing. "Just like the dictionaries," I muttered.

Shelly looked up. "Huh?"

"The word 'sociopath,'" I said. "It's not even in some dictionaries."

"Really?"

"Really. But the word obviously exists, right? I mean, we just had a lecture on it in my psych class."

"It definitely exists," Shelly said, nodding. She ran a hand across several books before pulling another copy of the DSM from the shelves. "This is an older edition. I bet it's in here." She scanned its index, then flipped the pages until she found it. "Yup." She handed the open book to me.

"Sociopathic Personality Disturbance" gleamed in bold black print at the top of the page and I looked at Shelly, confused. "So it *used* to be in the DSM, but now it's not?" I shook my head. "Why would they take it out?"

"It was replaced with 'antisocial personality disorder,'" she replied. "But I don't think the diagnostic criteria are the same." Shelly pointed to an empty table. "Have a seat," she said. "I'll see what else I can find."

I sat down, set the open book in front of me, and began to read.

This term applies to individuals who manifest disregard for the usual social codes, and often come in conflict with them, as the result of having lived all their lives in an abnormal moral environment. They may be capable of strong loyalties. These individuals typically do not show significant personality deviations other than those implied by adherence to the values or code of their own predatory, criminal, or other social group.

I took a short inhale. The description may as well have had my picture next to it. But what did it mean? Was I really a sociopath? I'd suspected as much. But now that I had an actual definition, what was I supposed to do about it? My mind was racing with the implications of my self-diagnosis when Shelly returned with another book. "*The Mask of Sanity*," I said, reading the cover. It had been written by a University of Georgia psychiatrist named Hervey Cleckley in 1941.

"I'm still looking," said Shelly, "but check this out." She opened the book to a section near the back. "This one's technically about *psycho*-paths," she said, "but the checklist inside is used a lot for sociopaths. They're sort of the same."

"Wait," I said shaking my head. "So psychopaths, sociopaths, and antisocial people are all lumped together?"

"I'm not really sure," replied Shelly.

"But antisocial personality disorder is the only one in the diagnostic manual."

"The current edition, yes." She set the latest DSM on the desk. "I grabbed it for you."

I looked at the thick manual. "This thing is huge."

"Well, it covers hundreds of mental disorders. Plus, there's a glossary."

"But nothing about sociopaths," I said.

The librarian frowned. "It is strange, I'll admit." She pointed to *The Mask of Sanity*. "Start with this, and I'll keep looking."

Shelly left me alone with the new book. On top of one page about psychopathy, the words "Clinical Profile" were printed in bold. Beneath them was a list of personality characteristics. I scanned the list quickly, my confusion growing with each tinge of familiarity.

1. Superficial charm and good intelligence.
2. Absence of delusions and other signs of irrational thinking.
3. Absence of nervousness or psychoneurotic manifestations.
4. Unreliability.
5. Untruthfulness and insincerity.
6. Lack of remorse or shame.
7. Inadequately motivated antisocial behavior.
8. Poor judgement and failure to learn by experience.
9. Pathologic egocentricity and incapacity for love.
10. General poverty in major affective reactions.
11. Specific loss of insight.
12. Unresponsiveness in general interpersonal relations.
13. Fantastic and uninviting behavior, with drink and sometimes without.
14. Suicide rarely carried out.
15. Sex life impersonal, trivial, and poorly integrated.
16. Failure to follow any life plan.

"What the hell?" I wondered aloud. These traits were even *more* descriptive of me. Did that mean I was a psychopath . . . or a sociopath? None of this made sense. What was the difference? I returned to the current version of the DSM and found the section on antisocial personality disorder. The delicate pages made sharp snapping sounds as I turned them.

"Diagnostic Criteria for Antisocial Personality Disorder," I read. "A pervasive pattern of disregard for and violation of the rights of others occurring since age 15 years, as indicated by three (or more) of the following:"

1. Failure to conform to social norms with respect to lawful behaviors as indicated by repeatedly performing acts that are grounds for arrest

2. Deceitfulness, as indicated by repeatedly lying, use of aliases, or conning others for personal profit or pleasure

3. Impulsivity or failure to plan ahead

4. Irritability and aggressiveness, as indicated by repeated physical fights or assaults

5. Reckless disregard for safety of self or others

6. Consistent irresponsibility, as indicated by repeated failure to sustain consistent work behavior or honor financial obligations

7. Lack of remorse, as indicated by being indifferent to or rationalizing having hurt, mistreated, or stolen from another

Shelly was right, I thought. Antisocial personality disorder *was* different from sociopathy, at least based on its diagnostic list. Certainly there were similarities between the two, but the criteria for each was distinctive. While I could easily identify with most of the traits on the sociopathic and psychopathic checklists, I was only able to relate to about half of the antisocial ones.

So why? I wondered. What was the point of replacing sociopathy with antisocial personality disorder if the two aren't diagnostically the same? *Why isn't sociopathy in the manual? And* how *are sociopaths different from psychopaths?* I sat there wondering where I might find the answers. Then it dawned on me.

Dr. Slack. She taught a course about psychology. At the very least she could point me in the right direction.

Scooping up the books, I walked back to the information counter, where Shelly sat preoccupied behind the desk. "Hey," I said, setting the books on the ledge. "Thanks for getting these for me. I'll probably be back. I just want to run a few things by my professor."

The librarian shook her head slowly, then gave me a confused look. "It's the craziest thing," she said. In front of her were several old dictionaries. "'Sociopath,'" she said. "You were right. I can't find the definition anywhere."

The following week I made an appointment to meet with Dr. Slack. Her small, cozy office was located on the ground floor of the psychology building.

"Thanks for coming in, Patric," she greeted me warmly. "How can I help you?"

"First of all," I said, returning the smile. "I loved your lecture on sociopathy. It was fascinating. In fact, I've decided to write my term paper on it."

The compliment, although calculated, was sincere. I liked Dr. Slack, and I enjoyed the feeling I got from letting her know, as if I was peeking out from a hiding place. "The problem is, I'm having trouble narrowing my focus. The research on sociopaths is extremely limited. I went to the library and they told me it isn't even in the DSM anymore."

"That's right," she confirmed. "They replaced it with antisocial personality disorder."

"But why? If the diagnostics aren't the same?"

She nodded appreciatively and leaned back in her chair. "It's a good question," she said, a hint of surprise in her voice. "Why don't you tell me what *you* think?"

I reached into my bag and pulled out the DSM I'd lifted from the library. "Here," I said, opening the book. "These are the diagnostics for antisocial personality disorder, right? But look at them." Dr. Slack scanned the page.

"The only one based on *personality* is lack of remorse," I continued. "Everything else is *behavioral*. Failure to conform to social norms, deceitfulness . . . all of these are about behavior."

"So?" she asked.

I tipped my head forward, as if the answer was obvious. "So it seems unreliable. Like, how do we know all sociopaths act like that?"

"Well," she said, after a significant pause, "having an antisocial personality diagnosis doesn't automatically mean that someone is a sociopath. It's more of an indicator. Most psychologists agree that an antisocial personality assessment is only the first step in diagnosing someone as a sociopath."

"But that doesn't make any sense," I said, shaking my head.

"Why not?"

I took a deep breath. "Because," I said, "in order to be diagnosed as antisocial, you need to have been labeled a criminal, and at a very young age. You have to have been arrested or been expelled from school, not just once but multiple times. It says so right here." I pointed to the book. "There has to be evidence of conduct disorder. But in order to have evidence of conduct disorder, you have to get *caught* exhibiting bad conduct."

"Right," said Dr. Slack.

I threw out my hands. "Well, what about the ones not getting caught?" I asked. "What about sociopaths who are more disciplined? Better at controlling themselves?" When she didn't answer, I continued, "You're telling me the only way to get diagnosed as a sociopath is to first be diagnosed with conduct disorder?" I frowned. "That doesn't make sense," I said again. "That would mean all sociopaths would have criminal records, and there's no way that's true."

Dr. Slack thought about this, then nodded in agreement. "It's an interesting observation."

I pulled some notes from my bag. "You said in class that many mental disorders are diagnosed on a spectrum, right? I wrote it down. Like autism? Some cases are more extreme than others?"

"Right."

"Well, what if sociopathy is like that, too?" I asked. "What if only a handful of sociopaths are the extreme type, the ones getting arrested and expelled?"

"Sociopathy as a spectrum disorder?"

"Yes."

"It's a unique theory," she said, smiling. "At the very least I think we've narrowed the focus for your paper."

Only I wasn't done. "And what about this?" I said. Again, I reached into my bag. I took out *The Mask of Sanity* and flipped to the list of traits I'd read in the library. "This book is about psychopaths," I said, tapping the page. "But the librarian told me these traits are used to diagnose sociopaths."

"Yes," said Dr. Slack. "That's true."

"So I don't understand," I said. "What's the difference?"

"Biology," she told me. "At least, that's what many researchers think. Psychopaths are believed to suffer from brain abnormalities. It's why they make the same mistakes over and over. They are biologically incapable of learning from punishment or understanding remorse or even experiencing anxiety. But sociopaths are believed to be different. While their *behavior* is often just as bad as psychopaths', they appear to be more capable of evolution. Their issues seem to be more environmental than biological." Dr. Slack shrugged. "At least, that's one of the theories. But there's a lot of disagreement in the field."

"Well, have you ever read anything about sociopathic pressure?" I asked. "Because I read somewhere that sociopaths experience this feeling of tension," I lied, "like a pressure rising. And the only way for them to make it stop is to do something bad."

Dr. Slack reached for a pen. "That's fascinating," she said. "Where did you read that?"

"I don't remember." I shrugged. "I just thought it made sense. Maybe this pressure is the same as that subconscious drive you discussed in class, that it's caused by a sociopath's desire to feel. If that's the case, then it makes sense that the destructive behavior of a sociopath might be motivated in the same way as the repetitive behavior of someone with OCD." I paused and asked, "Don't you think?"

"You know, now that you mention it, I'm positive I've read research on sociopathy and increased anxiety," she said. "Something like that could make for a fascinating study. It would be interesting to know whether there is a correlation to destructive acts."

Stuck stress, I thought.

"But, again," she added, "anxiety would most likely only be present among sociopaths—not psychopaths. We think psychopaths aren't capable of psychoneurotic manifestations. At least, according to Cleckley's list."

"So how can you tell whether someone is a sociopath or a psychopath?" I tentatively asked. "Is there a test or something?"

The professor nodded. "Yeah," she said. "Clinicians use the PCL if they think they're dealing with a psychopath."

"What's that?"

"The psychopathy checklist, sometimes called the 'psychopath test.'" She pointed to *The Mask of Sanity*. "The criteria is based on that book, actually. Lack of remorse is an obvious indicator. But social emotions play a key part as well."

I furrowed my brow, confused. "What do you mean?"

She stood and crossed to one of the bookcases that framed her desk. "Do you remember in class when we talked about Plutchik? And the primary emotions?"

I did. Robert Plutchik was a psychologist who identified eight fundamental feelings he termed the "primary" emotions: anger, fear, sadness, disgust, surprise, anticipation, trust, and joy. I recalled the day we learned about them. I'd written them on a piece of paper and later forced myself to match an experience of my own to the corresponding feeling. In the end, when I was able to successfully complete the entire list, I'd felt relieved.

"Yes," I said, nodding. "Everyone is born with a set of basic emotions."

"Right," she continued. "Even psychopaths. These emotions are automatic, inherent." Dr. Slack selected a binder and returned to her desk. "But there is another set of feelings that is *not* inherent." She set the binder down in front of me, gesturing to the open page. "Empathy, guilt, shame, remorse, jealousy, even love—these are considered social emotions," she said. "We're not born with them. They're learned."

"Okay . . ."

"Well, sociopaths and psychopaths both struggle to connect with the social emotions," she said. "Some researchers believe they aren't capable."

"Wait," I interrupted. "Aren't capable or are limited?" I shifted in my seat, eager to ask the right questions. "You said sociopaths *don't* have the same biological limitations as psychopaths," I pressed. "So, could it be that sociopaths aren't *in*capable, but just have a harder time? Like an emotional learning disability?"

"Emotional learning disability?" Dr. Slack gave me a quizzical glance. "Where did you hear that?"

"Nowhere. I just . . . I figure if there's nothing *physically* wrong with sociopaths, then maybe their problems are related to learning. Like dyslexia, but with feelings."

"It's definitely a unique take," mused Dr. Slack, "but I'm not sure it matters with regards to treatment."

"What do you mean?" I asked. "Why not?"

Dr. Slack leaned forward slightly. "Human beings have a hard time living without access to emotion," she said. "Apathy has an apparently profound, although dramatically under-examined, impact on the psyche." She tilted her head. "Think about it: What happens when a brain—which has evolved over millions of years to thrive based in no small part on its ability to acknowledge and feel emotions—cannot access or interpret them? It must be frustrating, like phantom limb syndrome."

"I don't follow."

"It's something that frequently occurs with amputees," she explained, "a sensation coming from a part of the body that's no longer there." She waited for me to make the connection before continuing.

"Sociopaths aren't missing a limb, but we think the neural pathways that handle processing the more complex emotions are somehow misconfigured. It's as if the emotions are there, just a little bit out of reach." The professor raised her eyebrows. "Wouldn't that be as maddening as trying to scratch a foot that isn't there?"

I nodded slowly as my thoughts drifted to the pressure I'd experienced my whole life. "Maddening," I said.

"Psychopaths and sociopaths are in the same boat because they're constantly looking for a way to connect those pathways. To *feel*. It's why they behave so destructively. It's why they're so dangerous. Eventually, the constant weight of apathy becomes too much to take."

"And then what happens?"

Dr. Slack frowned. "They snap."

Later that night, I sat alone and motionless at my desk. It had been hours since I'd returned from meeting with Dr. Slack and the sun had long since disappeared behind the west hills. Streetlights from the avenue below bathed the room in shadows as I stared blankly though the glass panes of my balcony doors. I felt hopeless.

I stood and walked to the doors, pulling them open. The balcony was decorative—barely a foot wide—and yet I stepped forward, grasping the rail with my hands and squeezing my foot onto the ledge.

A cool breeze whipped my hair and, while I stood there, I became aware that my hopelessness was transforming into something more familiar.

"Surrender," I whispered.

However actively I was experiencing it, I was also separated from it. Detached and attached at the same time. It was the way I'd felt after I'd locked the girls in the elementary school bathroom. That experience had always made me curious. Just how far could I go with such detachment? I had a sneaking suspicion I already knew. I could snap.

I'd always known I was capable of violence, and—worse—that I was internally rewarded for it. I'd known it ever since the day I'd stabbed Syd and felt that rush of feeling course through me. The temptation to hurt was always there, a blinking cursor on a computer screen waiting for input. But, like with the cat in Virginia, I'd always pushed back. I'd always resisted because I'd always had hope. But Dr. Slack had said there was no hope.

So what if that's true? I wondered. *What then?*

Dr. Slack was right. This life—this endless quest for feeling against the crushing weight of apathy—was exhausting. It reminded me of the title of one of my favorite albums: *Little Earthquakes* by Tori Amos. That's what my behaviors were, little earthquakes, generated to relieve pressure and prevent "The Big One." Normalization or not, the management of my "symptoms" was a continuous balancing act of light and dark that needed constant discipline, and I wasn't sure how long I could do it if there was no hope.

Everyone else had access to hope. Schizophrenics, alcoholics, bipolar depressives—there were treatment plans and support groups for all of them. The DSM was full of mental disorders and personality types, all of which included specific information and diagnostic insights, no matter how strange. There was even a term for people who compulsively ate things like couch cushions or paper clips. We'd learned about it in class. It was an eating disorder called pica and it had its own 1-800 number. But sociopaths?

"Nothing," I whispered to myself.

I'd gotten my wish. I was invisible, at least as far as my diagnosis was concerned. But I was also alone. While my dormmates were in class, I was breaking into their rooms and rifling through their belongings to see what secrets they were keeping. While my "girlfriends" were going on dates, I was stealing cars. *Is this all there is for me?* I thought helplessly.

My destructive urges hadn't gone away when I got to college. The pressure and the stuck stress hadn't receded. I was no closer to "normal." If anything, my problems had become magnified. Was this all I had to look forward to for the rest of my life? Intimate isolation and a steady increase of amoral behavior just to keep more dangerous impulses at bay? All the books in the library pointed to antisocial behavior as a symptom of my personality type, but none of them explained why. *Why* was I superficially charming and prone to lying?

Why did I feel the constant pressure to do bad things, and *why* was there so much stress attached to that pressure? *Why* did unacceptable behavior restore my internal equilibrium? *Why* was I so frequently apathetic?

The researchers and psychologists responsible for the diagnostics hadn't provided a single theory to explain the apathy. Did they not know? Did they even *want* to know? Was their decision to remove sociopathy from the reference books the only evidence I needed that my personality type was a lost cause? I was nauseous just thinking about it.

I fixed my gaze on the ground, then adjusted my grip on the railing and swung my legs over it so my body was on the other side. My arms stretched behind me as I leaned forward. I didn't know where my apathy ended any more than I knew where it began. But I knew where it would take me, certainly if I ever gave in to one of my more violent impulses. It would be no little earthquake, that I knew for sure. When it was all over, after the blood had settled and the rush of feeling was gone, it was likely that I would either be dead or in jail. Either way, though, I would no longer have to fight.

"Fuck it," I said.

I let go of the railing and for a second I was weightless. An eternity of stillness flashed across my consciousness before gravity took hold, and I started to fall. Although it was brief in reality, the descent seemed to take a lifetime. The street below rushed toward me. Instead of bracing myself for impact, I simply closed my eyes.

So be it, I thought. And then I hit the ground.

Directly beneath the balcony was a small patch of grass that separated the concrete walkway from the carport. I landed with a thud, the sod absorbing most of the shock and knocking the air out of my lungs. I rolled from my chest onto my back to catch my breath. Staring up at the stars from my now horizontal position, I shook my head at the absurdity of my dramatic display. I hadn't even broken a nail.

"Jesus Christ," I said, struggling to sit up. Then I remembered *The Mask of Sanity*, and a certain trait on its checklist:

14. Suicide rarely carried out.

I took a deep breath and lay still for a few minutes, surrendering to the mediocre predictability of what I'd done. After a while a car sped by, and I came to my senses. I collected myself, stood up, and walked to the back of the building, shaking my head at my ridiculous behavior. I found the maintenance window and pushed it open. Lowering myself inside, my internal climate returned to its all-too-familiar state of ambivalence. Only this time, I didn't fight it. *So maybe I am a sociopath*, I thought, as I stood inside the closet and closed the window behind me. *Maybe I'm a psychopath. Maybe I'm destined to spend the rest of my life dealing with earthquakes.*

I emerged from the maintenance room and strode down an unlit corridor. *Maybe I'll have to work a little harder to do the right thing.* I climbed the stairs to my floor. *Maybe I won't get to live a normal life with normal people in a normal house doing normal stuff. Maybe I won't get to make "meaningful relationships."*

I reached the top of the landing and marched to my room, unlocking the door with a spare key I kept hidden on top of the doorframe. *Maybe I won't experience college the way I'm "supposed" to.*

I stepped inside. The stillness of the room was as thick and soothing as a healing balm. I focused on the open French doors framing the balcony. They seemed less hopeless than they had a few minutes ago. *Maybe I won't experience anything the way I'm supposed to.* I walked to the ledge and stepped outside again. I caught a glimpse of my reflection in the window and paused for a second, staring at the girl on the other side. "So what?" I asked her.

If no one else can figure out what sociopathy is, then I'll figure it out for myself. "And if that makes me hopeless and tired or if that makes me a lonely little sociopath . . ." My voice trailed off. I stared into the sky and smiled.

So be it.

CHAPTER 9

Prescription

A few months later, I finished my first year at UCLA.

"You should come home," my mother had urged over the phone.

I'd wanted to. After all, I would have nowhere to live when the dorms closed for the summer, and it had been a long time since I'd seen her or Harlowe. But with the seriousness of my behavior at the front of my mind, I knew it wasn't a good idea.

I need to learn more, I thought, *so I can get myself under control.*

Instead, I decided to move in with my dad. His Coldwater Canyon Cape Cod–style house was the most logical solution. With its tall white gates and sparkling backyard pool, I found peace there, safe inside my own secret fortress. At least, I did at first. But—just as it had shortly after I arrived at school—my restlessness quickly returned.

I should get a job, I thought one afternoon, as I eyed the set of keys my neighbors had dropped next to their car, *so I don't wind up in jail.* It wasn't the first time I'd considered it. Summer break stretched from June until September, a veritable workshop of idle hours my devil side wanted nothing more than to get her hands on. These long months, with their lack of structure and responsibility, represented a cornucopia of potential disasters for someone like me. And I needed to set some guardrails.

Although my meeting with Dr. Slack had been initially disheartening, it resulted in an unexpected resolve. The day after the balcony incident, I returned to the library. But that time I stayed for hours, poring over every psychology book and research study I could find related to sociopathy.

Days spent in the library after school turned into weeks as I marveled at the dearth of resources available to sociopaths. Much of the information I found was disappointing. Descriptions of the disorder were vague at best and misleading at worst. Mass media references rubber-stamped sociopaths as loathsome villains with few exceptions. Some even promoted sociopathic isolation, an argument I found to be particularly dangerous. "These people should be avoided at all costs," one infuriating magazine article stated.

Where are sociopaths supposed to go for help? I wondered. These were human beings after all. They were people who desperately needed treatment. Yet most of the literature depicted them as monsters who should be banished. Pop culture, primarily based on sensationalized composites and secondhand stories, repeatedly described sociopaths as "evil," "terrible" people. They were said to have no conscience. They were said to have no soul. The books I found said sociopaths couldn't be treated and couldn't be controlled. They were completely unpredictable, unemotional, and dangerous to society. They lacked self-awareness and the capacity for emotional development.

But the data told a different story. Deep in the research racks I found multiple studies indicating that all sociopaths were *not*, in fact, monsters hell-bent on destruction. Rather, they were people whose default temperament made the learned social emotions—like empathy and remorse—more difficult, but not impossible, to internalize. This made sense to me based on my own experience.

Everything I read indicated I was a sociopath. I was lacking in empathy. I was fluent in deceit. I was capable of violence without remorse. Manipulation came easy. I was superficially charming. I engaged in criminal behavior. I struggled with connecting to emotions. I never felt guilty. And yet I knew I wasn't the monster the media described. I also recognized that my symptoms didn't *exactly* match those on Cleckley's psychopathy checklist.

"Unreliability" and "failure to follow any life plan"—numbers

four and sixteen on the list—were supposedly universally charac-
teristic of the sociopathic personality. But they couldn't be applied
to me. I was incredibly reliable when I wanted to be. I was a decent
student and had been rigorously disciplined when it came to getting
into UCLA. Yes, I was frequently untruthful and insincere (number
five). I also lacked empathy and could tell I wasn't working with a
full emotional deck. But that was the point. I *noticed* these things. I
was aware. I didn't experience any "specific loss of insight" (number
eleven). That meant I was not only capable of self-awareness but also
of evolution, other developmental milestones the literature said sociopaths couldn't experience.

Something was wrong. From where I stood, the research was
woefully inadequate. If everyone was using Cleckley's psychopathy
checklist to diagnose sociopathy, too, it could only mean that important nuances were being overlooked. Determined to get to the bottom
of it, I began spending nearly all my free time researching sociopathy in an attempt to better understand myself, to normalize myself.
Eventually the seeds of this self-normalization became more firmly
planted as I came to realize—not just anecdotally but empirically—
that I wasn't "wrong" or "bad," just different. Like Jessica Rabbit.
And nowhere was this distinction more important than in my understanding of love.

According to number nine on Cleckley's list, psychopaths had
an "incapacity for love," which was a tough pill to swallow. My lack
of any meaningful relationships to date (outside my family), sadly
seemed to indicate that this trait might apply to me. But when I started
to really think about it, I knew it couldn't be. *What about David?* I
wondered.

I remember the night I realized this and the flood of relief that followed. It was a few weeks before spring break. I'd been sitting in my
dorm reading a book about psychopaths, when suddenly it struck me.

"DAVID!" I shouted.

I slammed my hand down on the desk, startling Kimi, who'd just
returned from a shower. She stared at me.

"David!" I said again. I jumped up and rushed to her, putting my hands on her still-damp shoulders. "David was my boyfriend! And we were in love! *Really* in love!"

I was laying it on thick, the intensity of my outburst more than slightly exaggerated. I loved making Kimi freak out. Something about it delighted me past the point of rational thought.

"That sounds nice," Kimi said.

In the months since our first meeting, my roommate had become better at communicating in English. To my disappointment, she had even stopped using Machine, insisting, as she put it, on "full immersion" whenever she was at the dorm. She still wasn't entirely comfortable with the language, of course. Or with me, for that matter. Kimi's eyes darted back and forth, as if hoping to find something in the room to hit me over the head with. Meanwhile, I cupped her face in my hands.

"Don't you understand what this means?" I whispered. "Psychopaths aren't capable of love. But *I* was in love once. That means I'm definitely *not* a psychopath." I paused for effect. "It's a big deal."

Kimi swallowed hard and nodded. "That sounds nice," she said again. Then she retreated into the back of her side of the closet, where she liked to go when she felt "overwhelmed."

"David," I said again, after she'd disappeared behind several winter coats, "is all the proof I need."

This realization filled me with hope. That I had once been in love was evidence that I was capable of learning the social emotions. The relationship may have been short-lived, but it had happened. The emotions had been real. They still were. Despite the distance and time that had passed, my feelings for David had never diminished. I liked thinking about him. I liked talking to him. It made me feel normal. Which is why I never lost touch with him.

The first time I'd called, it was on a whim—a spontaneous chat a few months after summer camp to see what he'd been up to. I figured we'd only talk for a few minutes. But we didn't. That first phone call lasted hours. After that we talked all the time. David was the only person in the world with whom I felt I could be simultaneously honest and safe. This, for me, was a coveted dynamic. It reminded me of those early years in San Francisco, when I'd sit under the table and happily confess secrets to my mother. That type of safety had long been abandoned, traded—with good reason—for the protection afforded by deception. But what I gained in security I lost in companionship. It was isolating. And a part of me yearned to be *seen*, to experience safety through the lens of authenticity. That's why I loved talking to David. I never lied to him.

"Guess what," I said later that night. "I'm not a psychopath!"

He laughed. "Are you sure about that?" he said. "Let me talk to Kimi."

"Stop," I said. "This is important," I told him, explaining my most recent revelation.

"I'm confused," he admitted when I was done. "If sociopaths and psychopaths are so different, why do they always get lumped together?"

I'd had the exact same question. And the answer, I theorized after a few more trips to the library, was (once again) because of the literature. The standard books on sociopathy and psychopathy weren't uniform in their distinctions. One book would claim the two were the same. Another would say they were different. There was no consistency. The field of psychology had a habit of changing the names of mental disorders when they became tainted by slang-appropriation. Terms like "mental retardation" and "multiple personality disorder," for example, were replaced with "intellectual disability" and "dissociative identity disorder" to minimize the stigma attached to them. The problem is that updating terminology to fit the times, while well-intentioned, seriously complicates scientific research on these topics.

The word "sociopath" was popularized in 1930 by the psychologist G. E. Partridge, who defined the disorder as a pathology involving the inability to conform behaviorally to prosocial standards. In other words, these are people who don't act in ways beneficial to society and, rather, intentionally provoke discord. Subsequently, sociopathy was added to the first version of the DSM in 1952. With the publication (and popularity) of the fifth edition of Cleckley's *The Mask of Sanity* in 1976, however, the term "psychopath" became a catchall for both disorders. But because there was no official changing of the guard concerning the name, researchers and clinicians continued to use "psychopath" and "sociopath" interchangeably. This led to a great deal of disagreement in terms of diagnostic criteria and general understanding.

I sat at my desk at Dad's house that summer, reeling over statistics I'd uncovered after another visit to the library. Despite the confusion related to the name of the disorder, one thing researchers did seem to agree on was prevalence. According to several studies, sociopaths comprise nearly five percent of the population, about the same percentage of those who have panic disorder. It seemed crazy that a condition affecting millions wasn't given greater attention by the psychological association, particularly when the primary trait of sociopathy is apathy, and the primary consequence of unabated apathy is destructive behavior. *What are all these people doing*, I wondered, *to keep themselves in check?*

It was a question I desperately wanted to answer for myself. In the months since school ended, I'd been struggling with new ways to offset my growing restlessness. With only so much time I could spend at the library and without the steady stream of fraternity parties and stolen cars to jolt myself into feeling, I had to resort to other methods of apathy reduction. Luckily, the City of Angels provided plenty of opportunities.

I learned that breaking into houses was a lot like riding a bike. I hadn't done it since high school, but I found that it was still second nature, and still just as effective. Lounging in strangers' homes while they were at work, I was less restless. I *felt* relaxed. But without my mother's real estate lockboxes code, getting into houses was much trickier than it had been when I was a kid. I spent countless hours stalking residents to figure out exactly when they were routinely out of the house and for how long. I went to painstaking efforts to get inside properties without drawing attention to my access points. I became expert at picking locks and assembled my own set of tools.

I sat on Dad's living room couch one afternoon with an assortment of old padlocks and a tension wrench in my lap. I'd taught myself how to pick locks years before but had only recently begun to practice in earnest. The exercise was cathartic. In many ways, the manipulation of a lock was a lot like the search for my own apathetic pressure valve. I liked working it out.

I just have to find the right combination of behavior and distraction, I thought to myself, as I worked on a challenging old padlock, *and I can find my equilibrium.*

I closed my eyes as I felt my way around the inside of the lock. Moving the hook through the cylinder, I pushed up against the pins. I could feel the tension wrench give slightly against my thumb. "Almost there," I whispered. After a bit of gentle prodding, I felt the release of the final pin as I pushed it above the shear line. The lock made a satisfying *pop* as the shank snapped open. "Gotcha." I opened my eyes and smiled at my handiwork. *I wonder if I should be a locksmith*, I thought. Then, for reasons I still can't explain, an even better idea popped into my head.

I wonder if should be a nanny.

Working as a childcare provider might have seemed like an odd choice for someone who had recently realized she was a sociopath. But children, I reasoned, weren't as likely to notice that I wasn't normal. They weren't as likely to out me for refusing to play by the rules. As long as I was fun and creative, kids would overlook any transgressions. I thought it was an inspired way to keep myself occupied.

Granted, I wasn't what anyone might consider a "kid" person. Nor was I bubbly, expressive, affectionate, or any of the other things one might expect of a traditional nanny. Yet—surprisingly—I was hired almost immediately by a famous actor in the posh Los Angeles enclave of Brentwood. And perhaps more surprisingly, I loved the job. The three children I was charged to manage, with their quirky dispositions and charming temperaments, were like delightful interactive puzzles. I enjoyed getting to know their individual personalities. In my own way, I loved them. My intense feelings for those kids and instinct to protect them at all costs gave me an additional boost of hope. Maybe I wasn't such a lost cause after all.

As the months passed and I settled comfortably into my job, my dark urges became easier to manage. With my free time limited, I had fewer opportunities to get into trouble. I knew that simply distracting myself was not a fail-safe measure against the destructive urges, but at the time I was grateful for any help I could get.

My internal climate was like a balloon. Things that kept me occupied, like school and work, were my helium, lifting the balloon and pushing it above its apathetic baseline. But it wasn't permanent. The instant I wasn't distracted by some responsibility or coasting off the aftereffects of bad behavior, I became listless. The balloon would lose its buoyancy, and before long I would start looking for ways to jolt myself into feeling.

What I need is a trouble schedule, I thought.

It was my sophomore year, and I was sitting in my usual spot at the UCLA library during a break between classes, reading research materials. My latest find, "A Study of Anxiety in the Sociopathic Personality," in *The Journal of Abnormal and Social Psychology*, had taken me weeks to track down. It was written by Dr. David Lykken, a psychologist who claimed to have discovered a link between sociopathy and anxiety. After testing the anxiety levels of dozens of sociopathic subjects, he concluded there was a subcategory of sociopathy, which he labeled as secondary or "neurotic." He later theorized that this type of sociopathy may not be genetic, but was instead associated with stress caused by emotional frustration and inner conflict.

Stuck stress.

It was something I remembered experiencing as early as elementary school, a claustrophobic type of anxiety that seemed to rise and fall in lockstep with what I always called "the pressure." And now—finally!—I had an inkling as to why.

"If this pressure is caused by the brain's subconscious desire to jolt itself out of apathy," I reasoned, "then stuck stress must be an anxious *reaction* to apathy." It certainly made sense from my experience. Surrounded by "normal" people for most of my life, I was always working to conceal what made me *ab*normal. It was the only way I knew to fly below the radar and keep myself safe. That's why, at the first hint of pressure—at the first hint of rising apathy—I would start to get anxious. Knowing the pressure would ultimately force my hand, that the only way to get rid of it was to do something bad, I would start to feel powerless. I would start to feel trapped.

Unless I was alone, I realized with a start.

Indeed, my reaction to apathy wasn't always discomfort. Often, I'd even enjoyed the experience. Like the time I walked home from the slumber party and got inside that car; the hours spent at the abandoned house near Grandma's; the secret trips to the basement at the Rockefeller estate; the late-night drives in stolen cars. All of those times I was consumed by apathy, and yet I wasn't bothered at all. Quite the contrary. I felt free.

Because there was nobody watching me, I concluded. Without the risk of having to justify my lack of emotion, I could just . . . enjoy it.

This was a revelation, and as I left the library that day, another realization sprang to mind.

If I know that stuck stress is the result of my situational discomfort with apathy, I thought, *then why not be more proactive in neutralizing that discomfort?* In other words: If my anxiety is triggered by my discomfort with apathy, it might be possible to minimize that anxiety (and the destructive behavior that often resulted) by learning how to accept the apathy so it no longer made me uncomfortable.

The hypothesis made sense. Even though I now had a better understanding of what caused the pressure, as well as why there was so much stress associated with it, I still didn't know how to eliminate it. Nor did I understand under what circumstances I would or would not get anxious about being apathetic. Sometimes my apathy made me uncomfortable. Sometimes it didn't.

But the bottom line was this: In order to remain an active (albeit secretly dysfunctional) member of society and continue to enjoy all the perks of membership, I would have to alter my anxious response. I would have to *accept* my apathetic nature instead of being apprehensive of it. The longer I allowed my apathy to build, the longer I waited to dole out my "fix" of feeling, the more likely I was to become anxious and the *less* likely I was to properly control my response. *So why wait?* I asked myself. *Wouldn't it make more sense to engage in smaller acts of "bad" behavior more frequently*, I surmised, *than larger acts less frequently?* I decided to test my theory.

When I got back to Dad's that night I sat at my desk and attempted to log all the different types of "bad" things I'd done. Anything I could remember doing that I knew was "wrong," I scribbled onto the page. When I was finished, I reviewed my list.

These are all things that minimize my apathy, I concluded. *These things keep me from doing something really awful.* Attempting to be a researcher like Dr. Lykken, I ranked them in terms of efficiency.

I looked at the first item, "Physical Violence." I picked up my pencil and drew a sharp line through the words. No matter how effective it may have been at reducing apathy, I already knew that violence was not something I ever wanted to consider.

Besides, I reasoned, *the point is to find something that* isn't *extreme*.

Next was "Stealing Cars." Although fun, this was also too extreme. *Plus, it involves other people*, I thought, *and a very specific set of circumstances*. I reluctantly scratched it off my list. What I needed was something more versatile. Something I could theoretically do at any time and in any place, for the rest of my life, if necessary.

I moved to number three, "Trespassing/Stalking." I tapped the eraser against my chin. *That*, I thought, nodding, *I can work with*.

The next morning I woke earlier than usual. I poured myself some coffee, took a seat in the window bench in the living room, and looked at the house across the street. The people who lived there—a youngish couple from Tarzana—were executives at Warner Bros. They'd been married for a year and honeymooned in Cabo. I hadn't discovered this information accidentally. I'd acquired it by chatting them up during a Fourth of July block party that summer. I also knew they'd installed a state-of-the-art alarm system, but only activated it when they went "on vacation." And they had a dog named Samson who "only looked mean." Most importantly, I knew they were *always* at the office by 8:15.

Comfortable in my perch, I watched as they exited the front door and made their way to matching SUVs parked in the driveway. After they left—right on schedule—I went to my bedroom and got dressed.

Ten minutes later I stood at their back door. The deadbolt was old but a familiar brand. I made quick work of it with my tools and once I had it unlocked, stepped inside. When I crossed the threshold into the kitchen, I was momentarily hypnotized by the stillness.

The silence of a structure that has just been broken into is unlike any other. It's almost like the house can't believe what just happened and has gasped, taking all the air with it. There is unimaginable tranquility. I could spend an eternity in that silence, completely absorbed in the present moment and entirely at peace.

My moment was broken by the tap of canine paws trotting down the hall. "Hey, buddy," I said, kneeling to give Samson a handful of dog treats. "Mind if I hang out here for a bit?" Samson didn't mind. He clearly enjoyed the company. Together we wandered through the house. I scanned the knickknacks on the tables and the photos on the walls. I perused the books on the shelves and studied the clothes in the closets. I took nothing. I disturbed nothing. I simply existed in a world where I was not supposed to exist.

Samson whined and pushed against my legs when I tried to leave. I gave him one last squeeze, closed the door quietly behind me, and stepped into the backyard, marveling at the change in atmosphere. Though I'd only been inside the house a half hour, everything around me felt markedly different. The air was sweeter. The world, less hectic. I exhaled with relief and walked back to my house.

As I'd hoped, the rest of the day continued without incident. There was no stuck stress. There was no "emotional frustration or inner conflict." It was like I was a completely different person, a *whole* person and not one whose personality was at war with itself.

After that, I knew I never wanted to wait for the pressure to become overwhelming before I did something to alleviate it. Whether it was sneaking out my window to follow my neighbors home in the dark or methodically stealing cars from fraternity parties, I'd been haphazardly regulating my apathy with systematic destructive behavior since at least middle school. *But now*, I thought, *I'm conscious of it.* It made all the difference.

I approached bad behavior like a discipline. I was as responsible about it as I was about my job, and my routine was strict. Monday, Wednesday, and Friday mornings I sought a daily dose of sociopathic stress relief. Then I went to school.

After classes I would walk to the library and spend as much time as I could reading books on psychology and research studies on sociopathy until it was time to go to work. Then I'd collect the kids from their schools and take them home. I helped them with homework, readied them for dinner, and tucked them into bed before leaving at night. After that I'd go home, eat my own dinner, and study until I fell asleep. Then I would start over again the next morning.

My apathy was like a dragon that needed feeding. If I ignored it, it consumed me. So I put it on a diet. I did exactly what I needed to give myself necessary "jolts" of feeling. I never took it any further—even when I was tempted, which was often. I scheduled my mischief like I would have a doctor's prescription. And I never skipped a dose.

CHAPTER 10

Confession

I maintained this routine for years, and the consistency worked wonders. Eventually, I grew confident that my theory had been correct: Smaller, habitual "bad" acts were a safer choicer for relieving the pressure and abating my sociopathic anxiety than larger, more spontaneous ones. Premeditated transgressions were less likely to result in unintentionally revealing myself to the world and allowed me to adhere to my directive of not hurting anyone. I was a well-oiled machine of psychological and behavioral (however criminal) stability. Granted, I was still stalking people on a semi-regular basis, and I was still using unlawful entry as "treatment." But neither of these seemed harmful to me. Quite the contrary. Regular doses kept my darker urges from escalating uncontrolled. As a result, I was able to thrive.

I was on track to graduate. I'd accomplished a great deal in my research. I was a trusted nanny. I'd done exactly what I'd set out to do: I'd achieved some semblance of a "normal" life. Yet, despite my outward appearance as a responsible and well-adjusted, socially acceptable young adult, I still struggled with the one problem I'd had since I was a kid. I was alone.

Being on what I considered "the sociopathic spectrum" often felt like a life sentence in emotional solitary confinement. No one could relate to me. Nobody wanted to spend time with me. Not the *real* me, anyway. I was utterly alone. And loneliness, I had come to realize, could be dangerous.

My father had recently moved to a new place in Beverly Hills and let me stay in the house on Coldwater Canyon. For the first time in my life, I was entirely on my own. At first, I was thrilled. The complete lack of supervision and accountability was like a warm bath. After a few months, though, I noticed an uptick in my destructive compulsions. At first it was subtle. Savage fantasies would spring to mind out of nowhere. As time passed, these got stronger, and I started to get concerned. It wasn't just because the compulsions were more intense, but because they were more distinct. For the first time in a long time, I felt specific urges of physical violence, usually toward complete strangers. Desperate to understand, I started keeping a record of the dates and times when they arose. I soon noticed that they were most prevalent when I was alone for long periods. This was especially the case on weekends, when I would often go days without seeing anyone.

None of it made sense. Being alone was when I typically felt the *most* at ease, the *most* free to be myself. But after a string of uneventful weekends with no meaningful interactions with others, I realized I was more prone to violent fantasies after extended time alone with myself.

There's a big difference between the loners, I thought, *and the lonely*. It was past midnight, and I was heading home after a long day at work. *I wonder if some part of me wants to get caught*, I thought, as I pulled onto the freeway. *Or wants to be* seen.

As I drove, I considered the unique predicament being a sociopath presented. Were the millions of others like me just as conflicted about wanting to stay hidden? Was there any way to give them hope? I wished I knew. I wished I had a giant megaphone to scream to the world: "ATTENTION ALL SOCIOPATHS AND ANTISOCIAL OUTLIERS! DON'T PANIC! DON'T HURT ANYONE! YOU AREN'T ALONE! YOU AREN'T CRAZY!"

It was the first time I'd ever considered addressing the problem of sociopathy outside of myself, and the experience was surreal. Cruising along in the car, thinking about the possibility of helping other sociopaths, I felt like I'd suddenly learned a new emotion without even trying. Indeed, the idea of educating people like me sounded interesting, even entertaining. I pulled off the freeway. *Who says sociopaths can't empathize?* I thought.

My plan was to get online and do some research, but when I turned down my street, I spied my father's car parked in the driveway. I could see the television in the living room was on and I hurried inside, grateful for the unexpected company. "Dad? You don't live here anymore, remember?" I joked.

He smiled and said, "What can I say? This place still feels more like home." He turned off the TV and gave me a hug. "You're not just getting home from work, are you?"

Our embrace was brief as I wriggled away to get something to eat. I was starving. "Yeah," I said. "They had a premiere." Dad followed me into the kitchen and I began rummaging through the pantry.

"Things okay at school?" he asked, taking a seat at the island in the center of the kitchen. His tone seemed misplaced, and I got wary.

"Yeah," I said slowly.

"That's good." He watched me for a second, then got to what I was already suspecting would be his point. "You know," he began, "I really don't like you working this late while you're in school."

Inside the pantry, I rolled my eyes at the carefully arranged shelves of food. "I don't normally."

"I don't just mean tonight," he said with a concerned look. "You're up before dawn, then you're off at work until late in the afternoon, sometimes late at night. When do you study? When do you sleep?"

We'd been through this before. I knew my father wasn't a fan of my decision to work while still in school. From his perspective, college was a time to cut loose and have fun. Attempting to keep things light, I sidled up to the island and grinned at him as I tore into a Charleston Chew. "Sleep is overrated," I said, but he would not be swayed.

"Be serious for a second, Patric. Nobody values hard work more than I do. I think it's admirable that you're a nanny, especially on top of all your classes."

"Thank you."

"But you're burning the candle at both ends. You need to slow down. Appreciate the college experience before it's gone."

I bit my tongue, starting to get annoyed. "You don't understand," I said.

He reached across the counter and took my hand. "Then do me a favor, sweetheart," he said. "*Make* me understand." He squeezed. "You've been here almost four years. Where are your hobbies? Where are your friends?" And then, "What's going on, honey?"

In the dim light of the kitchen, he looked so calm, so rational. I wondered, *What if I just told the truth?*

God, it was such a familiar temptation—one I'd struggled with my entire life. Even now, I still found myself oscillating between the security of deceit and the freedom of truth. "The truth shall set you free!" I'd heard the adage so many times and every time I did, I longed for it to be true. But this rule, like so many others, didn't seem to apply to people like me.

Truth didn't represent freedom for us. Quite the opposite. The only times in my life I'd ever been in trouble were when I told the truth. Lying was what kept *me* free. Yet, deceit, however effective at keeping me safe, was exhausting. I was a monotonous combination of counterfeit personality traits and falsified storylines, and I was sick of juggling. It was one of the reasons I'd become so isolated. It was easier to be alone than to constantly put on a show.

Maybe instead of working so hard to be invisible, I thought, *I should see what it's like outside the shadows.* I'd always been honest with David, and I'd never once regretted it. I'd never once felt unsafe.

I looked at my dad. His kind blue eyes reminded me of the Pacific. "I'll tell you what's going on," I said, surprising us both with my candor, "but you're not going to like it."

He squeezed my hand again. "Try me."

I nodded, took a deep breath, and started talking. I disclosed everything about my apathy and my destructive urges. I divulged the things I did, both as a child and as an adult, and the ways I tried to manage my impulses. I detailed my struggles at school and my conversations with Dr. Slack. Then I described my research and the reasoning behind wanting to stay so busy.

"It's why I need the job," I told him. "Because *I* can't have too much free time. I can't be bored. It's tough to explain, but when I'm bored it's like I *remember* that I don't feel. And that *feeling*—the feeling of *not* feeling—makes me want to do bad things." I shrugged slightly. "Sometimes, anyway."

Dad listened in silence, staring at the marble counter. Then he looked up. "Jesus, Patric," he whispered. "I mean . . ." He paused, uncomfortable. "I always wondered. When you were younger, your mother and I, we always thought . . ." He trailed off.

"I might grow up to be a serial killer?"

He looked sad and embarrassed. "Not exactly."

I smiled, attempting to put him at ease. "Dad, I was joking. And anyway, it's fine."

"Fine that my daughter thinks she's a sociopath? How is that fine?"

I shook my head and took the last bite of my candy bar. "Because being a sociopath doesn't mean what you think it means. It doesn't mean what anybody thinks it means, really." I stood up.

"Look at me. You'd never think I do the things I do. I'm a responsible student with a full-time job taking care of little children, for God's sake."

"Who steals cars and breaks into houses!"

"Right. See my point about free time?" I returned to the pantry.

"Honey," he said, "this is not sustainable. What about finding a therapist?"

"Didn't you hear what I said? No therapist is going to help me. Sociopathy isn't even in the DSM."

"Well, it might help to talk about your feelings."

"What feelings?" I replied.

"Don't be ridiculous, Patric," he said. "I know you have feelings."

I returned to the island, another Charleston Chew in hand. "Yes, you're right," I said, taking a seat. "Of course I have feelings. You just have to understand, my feelings aren't the same as other people's."

"Explain it to me, then," he said finally. "How does it *feel* when you feel?"

I thought about it, trying to find a relatable metaphor. "You know what it's like?" I said. "It's like having bad eyesight. I can see most stuff, but there are some things I have to squint to read. It's the same with emotion. Happiness and anger—those are clear. They come naturally. Other ones don't. Things like empathy and remorse—I can connect to them if I really try—but it doesn't happen on its own. Sometimes it doesn't happen at all." I frowned. "I really have to squint."

Dad nodded solemnly. "And these urges you have," he responded. "When does that . . . happen?"

"Whenever I go too long without feeling something," I replied. "The things I do are like a medication. I break into a house or steal a car and then the pressure just . . . goes away." I fluttered my hand like a butterfly. "It's a behavioral prescription."

"And have you ever . . . hurt anyone?" he asked softly.

"Not since middle school."

"But you've *wanted* to."

I sighed. "Sort of. It's not that I want to, as much as I feel like I *have* to." I shrugged. "But like I said, those urges are rare. They only come up when I've felt nothing for too long. Or if I spend too much time alone."

"What counts as 'too much time'?" he pressed. "You mean like weekends? What happens then?"

Unprepared for the question, I shrugged again and began to toy with the lazy Susan on the counter. "I keep busy."

In recent months, I'd come up with what I considered to be a harmless and effective way to fill time and avoid isolation during the weekends. In addition to keeping me distracted, this activity actually helped a great deal in keeping the pressure at bay. But I knew my father wasn't going to appreciate it.

"Honey?" Dad nudged. "What do you do on weekends?"

"I go to church," I said.

This wasn't the full truth. But I wasn't sure how honest I was prepared to be on such short notice.

"I didn't know you were going to church," he said. I could tell he was excited about the idea. Dad was raised a Southern Baptist in Mississippi and had never been able to fully resist the pull of the cloth. "Which one are you going to? I'd love to go with you, if you didn't mind."

I rocked my head from side to side. "I mean, *I* wouldn't mind. But I don't think you'd like it." I hesitated. "They aren't normal church services."

"What do you mean?"

"They're funerals."

It had started a few months before. A friend of Dad's had died, and he asked me to meet him at Forest Lawn Memorial Park for the service. I hadn't expected much. I'd only met the friend a few times and I figured the ceremony would mostly be pomp and circumstance. I couldn't have been more wrong. When we walked into the chapel, I was struck by the sound of a woman weeping. Not just crying, but howling, nearly hysterical with grief. It was the wife. As we took our seats, I could see her bent over one of the pews, her body shaking. I'd never seen such a display of raw emotion, and I was captivated. I looked around, wondering how others were reacting. I realized everyone else in the chapel was affected, too.

It was unlike anything I'd ever experienced. Certainly, I had witnessed my fair share of emotional expression, but this was something different. I was surrounded. Everywhere I looked, people were cloaked in emotion. Some were overt in their reactions. Others were subdued. But everyone was feeling . . . *something*. It was like they were all connected by some invisible emotional string. And then the strangest thing happened. My apathy started to dissipate.

I couldn't believe it. It was the same way I felt after I broke into a house or stole a car, except I hadn't done either. The sensation was a combination of acute awareness and utter relaxation. I wasn't feeling, per se, but I wasn't *not* feeling either. It was like I was floating, coasting off the energy of the people around me.

When the service concluded, I walked with Dad to the gravesite as if I was in a trance. Never in my life had I been surrounded by so much heightened emotion, and the effect was transformative. It was as though I was escaping apathy through osmosis. I couldn't get enough. I was like an emotional vampire. *Are all funerals like this?* I wondered. I had to find out.

After my father left, I wandered back to the chapel, where another service was beginning. I took a spot in the back row, sat quietly, and waited. The next ceremony was notably different. The deceased was an elderly woman who had suffered a long illness. The mourners, though numerous, were composed. Nobody appeared *overcome* with sadness and only a few people were visibly crying, but the energy inside the room was the same as it had been at the first funeral. If anything, it was even more powerful.

After that I was hooked. Nearly every weekend I began attending what I thought of as "stranger services." My preferred location was Forest Lawn, but eventually I expanded my territory to include cemeteries all over Los Angeles. My favorites were the services that took place at night. Though rare, these were typically the most emotionally charged, not to mention atmospherically evocative. I'd scan the papers and church and cemetery websites, then plan entire weekends around evening funerals.

I did my best to convey my enthusiasm to my father. "I'm telling you," I said. "Nighttime funerals are a totally separate deal. I wish I knew who was responsible for setting them up. Like, I wish I could meet those people before they died. I bet they're amazing. No joke. You should come with me sometime."

Dad stared at me, horrified. "Patric," he said, after a beat. "This isn't right."

"Going to funerals?" I snorted. "Give me a break."

"Hear me out," Dad said, as I started to protest. "You might not be taking anything tangible from these people, but make no mistake: You're stealing. You're using their pain for your own gain. That's wrong, honey."

"It's not against the law," I argued. "I mean, I know stealing *material* things is. But who says going to strangers' funerals is wrong?"

"Honey, no," he said, exasperated. "Something doesn't have to be *illegal* to be wrong. You know that."

"Oh I *know*," I said. "I just don't *care*." I tried to think of how to explain it. "You say it's 'wrong' because it feels wrong to you."

"Yes," said Dad. "Because you're exploiting someone else's pain."

"Right," I said. "So what you're saying, essentially, is that you wouldn't do it because you wouldn't like the way that it would make *you* feel."

He considered this and then reluctantly agreed. "Yes," he said.

"See?" I said. "That's what I'm trying to tell you. I don't have that feeling. That shame. So, there is literally nothing, internally or externally, to stop me from doing it. Going doesn't make *me* feel anything. If anything, it makes me feel *okay* about the fact that I don't feel anything. It helps me accept not feeling. And that acceptance, I think, is what keeps my 'sociopathic anxiety' at bay." I smiled, expecting him to be impressed with my reasoning. "It's not like I'm being disruptive or disrespectful or anything."

He sighed, steadying himself. "Well, one could argue that your very presence is the disrespectful part."

"Look," I said. "I can't help that I don't feel things like normal people. But I have to choose the lesser of two evils. These funerals, for example," I explained. "I understand the people around me are sad. I get that. But it *helps* me. So when I go, I'm very respectful. I don't know how else to explain it. It's sort of like my way of keeping things organized. It's why I bring flowers."

Dad blinked. *"What?"*

"I mean, unless the family requested donations. Then I write a check."

My father shook his head, unable to process what he was hearing. "You write checks . . . to the families . . . of the people whose funerals you . . . crash?"

"Well, usually it's to some sort of charity. But, yes." I took a sip of water and stared at him. "It's the same thing with the cars I take. If I see they're out of gas, I fill them up. And the houses, too. One time someone left the stove on, so I turned it off. It's my way of trying to balance the karma."

Dad buried his face in his hands. "So, what is it you're *saying*, Patric?" he asked, his voice muffled. "That you're some sort of sociopathic Buddhist?"

My eyes widened. I was enchanted by the idea. "Yeah!"

He struggled to maintain his composure. "I was kidding."

"Oh."

"Honey," he continued, dropping his head, "this is crazy. What if someone wants to know who you are at these funerals? Has that ever occurred to you? That someone might want to know who the tall blonde sitting alone in the back of the church might be?"

"Trust me, Dad. Nobody ever pays any attention to me. Which is fine because I'm not there to interact with anyone."

He shook his head. "Then why go in the first place? If you don't like interacting with people?"

I closed my eyes and rubbed my temples. "It's so hard to explain," I said, "because I don't relate to other people the way you do, the way most people do. I don't care about things normal people care about. I don't like interacting with people because they don't connect to me. And I can't connect to them." I took a deep breath. "But just because I *can't* connect doesn't mean I don't *wish* I could." I shook my head sadly.

"I didn't choose this," I said helplessly. "I didn't decide to be someone who doesn't feel the same way as everybody else. And I think I'm getting better at accepting it, but it still sucks. I'm isolated. Physically, socially, emotionally, all of it." I exhaled angrily. "Everything about me is a fucking contradiction."

Dad looked sad. "Oh, honey," he said.

I gazed at the floor, my thoughts disappearing into the Mexican tiles. "You know what the worst part is? The worst part about being a sociopath?" I said. "It's the loneliness. You wouldn't think so, but it is. I want friends. I want to connect. But I can't. It's like I'm starving, but food makes me sick."

Dad didn't say anything, and I could tell he was trying to remember something. "Hey," he offered, after a long silence. "What about David? Aren't you two still friends?"

Just hearing his name made me smile. "Yes," I said.

Dad was right. David was my friend, and a close one at that. Hardly a month went by that my high school sweetheart and I didn't talk on the phone. We'd even hung out occasionally, at holiday parties and random events over the years, usually when I flew home to visit Mom and Harlowe. But despite our undeniable bond, that relationship felt intangible to me, long distance. I wasn't a kid anymore, and neither was David.

"You had feelings for him, right?"

I shrugged weakly. "Yes," I said, "but David doesn't live here, Dad. He's got his own life three thousand miles away. His own *normal* life. That's what I want. *My* own normal life. Y'know, relatively speaking."

Dad leaned against the island, a curious expression on his face. "So let's talk about it," he said.

"Talk about what?"

"You graduate in a few months," he said. "What do you want to do?"

I sighed; the enormity of the question exhausted me. "Jesus, Dad," I said. "I have no idea."

"Well," he said, "can *I* make a suggestion?"

"Can I stop you?"

"I think you should come work for me."

Dad had frequently worked with one of the largest talent management firms in the industry. He'd recently decided he wanted to open his own company, and had pitched me the idea of helping him start it a few times. I'd never taken him seriously.

I looked at him as if he was crazy. "Work for you and do what?"

"You can be a music manager."

"Oh, I *can*?" I shook my head, laughing. "What idiot would hire me to be their manager?"

"I would."

I smirked and tilted my head. "Daddy," I said, touched by his offer to help. "I love you, but that's crazy. Haven't you been listening? I'm a *sociopath*, for God's sake."

"Says *you*," Dad responded. "I still want you to talk to a therapist about it. In fact, I insist."

"Fine," I relented. "But I don't need you to give me a job to keep me out of trouble."

"I'm not," Dad said. "I've been thinking about it for months. You've got great instincts when it comes to music, Patric. And besides"—he looked around—"what else are you doing? You want to be a nanny for the rest of your life?"

My eyes fell once again on the lazy Susan. I tugged at the bowl that rested on it and admired the perfectly symmetrical tower of apples that sat inside. I'd bought the apples at the weekend farmers' market. When I got home it had taken me an hour to get them exactly the way I wanted, sort of like playing *Tetris*. For me, it was an excellent use of time, like meditating. Just looking at them gave me a tremendous sense of detached peace and satisfaction.

"So?" Dad pressed. "What do you think?"

I stood and pushed away from the counter. "I think I'm exhausted. I have a ton of stuff I need to do for class, and I want to spend as much time as I can at the libraries before graduation." I shrugged. "I'll need some time to think about it."

Dad grabbed an apple, shifting the bowl and skewing the

arrangement. My once symmetrical fruit installation now needed serious reconstruction. He smiled and bit into the crisp Granny Smith, the loud crunch sending shivers down my spine.

"You have two weeks," he said. Then he kissed me on the cheek and left.

CHAPTER 11

Borderline

Just off Mulholland Drive, on the way to my father's house in Beverly Hills, sits a cottage. Unlike the many mansions that line the fabled thoroughfare, this home is small and antiquated. On visits to Dad's, I'd slow down to catch a glimpse of the little old woman who was almost always outside tending her rose garden. She was rarely alone. An old man I assumed was her husband usually sat in a lawn chair nearby, watching her work while he read. He balanced a coffee cup on a collection of books stacked in the grass next to him.

"I'm going to buy that house someday," I murmured.

It was several months later and I was sitting in an office on San Vicente Boulevard. The afternoon sun had started to dip below the horizon and if I angled my head the right way, I could just make out the curve of the ocean through the window.

"You're changing the subject again, Patric," Dr. Carlin said.

At my father's insistence, I'd finally started seeing a therapist. Dr. Carlin was a psychologist who came highly recommended. After telling her my history and stories of my bouts of apathy and destructive behavior, she, too, suspected that I suffered from sociopathic personality disorder. So she asked to administer the psychopathy checklist, the PCL test.

I squinted out the window. "That's because your subjects are so annoying," I said.

"I think it's a good idea," she prodded gently.

My gaze emptied into space, and my thoughts returned to the

cottage. We sat in silence for a few seconds before I turned back to her. "I just don't understand," I said, shaking my head. "Why do you want to give me the PCL? I'm not a psychopath."

"Diagnostically, I'm inclined to agree," said Dr. Carlin, shifting in her chair. "But even though the PCL was designed to assess psychopathy, many researchers use it to test for sociopathy . . . off-label, so to speak." She added, "There's no official separate diagnosis for sociopathy."

"Okay," I said cautiously. "So how does *that* work?"

"Well, even though they're essentially the same disorder, many clinicians—myself included—believe sociopathy is something of a milder form of psychopathy. The maximum score on the PCL is forty," explained the therapist, "and psychopathy is indicated by a score of thirty or higher. But sociopathy is generally assumed to register at twenty-two or more."

"Generally assumed?"

"Well, again, the test is technically structured to assess for psychopathy. And there's a lot of disagreement about how to diagnose those who fall at the low end or just below the psychopathy cutoff."

"So what do normal people score?" I asked.

"It varies," said Dr. Carlin. "But I think the consensus is around four."

My jaw dropped. *"FOUR?"* I leaned back in my seat. "So let me get this straight," I said. "If you're a psychopath, you score a *thirty* or higher. But if you're a 'normal' person you score a *four*?" Dr. Carlin's eyes widened slightly, and I laughed.

"I'm sorry," I continued, "but that's insane. You're telling me there's no clinical diagnosis for people who score *between* a four and a thirty? What about someone who scores a fifteen? Or a twenty-one? You're telling me the PCL doesn't say anything about them?"

"Well, like I said, we think sociopaths score between twenty-two and twenty-nine," the therapist clarified. "And, to be fair, a 'normal' person would never take the PCL. It's meant for criminal offenders. Recorded criminal history is a requirement."

"Then how can you give it to me?" I asked.

Dr. Carlin explained, "Because I'm going to use the PCL:*SV*. It's similar, but it's designed to be used in clinical settings."

"So there are two versions of the same test?" I asked. "One for criminals and one for everyone else?"

Dr. Carlin nodded. "Both tests use the same criteria. They look for symptoms across four categories: interpersonal style, deficient emotional experience, impulsive behavior, and antisocial conduct. The difference is that the PCL:SV doesn't require a criminal record. So it can be used on anyone."

"Christ," I muttered. "Why is all of this so complicated?" I shook my head. "And what's the point of testing at all if you can't *officially* diagnose a sociopath?"

"What do you mean?"

"There's no treatment for sociopathy, correct?"

"Not currently, no."

I threw up my hands. "So what are sociopaths supposed to do with their diagnosis? Smoke it?"

The doctor shifted anxiously. "Well, psychopathic and sociopathic diagnoses are primarily used by clinicians," she paused, "to gauge the propensity for criminality."

I laughed. "In other words, this test is only used to see how likely it is that someone *might* commit future crimes?"

"More or less."

"Well then let me save us both some time, because I'd say my 'propensity for criminality' is sitting at a strong one hundred percent."

Dr. Carlin simply said, "Let's find out."

The PCL:SV interview was exhausting. For hours I sat across from the therapist and we talked about everything from my criminal impulses to my sleep patterns to my sexual history. Then I had to wait an entire week—until our next appointment—to get the results.

The following Tuesday I was early for our session. "How'd I do?" I blurted out.

Dr. Carlin closed the door and calmly took a seat. "Well," she said, after getting settled, "I thought maybe we'd talk about the test itself first. You seemed pretty tired afterward. How was that experience for you?"

"Oh, come on," I responded. "What'd the test say?"

Instead of answering, she asked, "Why is that so important to you?"

I tilted my head forward. "Why are the results of the test that will confirm my sociopathic diagnosis important to me?" I asked incredulously.

"Yes."

I exhaled. "I don't know," I said, thinking about it for the first time. "I guess it would just be nice to have an answer once and for all. At the very least I think it would be easier for me to explain to people that I'm a sociopath. There'd be a lot less confusion, that's for sure."

Dr. Carlin was intrigued. "You'd tell other people about your diagnosis?" she asked. "Why?"

I shrugged. "So I wouldn't have to pretend to be 'normal' all the time. People pick up on stuff. They have since I was a kid. I think coming clean right off the bat would head off a lot of questions. It would definitely make *my* life easier, that's for sure."

"It seems odd," Dr. Carlin observed, "that you would care what other people think."

"That's the thing," I told her, "I *don't* care what people think. I've never cared. I do have a survival instinct, though, some need to stay hidden to keep people from finding out who I really I am. That way I could keep acting out without getting caught, without being revealed. But now, I don't care about being found out. I accept who I am." I paused, then added, "I've tried to, anyway."

Dr. Carlin looked pleasantly surprised. "Hmm," she said.

I was starting to lose my patience. "Great," I said. "Now that that's settled, can we get to the test, please?"

The therapist held up her hands in reluctant agreement. "Okay," she said, looking down at her notes. "Well, if you remember, the test covered four clusters. Your scores indicate an above-average range of psychopathic symptoms across all four." Dr. Carlin frowned. "It's interesting, though," she continued, "because your interpersonal style doesn't consistently correlate with the PCL criteria."

Acknowledging my befuddled expression, Dr. Carlin explained, "According to the PCL, psychopaths and sociopaths all demonstrate a very specific type of social aggression. I describe it as the pushy-salesman symptom. There's a lot of overt arrogance and antagonism." She continued, "It's the primary way sociopaths establish social dominance. It's how they assert control."

"You're saying I'm *not* like that?" I asked.

"No, you are," Dr. Carlin replied, "but the way you establish dominance is through manipulation and charm. Which makes sense, because you're a woman." Then she added, "A female sociopath isn't necessarily going to use the same interpersonal techniques that a male one will. It's one of the problems I have with the PCL, actually," the therapist said. "I feel like there's a lot of gender bias."

"So what does that mean?"

"It means that the place where your score is lowest, relatively speaking, is specifically on that interpersonal style scale," she replied. "But it's still elevated. Everything, in fact, is elevated across the board. As I suspected, the levels aren't high enough to put you in the extreme psychopathy category, but they definitely indicate sociopathic personality disorder."

At first, I didn't say anything, just shifted my gaze out the window. On the opposite side of San Vicente was a park. A group of people entered the gates and began a leisurely walk across the grass. It was a yoga class or a field trip or something. There were a couple dozen of them. "One in twenty-five," I mused.

"Patric," said Dr. Carlin, "talk to me."

I turned back to her while tapping a finger on the glass. "Did you know that?" I asked. "Roughly one in twenty-five people is a sociopath. That's what the research says." I looked again at the people in the park. "So do you think there's another sociopath at the park or is it just me in this sample?" I glanced back at Dr. Carlin, who had cocked an eyebrow at me. "I'm serious," I said.

She considered this and then said, "It sounds to me like you're wondering if you're alone." She paused. "What does that feel like?"

I looked down, slowly shaking my head as I thought of what to say. "It feels like something I *know*," I said at last. "It doesn't feel like something I feel."

"And is that your normal reaction?" she asked. "When you think about your relation to other people?"

I shrugged. "Yeah."

She furrowed her brow as she glanced again at her notes. "What about the guy in Florida? You said you experienced feelings for him."

"David?" I asked, surprised. "Yeah, I love David. Or, *loved* him." I bit my lip. "I don't really know."

"What do you mean?"

I thought about it. "Well, it just seems silly at this point. I mean, we dated when I was fourteen. And since then, I've never felt the same way about *anyone*? That seems unbelievable to me. I've been starting to think it was all just something I made up." I shook my head sadly. "Like . . . I wanted to feel love, but I actually didn't."

Dr. Carlin nodded slowly. "And how does *that* make you feel?"

"It's a bummer," I said, thinking about the boyfriends I'd had. Number fifteen on Cleckley's list sprung to mind: "Sex life impersonal, trivial, and poorly integrated."

"Though, I guess it would make sense, right?" I continued. "I'm not good at connecting to people or to myself. I'm a sociopath." I paused for a second, listening as the word left my mouth. It seemed different now.

"True," said Dr. Carlin, looking me in the eye. "But do you know what I find interesting?"

I shook my head. She set her paperwork to the side and leaned forward. "In spite of your difficulty connecting with others, your first impulse—after being told your diagnosis—was to look out the window to find someone else like you." She allowed her words to settle. "Now, why do you think that's the case?"

I looked out the window again. By this time the group of people had crossed the park and was out of view. I was disappointed that I could no longer see them. "I don't know," I said softly. "I guess it would be nice to meet someone like me. To not have to explain why I feel or don't feel. To not constantly have to justify my actions or try to speak an emotional language I don't understand.

"I think it would be nice to just feel normal around someone," I said. "I can't explain it. I feel like if I met someone like me, then I'd feel like . . ." My voice trailed off. "I don't know."

"No," Dr. Carlin pushed gently. "Finish the sentence. Then you would feel . . . what?"

"Hope," I said, exasperated. "Though that doesn't make much sense."

Dr. Carlin leaned back. "I disagree," she said. "I think it makes lots of sense. It means you're looking for someone with whom you can relate. And that's *good*. Between your curiosity about other sociopaths and your willingness to share your experiences, I'd say there's lots of hope for you."

I snorted at the thought, then turned away from the window and gave her a sarcastic grin. "Hope for what? A sociopathic friend?" I rolled my eyes. "Lucky me."

"You're not looking for a friend," she said.

"Then what am I looking for?"

Dr. Carlin cocked her head, a small but confident smile on her lips. "Empathy," she said.

My therapist's observation that I was an empathy-seeking sociopath was insightful, if not entirely surprising. In many ways I was like the lost duckling in the children's book *Are You My Mother?* Except instead of a brave little bird with a kind heart and identity issues in search of its mommy, I was an antisocial outlier with a limited emotional range and a habit of lying in search of a buddy. Despite my diagnosis, I wasn't any closer to figuring out why I was the way that I was.

Not that I had much time to think about it. After a brief post-graduation respite, I accepted my father's offer and joined his new company. Shadowing him and several of his associates for those first few months on the job, I made it my mission to learn every aspect of music management. And what I discovered was surprising. The music industry, I quickly realized, was a sleight-of-hand macrocosm for which I was perfectly suited. Distracted by the allure of the music and carefully crafted mystique of the artists, few paid much attention to the shadowy figures lurking behind the scenes. Yet this was where the real magic was taking place. The *dark* magic.

From backroom payola deals and side-hustling A&R scouts to shady producer agreements and double-dipping management firms, the music business was "a cruel and shallow money trench, a long plastic hallway where thieves and pimps run free." At least, Hunter S. Thompson seemed to think so. It was hard to argue.

From the moment I started working as a talent manager, my psychological horizons began to expand. Suddenly, I no longer felt like the only sociopath in the world. Not only did most of the people I met appear to embrace my personality type, many seemed prone to co-opt it. Indeed, I was shocked by the number of people I encountered in the entertainment business who, after hearing about my diagnosis, professed a similar disposition.

"Oh, I'm totally a sociopath," said Nathan, a music producer, shortly after we met. "I don't give a fuck about anything."

One look at his production contract indicated this wasn't entirely accurate. Nathan seemed to care a *lot* when it came to royalties—so much so that any artist signed to his production company had to surrender almost all of their creative ownership.

"But that probably explains why I'm so good at my job. I like to do bad things," he added with a sly grin. "I like being a sociopath."

Before diving into the music industry, I'd always struggled to find people willing to accept the type of person I am—much less admit to having a similar personality type. But now I was surrounded! The effect was hypnotizing (and initially blinding). So enthralled with the prospect of like-minded company, I gave zero thought to the credence of the sociopathic self-diagnoses of my so-called cohorts. Like a dehydrated traveler, I simply guzzled every last drop. At least, I did at first. And then I met Jennifer.

Jennifer was a record label executive tasked with handling the sophomore album release of one of my father's most lucrative clients. Because Dad wanted to make sure the new record was successful, he encouraged us to meet.

"The rock world is nothing like the pop world," she explained to me one night. It was a year after I'd started working as a manager and we were having drinks at Casa Vega, my favorite Mexican restaurant in the Valley. "You've gotta be tough to survive," she added, "especially if you're a girl."

I smiled and stepped quickly into the opening she had unwittingly provided. "Well, that's perfect for me because I'm a sociopath."

She grinned, thinking I was joking, but then listened closely as I gave her a brief explanation of my history and diagnosis.

"Whoa," she said when I finished. "That's *amazing*." She lowered her voice and leaned in conspiratorially. "To be honest, I've always sort of wondered if *I* was a sociopath."

"Huh," I replied. I'd been hearing that a lot lately.

"No, but you know what I *mean*?" Jennifer pressed. "Things that make other people cry don't make me cry at *all*. Like, true crime stuff. I'm obsessed with it!" She looked around again. "And I have totally fantasized about killing people."

I shook my head. "Well, that's . . . Wanting to kill someone doesn't

automatically mean you're a sociopath," I said. "That's sort of a mis-
conception. Sociopathy in general is actually way misunderstood—"

"No, but you know what I mean?" Jennifer repeated, cutting me
off. "I love dark stuff, like vampires." She smiled. "It's probably why
I got into marketing for rock bands!"

I was starting to wonder if I should revisit my policy about revealing my personality type. But I'd hardly had time to consider it before
she rested a hand on my forearm. "I get you, girl," she said, nodding.

I glanced down at Jennifer's hand and saw her baby finger was
wrapped in surgical bandages. "What happened there?" I asked,
happy to change the subject.

Jennifer pulled her hand away. "Oooooh," she said. "I rescued this
dog, a pit bull. She's the sweetest thing, but last month she started a
fight with my other dog. When I tried to separate them, she bit my
finger off."

This gruesome admission made me choke on my cocktail. I coughed
and took a deep sip. "I'm sorry," I said. "She bit your finger *off*?"

Jennifer nodded. "Yeah. My neighbor had to drive me to the emergency room. Luckily, the doctors were able to sew it back on." She
smiled. "Do you have any doggies?"

I was speechless. "Uhm, no, I don't have—hold on a sec," I said,
trying to get my bearings. "What happened to . . . your *other* dog?"
I asked.

Jennifer grimaced. "Yeah, that's an ongoing issue. Lady's only aggressive with other dogs, so I have to keep them separated all the time."
She paused to signal our waiter for another drink. "Doggies are the
best. Especially now that I'm divorced. Did you know I'm divorced?"

I shook my head. Jennifer didn't seem to notice.

"I was married for ten years and all I have to show for it is my
shitty little house in the Valley. Next time, I want someone to take
care of *me*, y'know? Like a rich guy." Jennifer drained the rest of her
margarita. "That's what I have now—a rich guy. His name's Joel and
he's *so* rich." Her eyes widened. "He knows other rich guys, too, you
know. We could set you up, and we could go on double dates!"

I shook my head. "I'm not really—"

"He's got this huge place in Beverly Hills flats," she interrupted wistfully. "I feel, like, that's where I should live, too, y'know?" Her expression darkened briefly as she stared off into space, then added, "I *deserve* it."

I was confused. Not knowing what else to do, I started modeling her behavior. I put on my most sympathetic expression and rested my hand against her forearm, careful not to disturb her reattached finger. "I get you, girl," I said.

But I *didn't* get her. And the more I got to know her, the more confused I became. Like many of the self-diagnostic "confessions" I'd been hearing from people in the entertainment industry, Jennifer's speculation that she was a sociopath *almost* made sense. She regularly complained about feeling "empty." She was frequently impulsive, and her behavior, like mine, was often destructive. She was also highly insensitive, demonstrating either impunity or indifference to other people's boundaries. But this, I quickly discovered, was where the similarities stopped.

Whereas I suffered from a lack of feeling, Jennifer seemed to have a surplus. For starters, she had terrible mood swings. She would switch from euphoria to agitation for no apparent reason. She also had a terrible temper and limited self-control, frequently storming out of meetings or screaming at staff members when she didn't get what she wanted. But perhaps most different from me, Jennifer seemed to be highly erratic. This was particularly true when it came to her romantic relationships. Even the slightest perceived rejection would send her into a cognitive dissonant meltdown.

"She sounds borderline," Dr. Carlin surmised.

I was at the therapist's office for our weekly session. Curious about Jennifer's personality type (and its similarities to mine), I'd asked for her take.

"Borderline personality disorder is often confused with sociopathy," she explained, "because a lot of the *behavioral* diagnostics are similar, the observational stuff. Unstable relationships, impulsivity, self-destructiveness, habitual emptiness, anger, hostility—many of those traits overlap. Same with narcissism, actually."

"But why is that the case," I asked, "if we're so different?"

"Because your behavior is motivated by different things," said Dr. Carlin. "Borderlines act out due to an abundance of feeling. Sociopaths act out because of a deficit.

"It's all about attachment," she continued after a beat. "People who suffer from borderline personality disorder are desperate for love. It's why they tend to be hyperemotional. They will go to any length to avoid loss of affection, even if it means disrespecting boundaries or engaging in destructive behavior. They don't care about anyone else's needs or feelings. All that matters to them are *their* needs and *their* feelings. Other people are perceived as self-objects. In other words, borderlines don't view others as separate individuals but as extensions of themselves. Their perception of the world is therefore purely egocentric and one-dimensional.

"Sociopaths, on the other hand, are *not* motivated by attachment," Dr. Carlin continued. "If anything, their view of the world is shaped by a *lack* of attachment. But that worldview is similarly egocentric and one-dimensional. It's why people always get them confused."

The more I paid attention, the more I agreed. On the surface, Jennifer *was* a lot like me. Her emotions—although far more bombastic than mine—were fairly limited. She appeared incapable of empathy and immune to shame. She was frequently dishonest. Her behavior seemed to vacillate between extreme periods of good and bad, and her attachments to other people were not symbiotic, but based on self-interest.

So why wasn't I relieved? Given my psychological isolation, I should have been happy to have met someone moderately similar, even if our specific diagnoses were different. After all, Jennifer was certainly happy to have met *me*. *I'm so glad we met. I feel like you're my soul twin!* she texted several days after our initial meetup at Casa Vega.

But the feeling wasn't mutual. I loathed Jennifer. Her excess emotion made me uneasy. While there was a method to *my* madness, she struck me as unhinged. Her turbulent behavior was ruled only by whatever self-serving sensation was rearing its ugly head. *She reminds me of Syd*, I thought with disgust. *As if sociopaths don't have a bad reputation already, we've got people like Jennifer making things worse.*

Jennifer was no sociopath. She was worse. A knockoff. A sheep in wolf's clothing. It made me angry. The more I thought about it, the angrier I became. I found myself thinking about Jennifer all the time, and not just casual ruminations but specific fantasies of violence against her. And I *liked* it. It was almost soothing to have a fixed point on which to focus my attention. Even though, thanks to my "prescriptions," it had been a few years since I'd felt any serious rise in "pressure," I was always looking for an opportunity to feel.

Working as a manager, trying to be "good," going to therapy, even meeting up with "friends" for drinks, all of these things were normal on the surface. All of it was healthy, in *theory*. However, the reality of my situation remained the same. No matter what was happening on the outside, my internal climate was always at risk of stagnating. Fortunately, once I met Jennifer, I no longer had to worry. Hating her not only helped to keep my apathy in check, but my behavior as well.

"Patric!" Jennifer shouted. "I have *got* to talk to you!"

It was the morning of the album release, a month after our first meeting at Casa Vega, and I had just arrived at a radio station where she'd arranged a live interview with the band. Stepping out of my car, my shoulders slumped at the sight of her waiting for me in the parking lot. *Ugh*, I thought. I could see she was agitated and disheveled.

"Why haven't you returned my calls?" she asked frantically,

gasping for breath as she trotted across the lot. "Something really bad happened, and I need to talk to you," Jennifer insisted.

I shook my head. "No chance. The interview is in ten minutes."

"You don't understand. It's important!" Jennifer put her hand on my arm and gently pulled me close. "You know my dog Lady?"

Sighing impatiently, I looked to see the lead singer entering the lobby of the radio station. "Are you serious? I'm not listening to a dog story right now."

"She killed my neighbor's dog!"

I was shocked. *"What?"*

"You know I have to keep her away from my other dog, right? So I've been putting her in the backyard. Well, my neighbors keep their dog in *their* backyard. Anyway, Lady must have dug under the fence or something because she got hold of their dog and killed it! I saw the whole thing happen."

Now it was my turn to grab *her* arm. Jennifer's elbow made a satisfying pop as I yanked her out of my clients' line of sight. "You watched your dog dig under a fence, attack another dog, and kill it?" I demanded.

She nodded.

"Why?" I asked. "Why didn't you stop her? Why didn't you *do* something?"

In response, she weakly presented her recently reattached finger.

"Oh, you've gotta be fucking kidding me," I snipped, genuinely disgusted. "What did your neighbor say?"

"That's the thing," Jennifer said, her voice rising in a panic. "After Lady was, y'know, *done*, I panicked. I knew I had to hide the body, so I took it out to the street and left it there. They'll think it was *their* fault it got out, right? They'll think it got hit by a car?"

"What?!" I exclaimed. "What the fuck is wrong with you?"

"I had no choice!" Jennifer shrieked, starting to cry. "She took me to the hospital last time. She knows Lady's aggressive! If she finds out, she'll make me put her down!"

"Oh my God," I said, when I made the connection. "This is the *same* neighbor who drove you to the emergency room? What the fuck is wrong with you?" I asked again.

"I told you," Jennifer insisted. "I'm a sociopath!"

"You're not a sociopath," I said, furious. "You're a fucking *moron*."

She sobbed, and her wails were attracting attention in the parking lot. "Oh my God, what if I get caught?" She moaned again. "I feel so *baaaad*," she sputtered between tears. Grabbing my wrists, she pleaded with me, "Patric! You have to help me! You have to tell me what to do!"

I wrested myself from her grasp. "You want my advice?" I hissed. "Go home. Get yourself cleaned up and stop spinning out. I'll handle the fucking interview on my own."

That seemed to snap her out of her hysteria. "Yes," she said, sniffling. "You're right. I should just take a deep breath and be kind to myself." She made an exaggerated display of inhaling and exhaling, then said, "I'm not going home, though."

"Why not?" I asked, immediately regretting the question.

"The guy I'm seeing, Joel," she said. "I'm just gonna go to his house. I deserve some retail therapy after the week I've had!"

I actively resisted the urge to stab her with my keys. My nails were sharp and they pierced the flesh of my palms. "Fine," I said evenly. "I don't care. Just get it together."

I turned for the station, but Jennifer wasn't done.

"Patric? Can I ask you something?" The tears and hysteria were gone now.

I spun around. "What?"

"So, Joel gave me one of his cars to drive, right? It's nice. It's a Porsche. But he didn't give me his credit card or anything. I sort of feel like that's dickish." She paused. "That was dickish, right?" she asked again. "Like, we've been seeing each other for a while now, and I'm at his place all the time. I feel like he should have offered me his card to go shopping."

I took a moment to fully appreciate my hatred. "Totally," I said finally. Then I headed into the station.

I made it in time for the interview. After dispatching the band to the DJ booth, I took a seat in the listening area. The room was fortunately empty, and, as I stared into space, I could feel apathy—blissfully—start to rise. But I couldn't zone out for too long. Something was bugging me, a feeling of discomfort. I glanced down at my hands. My palms were bleeding.

CHAPTER 12

Fauxciopath

A couple weeks later, I sat in my bedroom putting the final touches on my makeup. It was the night of the Midsummer Night's Dream party at the Playboy Mansion, an evening of debauchery I eagerly anticipated every year. But as I stared at myself in my vanity's mirror, I realized I didn't feel very excited. If anything, I felt claustrophobic. I lifted a makeup brush absentmindedly to my cheek as my thoughts wandered to the therapy appointment I'd had earlier that day and what I suspected was the cause of my stress.

It had felt like a normal session at first. Normal for me, anyway. I'd spent the first few minutes recounting Jennifer's dog story and my disgust that she'd used her sociopathic self-diagnosis as an excuse for her actions.

"It made me *sick*," I fumed. "She's no fucking sociopath. She's a dumb-fuck road-whore who deserves to have her ass kicked." I shot the therapist a defiant glance. "I swear to God, if I met her in a dark alley, I'd take her out."

Dr. Carlin nodded thoughtfully. "It sounds like it was disappointing for you, realizing that she wasn't the person she said she was."

I snorted sarcastically. "It was disappointing I didn't get to stab her with my keys in the parking lot."

"I agree that what she did was reprehensible," Dr. Carlin acknowledged. "My guess is she knows it, too. That's why she wanted to talk to you about it, because she was traumatized."

"HA!" I replied. "That woman wasn't traumatized by *shit*. She spent the entire weekend hanging out in the flats, cash-fucking her sugar daddy."

Dr. Carlin raised an eyebrow. "Really? How do you know?"

"Because I watched them."

A few days after the dog incident, we hosted an album release party at a local bar called Lola's. Watching from a window close to the entrance, I sneered when Jennifer arrived in Joel's Porsche. *Asshole*, I thought.

Jennifer said, "Hi," as she walked through the door.

"Hey there," I replied, giving her an unexpected hug. "Were you able to relax?"

She smiled, relieved by my friendly demeanor. "Something like that," she said slyly. I giggled with her as if we were old girlfriends.

"Well, you seem . . . better," I offered.

She looked at me, confused. Then her face contorted into something resembling sadness. "Yeah, but I'm still so sad about that doggie, though!" she wailed, a bit too forcefully. "You know?"

"For sure." I put my arm around her back as I led her to the bar. "So, tell me about this guy's house," I said. "I'm dying to see it."

"Oh my God, Patric, you'd *die*," she replied, as all traces of sorrow disappeared from her face. She told me the address and explained, "It's right off Beverly. It's got five bedrooms *plus* a studio. And between you and me"—she looked around before lowering her voice—"I'm gonna fuck him in all of them!" She laughed and said, "Like Goldilocks, y'know?"

"You are *bad*!" I shook my head playfully, fighting the bile rising in my throat. "So tell me," I said, pulling her close, "about *Joel's* bedroom."

It was the room off the pool. I took my time finding it. I left the party early and enjoyed a leisurely dinner at home before taking a long bath. By midnight I figured the coast was clear, so I got into my car and drove to Beverly Hills.

The upscale neighborhood's streets were empty, and I easily found a place to park on the side of the road. Creeping alongside some low hedges, I made my way to Joel's house and hopped his small fence. I couldn't believe the lackluster security for such a posh part of LA. I reached the back of the house and flattened my body against a wall near the main bedroom. Hidden from view, I inched closer to a set of patio doors and peered through a small pane of glass.

They hadn't bothered to close the curtains before drifting off to sleep, so I could see the whole room. On the right was a bureau and television that took up most of the wall above it. At the far end of the room, a set of double doors opened to a hallway. On the left was the bed, a large four-poster monstrosity with equally ugly mahogany end tables. Something caught my eye, and I saw Jennifer rolling over in her sleep. She was topless, with her wrist bent across her chest. Joel lay next to her with his back to me. *Bummer*, I thought. I'd wanted to know what he looked like.

I stood on my tiptoes and grabbed a door handle to balance. I hadn't expected it to move but, to my surprise, it did. *Seriously?* I thought. I pushed the handle again to confirm it. The door was open, all right. All I had to do was push. So, without giving it much thought, I did. Three quick beeps chimed from an alarm system, and I froze. My focus darted to the bed, certain the noise would wake one (or both) of them. But, no. The alarm hadn't been triggered. The beeps were simply an open-door chime. I paused to gather my senses. Then I stepped inside.

Like so many places before, the stillness of Joel's house felt like it was bursting with frenetic energy. I stood there for a few seconds, basking in it. Then I took a deep breath and relaxed into apathy. After a few seconds I crept closer toward the bed. I stared down at Jennifer. *She's a lot less repulsive when she's asleep*, I thought. *Still, how nice it would be to rid the world of her.*

I knew this thought was extreme, but I allowed myself to think it. I'd never done something so audacious before, broken into an occupied house to watch its sleeping residents—even if it was only an accident. For a minute I just stood there, imagining all the things I could do. But then muscle memory took over, and some part of me registered the foolishness of my position. I remembered my childhood list of rules and the words written in bold print at the top:

NO HURTING ANYBODY

This is a bad idea, I thought.

Moonlight bounced off the pool, causing a ripple of light to move hypnotically across the bedspread. I gazed at it, wishing I could lie down and go to sleep. Instead, I blinked hard and reminded myself I needed to leave. Making my way carefully across the bedroom, I slipped silently out the door.

Dr. Carlin sat quietly as I prattled on about my excursion. When I was done, she set down her pen and looked at me sadly. "Patric," she said gravely, "I'm not sure I'm the right therapist for you."

Her words took me by surprise, and I found myself reeling. "What?!" I exclaimed. "What are you talking about?"

"Behavior like this," she replied. "I'm afraid we're getting into Tarasoff territory." As a licensed psychologist, Dr. Carlin was bound by the Tarasoff rule. In school we'd learned about the Supreme Court of California's decision in *Tarasoff v. Regents of the University of California*. It requires that all therapists must report to the proper authorities any patient who poses a serious risk of inflicting bodily injury upon a specific victim.

I threw up my hands. "Tarasoff? Are you serious? I didn't go there to hurt anybody. I didn't go there to do anything! The door practically opened by itself!"

"It's not just Tarasoff," she continued, her voice softening. "As your therapist, it's my ethical responsibility to *help* you. But we've been working together for a while now and your behavior only seems to be getting worse."

"Great," I said, my voice dripping with sarcasm. "So once again I tell the truth—to my own fucking therapist, no less—and I *still* end up getting punished for it."

"I'm not punishing you, Patric," Dr. Carlin insisted. "But it's not right for me to continue seeing you if I don't believe I can help you, particularly when you are breaking into people's homes."

"I'm not breaking into people's homes!" I nearly shouted. "I went into *one* home, and it was basically an accident." I snorted. "Besides, what do you care? That chick is a dog-killing clot-roach!"

"You sound angry," Dr Carlin said.

"I *am* angry!"

"Why?" she asked.

"Because she's a LIAR!" I erupted. "Jennifer isn't a sociopath. She's a *faux*ciopath. She'll tell anyone who'll listen how 'dark' she is, but it's only for attention. The truth is she doesn't know the first thing about darkness. None of them do! Jennifer, Nathan, all the other sleazebags I've met lately, bragging about being sociopaths. They're *all* full of shit. They're cheap fakes using *my* diagnosis so they can write off their disgusting behavior as some sort of symptom."

"Wait a minute," interjected Dr. Carlin. "What do you mean *your* diagnosis? What are you saying? That you're the only one allowed to be a sociopath? That you're the only one allowed to justify bad behavior?"

"Maybe I *am*," I said. "But not because I think I'm the only one who's a sociopath. I'm *not* the only one. THAT'S MY WHOLE POINT!"

I jabbed a finger at the window. "People like Jennifer? Those fauxciopaths? They're making it harder for *real* sociopaths to get help. Don't you see?" I said. "Those copycats don't know a thing about *real* sociopathy. They can't imagine the relentless, never-ceasing, all-encompassing fucking void of *true* apathy. All they *do* is care, and wish they didn't. Those people never have to worry they might hurt someone—that they might fucking *kill* someone—just so they can *feel* something." I stopped and took a deep inhale, forcing my breath to regulate. "So maybe I *am* sanctimonious," I told her. "Maybe I *am* being judgmental. But I don't care. Those people are *liars*. They're phonies. And I fucking *hate* them."

The therapist shook her head and looked down. "This is my concern," she said softly. "You are angry, and you are struggling. You can argue semantics all you'd like. But what you did, following that woman to her boyfriend's house and going inside? That is not okay."

"It won't happen again," I said quietly.

"How am I supposed to trust that?" Dr. Carlin asked. "Not five minutes ago you were telling me how much you wanted to hurt her. And now I find out you spent the weekend stalking her and breaking into her boyfriend's house."

"I didn't stalk her," I argued, then held up my hand as the therapist opened her mouth to protest. "Stalking applies to someone who willfully, maliciously, and repeatedly follows or harasses someone else with the intent to harm." Dr. Carlin didn't reply, but she shot me an incredulous glare.

"I had no malicious intent when I was following her," I continued. "I wasn't even mad when I decided to go. I was just . . . bored."

"You *weren't* bored," Dr. Carlin countered. "You were looking for a psychological release as a way to stabilize your mental process. You were engaging in a risk-driven act to reduce your apathy."

"Whatever," I said with a shrug. "Same thing."

"No," she argued. "It is *not* the same thing. People who are bored pick up a book or turn on the television. What you did was very different. You are hunting. You are escalating. It's a problem, Patric. This is inadequately motivated antisocial behavior."

Number seven on Cleckley's list.

"So tell me," she continued. "How long are you going to manage your apathy this way? How long until the hunting isn't enough?" She paused. "How long until you hurt someone?"

"How the fuck do I know?" I snapped. I sat back and folded my arms. "Look, I'm doing the best I can," I continued, frustrated. "You know as well as I do. There's no cure for this. There's no actual treatment plan. So what the fuck am I supposed to do?"

Dr. Carlin sighed. "This is why I feel like I'm not helping you."

I didn't respond. The two of us sat in silence as the sun started to set.

"You know," I said after a while, "there's this researcher, Linda Mealey. She's done some really interesting work on sociopathy. Have you heard of her?"

Dr. Carlin shook her head. "I haven't."

"Well, she wrote a paper on game theory and sociopaths. She said sociopaths are competitively disadvantaged individuals who use cheating strategies as a means of trying to make the best of a bad psychological hand.

"I memorized it," I said, "because she's right. That's what *I* am. That's what I *do*." I paused. "The stealing when I was a kid. My "prescriptions" in college. My fixation on Jennifer. All of it. Those are *my* cheating strategies. I'm just trying to make the best of the hand I was dealt."

Dr. Carlin pondered this for a moment. "But your choice to go into the house after you realized the door was unlocked wasn't part of any strategy. It was an impulsive escalation."

"So?"

"So how do I know something like that won't happen again?"

I shook my head. "Because it won't."

"That's not good enough," she said simply. "I think that if you mean what you say about wanting to get better and you want to continue working with me, then we need to have an agreement."

"What sort of agreement?" I asked cautiously.

"A contract," she said. "In writing. You agree to stop engaging in illegal activity—completely—and I will agree to continue to treat you."

I raised my eyebrows, dubious. "What's to prevent me from agreeing to stop, but then just doing it behind your back?"

"Nothing," said the therapist. "But I don't think that would be very helpful, do you?"

So we agreed. I would sign an agreement promising Dr. Carlin I would no longer engage in any illegal behavior, including following people without their knowledge. In exchange, she would continue to treat me.

I left the office that afternoon feeling okay, but as I sat in my bedroom preparing for the party, it was clear that something had changed. The contract I'd agreed to sign with Dr. Carlin was already making me uneasy. An authentic relationship with my therapist was now contingent upon a promise I knew I couldn't keep. I was trapped. It was a dynamic that was unsettling and familiar.

I kept my head down as I walked into the Playboy Mansion, through the foyer to the first bartender, hoping I wouldn't run into anyone I knew. Pushing through the crowd, I crossed the backyard to the pool, where the grotto was in full swing, and downed several cocktails on the way. I found an inconspicuous place to sit next to one of the grotto's caves and stared into the water, the lights beneath the surface giving everything a phosphorescent glow.

This sucks, I thought.

I wanted to be excited. I wanted to be hiding in plain sight, watching people and observing their mannerisms. Under normal circumstances I would be. But my thoughts kept returning to my session with Dr. Carlin and the nagging suspicion that I was a lost cause. The party seemed to shrink, and I could feel myself fading into hopelessness. It reminded me of the night I jumped from my balcony.

A splash from the pool startled me, and I took a sharp inhale. I felt my forehead. The world was spinning. The alcohol had kicked in and I knew I needed to leave. But I wasn't sure I could make it across the yard, much less back to my car. I swallowed hard and took another deep breath, steadying myself against one of the grotto's rock walls.

I'm just buzzed, I thought. *It's no big deal. I just need a quiet place to ride it out.* I looked across the yard again, scanning the property for an escape. I fixed my sights on the back patio and slowly took my hand off the wall. I took a careful step forward as I regained my balance. Then another. And another. The walk wasn't far but seemed to take forever. "Why'd I fucking drink so much?" I muttered. I'd always had a delicate relationship with alcohol. I liked being relaxed but certainly didn't like the idea of losing control. My destructive behavior was hard enough to keep in check under normal circumstances.

I slipped off my shoes. The cool grass under my feet improved my mood. I looked up at the bright lights of the mansion. *Getting there*, I thought.

There were people everywhere. I took my phone out of my purse and acted as if I was talking to someone. My steps were quicker as I approached the building and climbed the marble stairs. Finally reaching the patio, I grasped the door's handle as if it was the edge of a swimming pool. A wave of air-conditioning hit my face and I was happy for the relief. I walked slowly toward a giant split staircase and leaned against one of the immense wooden sculptures that formed its banisters. It was a statue of a man wearing a wide-brimmed hat. He was holding an orb in one hand and something like a spear in the other. It looked like Don Quixote.

"What's with the orb?" I asked him.

The massive room that separated the front and back entrances was awash in light. I shielded my eyes from the glare of the titanic chandelier that hung from the vaulted ceiling. *I just need quiet*, I thought. *I need darkness.* I glanced at the front door. *Maybe I should just start walking to my car.* I was parked a considerable distance away and, with the state I was in, I knew the idea was foolish. But I was running out of options.

There was an archway directly across from me, draped with thick black curtains. It framed a corridor, I knew, that led to Hugh Hefner's private office. Hef's office would be dark and quiet and empty. It was the perfect place for me to recalibrate and get myself together. I cut across the marble floor to the archway. There were a dozen people still congregating in the foyer, far too many for me to sneak into the office unnoticed. I turned my back to the room and decided to wait them out, watching their reflections in a window.

After a few minutes the crowd receded like a tide. I figured it wouldn't be long before the next swell, so I quickly pushed through the velvet curtains and slipped into the archway. The corridor was nearly pitch-black, and my discomfort was swiftly eliminated by the sensation of obscurity. Invisibility, once again, provided an immediate solution to my stuck stress. The rising pressure, exasperated by my anxious and claustrophobic reaction, had been neutralized. Now the apathy was a welcome repose.

Disappearing into Hef's office, I closed my eyes and leaned back against the door. I took a moment to embrace the stillness, then wandered around the cavernous room as my vision slowly adjusted to the darkness. A life-sized ceramic tiger sat next to a chaise lounge. Its eyes were sparkling as if every bit of the limited light inside the room had decided to congregate in their tiny apertures. I sat on the chaise and rested my hand on the tiger's head.

"I wonder what would happen if we tried to leave together?" I asked the tiger. "You, me, and Don Quixote." I smiled. "That would be fantastic.

"Fantastic and uninviting behavior, with drink and sometimes without," I said, reciting number thirteen on Cleckley's list. Then I rested my head against the plush fabric. "This would definitely fall under the former," I confirmed drowsily.

With noise from the party floating through the drapes in velvety muffled tones, I was so relaxed that I almost fell asleep. But my groggy spell was broken by the crash of a glass exploding onto the marble floor somewhere, and at once I was wide awake. I listened for a few seconds, then pushed myself up and off the recliner. I crossed the room and took a seat at Hef's desk. A notepad sat next to the telephone. Each page had the Playboy bunny embossed on the top and, below that, "from HUGH M. HEFNER."

I liked Mr. Hefner. I wasn't sure how he would feel about me sitting alone at his desk instead of socializing, but I imagined he wouldn't be terribly upset. Just to be sure, though, I scribbled him a quick a note:

> *Hi, Hef,*
> *In case you were wondering who was hanging out in your office tonight, it was Patric. I promise I didn't disturb anything even though I really wanted to.*
> *xxP*

I slipped the note under the corner of the telephone, which triggered a thought that had been gnawing at me for some time. In recent weeks there had been at least a dozen different times I'd wanted to make a call.

"What do you think?" I asked the tiger. "Should we see if he's home?" I lifted the sleek black handle and dialed the number I knew by heart. David answered on the second ring.

"Guess where I am," I said.

"Hey!" he said. "I was hoping it was you. Caller ID just said L.A."

"Holmby Hills, actually," I told him. "I'm at the Playboy Mansion."

"Get *out!*" David laughed. "I've gotta visit you someday. Your life is so crazy!"

The thought of David visiting made me so happy. Of course, I knew better than to put my faith in simple solutions. But still, it was lovely to imagine. Hearing his voice, thinking about being together again, it felt good. It felt honest. It felt *real*, even though I knew it was a fantasy.

"How long's it been?" he asked. "Two years now?"

"Closer to three," I said. It was the longest we'd gone without seeing each other since we'd met. "But who's counting?"

Neither of us said anything for a bit. David broke the silence. "It's weird," he said. "We haven't seen each other in years, we live on different sides of the country . . . but I still think about you every day. Like you live next door."

I smiled, glad I wasn't the only one. "Me, too."

"What do you think that means?" he asked.

"I don't know," I replied, absentmindedly rifling through one of Hef's desk drawers.

"Well, for what it's worth," he said softly, "you're still the coolest girl I've ever known."

I stopped fidgeting and smiled. "Yeah? Well, I think you're pretty cool, too."

After another pause, I decided to lighten the mood. "So I'm gonna send you a little present from Hugh Hefner's office. Think of it as a reward for being such a loyal subscriber."

"Please don't steal anything."

"Christ, will you relax?" I told him. "I swear to God, you're such a square."

"As in . . . not a THIEF?!"

"Ask forgiveness, not permission," I replied.

"That's terrifying."

"Well, it's my motto, and I'd say it's worked out pretty well so far." I could hear David laughing. "Address, please?"

He gave me his mailing address and we said our goodbyes. Then he added:

"I really love you, you know."

And I *did* know it. Even after all these years. "I love you, too," I said. Then I hung up.

There, in the dark, my ear still warm from the phone, I felt unbearably at peace. But—unlike when I'd first entered Hef's inner sanctum—my tranquility was not the result of invisibility or apathy. It was because I felt *seen*. I felt acceptance. I felt honest, and yet I still felt safe.

I slipped the notepad into my pocket and turned to leave. Halfway to the door I stopped myself. I returned to the desk, grabbed a pen, and added to my note:

PS—Not true, I actually took one of your notepads so I could send it to an old friend. I hope you don't mind. xx

David would be proud of me, I thought, as I walked away. Then I thought of my mother. The unexpected memory washed over me like a tidal wave. I recalled the way I used to feel when I would confess my crimes and she would call me her honest girl. For a second, I was transported to San Francisco and the smell of chocolate cake, to a time before I had to hide, to a time before I knew words like "sociopath" and "fauxciopath," to a time when my feelings for someone else were so powerful they were all I needed to try harder, to be better. To a time when self-acceptance wasn't a task but a given. *Before* I understood that I was different. Before I felt like I was all alone. *It wasn't always bad stuff*, I thought. Once upon a time there *was* another way to make the apathy disappear.

A flicker of light distracted me and I saw the tiger's eye glimmering in the darkened room. I winked at him, turned, and walked away. A few seconds later I left the mansion and started down the long and winding road back to my car, wondering if what I was feeling now was lingering inebriation or something else. I no longer felt drunk, though. This was something different. This was something . . . normal.

CHAPTER 13

Home

I was at home late one evening a few weeks later when I was startled by a knock at the door. I got up from the couch and peered through the peephole. My jaw dropped as I threw open the door.

David smiled nervously. "I wasn't sure if you were serious," he said, "but I figured I'd roll the dice."

I leapt into his arms, nearly knocking him over.

"How'd you get here?" I asked finally, my voice muffled against his neck.

He laughed. "I drove, silly. Packed up everything I own and just headed west."

I pulled back and stared at him, still in shock. "For *me*?"

"For you," he said. And then he kissed me.

It was exactly the way I'd always dreamt it would be, on the rare occasions I'd allowed myself to dream. In an instant, all my old feelings returned, splintering my apathy as they rose. David's strong arms and steady countenance felt like what I'd always considered "home" to mean.

There was no awkward adjustment period. It was like we'd never been apart. Overnight, I went from being an independent single woman to being half of a couple. I'll admit the change was quite abrupt. I'd never been in a conventional relationship as an adult, and I'd never been the type of person who rushed into things. I liked privacy. Secrecy. Discipline. I preferred to keep people at arm's length, and to keep my house an immaculate sanctuary. So I surprised myself when, from the moment David showed up unannounced on my doorstep, I traded it all to be with him.

"You're like a magician," he said.

We were relaxing in the Los Angeles sunshine the following weekend, sipping wine at Moraga Vineyards. The private winery was tucked away behind a thick gate in a canyon of the Santa Monica Mountains, and it was one of my favorite places in the city. I'd been invited to a tasting a few months before and was thrilled that I could now take David as my plus-one. "This place," he continued, looking around. "It's like a mirage. How'd you even find it?"

He was right. Moraga *was* like a mirage. A stunning vineyard hidden in the heart of Bel Air, I'd never known it was there until I stumbled upon it during a walk one afternoon. Astonished by the seemingly endless rows of pristine grapevines, I made my way to the street and looked around until I found the entrance. Then I knocked on the door and introduced myself to the owners.

"So you just knocked on the door?" David asked. "What did you say?"

"The truth!" I replied. "That this place is the Mecca of secret gardens and they deserve a medal for turning the land into a working vineyard."

"Wait," David interjected. "Who is 'they'?"

"The owners. Tom and Ruth Jones."

"Hold up," he said, his eyes wide. "This is Tom Jones's house? *The* Tom Jones?"

"No," I said, laughing. "I mean, yes, this is Tom Jones's house. But not the singer. Trust me, though: This Tom Jones is the best Tom Jones."

"So, you just walked up to the door and said, 'Hi.'" David shook his head. "Did they freak out?"

"No!" I said. "They were very sweet and told me all about the property and the history. Then they asked for my address to put me

on the list for tastings and stuff." I waved my hand around at the surroundings. "And voilà!"

"Like I said," he replied, his eyes twinkling. "You're a magician."

I felt the same way about him. Suddenly, I was no longer tor-
mented with the task of managing my apathy. The second David
arrived, it disappeared, eradicated by overwhelming feelings of love.
Mad, crazy, all-encompassing love that never seemed to diminish. I
no longer had to worry about prescriptions or cheating strategies or
pressure or sociopathic anxiety. I could just . . . be. With nothing to
hold me back, I set about exploring life as a "normal" person.

It reminded me of a show I used to watch on Nickelodeon called
Super Toy Run. In the show, kids were given five minutes to race
through a Toys "R" Us and grab everything they could. As a child,
I spent hours re-creating the circumstances in my mind, categoriz-
ing the aisles, and perfecting my own strategy for how to achieve the
best outcome in the shortest time. And now, I was doing something
similar. My plan was simply to run around life and grab as many normal experiences as I could. Going to dinner and a movie after work
was a joy. A Sunday morning walk around the neighborhood, sipping coffee and holding hands, was an adventure. The more mundane
the better. I embraced all opportunities to be conventional. Ordinary
things—like buying groceries or crawling into bed with him at the
end of the day—made me feel effervescent with contentment. For the
first time in my life, I wasn't just imagining a life free from emotional
detachment and shadow-self temptations. I was experiencing it. I was
free! I wanted to shout my excitement from the rooftops.

And I wasn't the only person grateful for David's influence. My
father, although surprised by the velocity of our relationship, welcomed the change in his daughter's lifestyle.

"You really seem to like this guy," he said.

Dad and I were having our weekly Sunday dinner at the Palm.
As usual, we'd met at the bar while waiting for our table. David had

quickly become a fixture at our "family" dinners, but he was running a bit late. I was happy for the opportunity to gush behind his back.

"Dad," I said, "I don't just *like* him. I'm like a crazy person. I am crazy, insane, madly in love with him!" The waiter set a freezing martini in front of me and I took a deep gulp, slurping up the thin chips of ice floating on top. "He makes me feel like all the bad parts of myself aren't bad at all; they're just misunderstood. I feel like the best version of myself when I'm around him. I'm serious, if he asked me to marry him tomorrow, I would."

"Whoa," Dad replied. "Maybe pump the brakes a bit."

"Why?" I asked. "David's the guy. I know it in my soul." I paused, then lowered my voice. "It might sound nuts," I said, "but it's like I found my missing half—my *good* half." I shook my head in disbelief as I considered it. "All the things I've always struggled with, empathy, emotions." I paused again. "It's like David has filled the space in my heart where those things are supposed to be. And he's such a *good* person, Dad." I sighed. "He gives me a reason to be better. He makes me feel like *I* can be a good person, too."

It was true. David was patient. Thoughtful. Calm. But unlike my sense of calm (which was often simply indifference), David radiated a serene stillness. This wasn't just evident in his demeanor, but also in his marvelous ability to recognize the sublime in the simple. Whether it was taking the time to consciously devour the perfect sandwich from Bay Cities Deli or stopping to point out a constellation in the night sky, David was masterful at savoring simplicity. Surprisingly, for the first time in my life, I was able to follow suit. Even household tasks, like cooking, now brought me immeasurable joy.

Though I'd always loved food, I'd never taken much interest in learning how to make it myself. But when David arrived, cooking became my passion. I embraced the role of happy homemaker and began making our dinners nearly every night. I started with basic stuff but eventually became more adventurous, spending hours mapping out menus and experimenting with different flavor profiles. After work, I'd head straight to the kitchen to chop ingredients and select the wine. Once the meal was planned, I'd remove layers of cakes from the refrigerator (where I'd left them to cool after baking them in the morning) and then take my seat at the dining room table. There I'd slice each layer in half using pieces of thread—just the way my mother had once done—and slather homemade icing between them, stacking the pieces into towers of decadence.

Sitting there, licking chocolate off my fingertips, I often thought of the man with the German shepherd I'd followed home to his perfect little family. The slice of life I'd captured though their living room window remained crystal clear, like a vintage Polaroid pinned for years in the dusty corner of a vision board. *One day I'm going to be just like them*, I'd imagined. And now I was.

Leaning hard into my vision of domestic utopia, I always made sure the house was perfect before David got home. Once dinner was prepped, I would carefully set the table, then light candles and walk around the house, double-checking that everything was neat and tidy. But all of these tasks were pleasure-delaying tactics that set the stage for my most cherished ritual: selecting the evening's soundtrack.

I kept the records in the living room on a bookcase near the fireplace. There were hundreds of LPs, most of which had belonged to my father, vestiges of his lifetime spent in radio. But lately I'd begun making contributions of my own. Jackie McLean, John Coltrane, Hank Mobley, Thelonious Monk, B.B. King, McCoy Tyner, Bill Evans, Duke Ellington, and Nina Simone were just a few of the recent additions I'd made to the shelves. I'd had the albums for years, but I'd never put them on display. I'd kept them hidden, and for a specific reason.

Jazz music had always had a profound, almost paranormal, effect on me. The rhapsodic notes never eased my apathy, but they did sit alongside it, like a silent companion or a perfectly paired glass of wine. I was always careful with the dosing. I think I was worried the music might lose its power if I listened too much. Or perhaps I would start to associate it with a particular memory or period. I wanted to keep it clean, potent, so I refused any risk of overindulgence. Instead,

I would wait until the pressure was nearing its unbearable peak and only then would I reach for my albums. With jazz blaring through my headphones, I felt less alone and more accepting of the nothingness inside. I never had to alter the lyrics to suit my vacancy. I never had to do anything but listen. In this way the music was its own reward, and I relished any opportunity to disappear inside it.

Living with David, however, I had no use for such rationing. Whether it was jazz or food or wine or sex, I could indulge in every-thing I wanted, *whenever* I wanted. I didn't have to always be in con-trol. I didn't have to be measured. I knew I was safe with him, and that meant I was free. I was free to be normal. I was free to make my dinners and drink my wine and seduce my boyfriend. And I was free to listen to my music . . . every night!

To be fair, I always made it a point to do so before David got home. Even though our musical tastes were near-perfectly aligned in every other respect, David *hated* jazz, and he made no secret of his disdain. "This music sounds insane!" he said one night, laughing. "It makes no sense!" I laughed along with him.

David worked in technology, and he preferred things that were linear. His devotion to logic was uncompromising. For him, there was only one way to do things: the "right" way. It's one of the reasons he'd become such a good computer programmer. He never made mistakes. *Ever.* He was methodical and patient, and he didn't cut corners. That's why it was no surprise when, soon after moving to LA, he was hired by an internet marketing start-up to spearhead the creation of all their digital initiatives. He got the job with little effort, and we settled even deeper into our life of blessed domesticity.

"Why do you have a lock-picking kit?" David asked.

It was several months after he'd arrived, and he was rearranging my closet to make room for some of his things. After a few half-hearted attempts at finding him his own place, we decided to acknowledge the obvious. "You should just move in with me," I'd said. And so he had.

"Do you actually know how to use this stuff?" he asked. He was holding up a clear plastic padlock, a teaching tool that allows you to see inside it while you're practicing.

"Yes!" I said proudly.

"Why?"

I stepped inside the closet and cocked an eyebrow as I leaned against the frame. "You know why," I answered.

David *did* know, of course. He knew all there was to know about me, yet he often acted surprised by my revelations, a reaction that confused me.

"What am I going to do with you?" he asked, wrapping me in a sexy embrace. "You're such a bad girl."

I smiled and kissed him. "Yup."

"But you're *my* bad girl," he said, breaking away to lock eyes with me. "Right? We're in this together now. So let's eighty-six the breaking and entering." He tossed my lock-picking kit into a nearby wastebasket. The tools made a clang when they landed in the metal trash can, and I winced.

"Geez, honey. Do you have to throw it *away?*"

His dark brown eyes were imploring and tender. "I'm just trying to keep you safe," he said. "So can you quit it, please? For me?"

I sighed, shook my head, and planted a kiss on his cheek. "Sure," I heard myself saying. "I can do that for you."

A few hours later, I was back in the closet, my arms full of dry cleaning. As I hung the clothes on the rack and stripped the plastic bags from the hangers, my eyes fell once again to the trash can and my kit still sitting inside it. I glanced at the bags in my hand and then again at the garbage can, where I intended to toss them. The thought of burying my tools beneath a fistful of plastic seemed strangely horrifying.

Fuck that, I thought.

I bent down and retrieved them. The soft clinking sounds they made inside their leather case was comforting. I shoved the plastic into the bin and turned to the drawer where I kept my favorite T-shirts. "You can stay here," I said to the kit, as I slid it beneath a stack of concert tees. Satisfied with the hiding spot, I closed the drawer and left the closet, snapping the light off as I went. The tools silently rested out of sight beneath a mountain of soft cotton, waiting patiently for their next adventure.

CHAPTER 14

Liberty

"You know this isn't going to last, right?" Dr. Carlin said.

It had been six months since David moved in, and I was in her office for our usual session. The park across the street was empty, and it occurred to me that the soft grass would be an excellent place for a picnic. It was similar to the park at the Rockefeller estate where we'd first met. Instead of answering Dr. Carlin, I started making a mental list of what I needed to create the perfect basket.

"Patric?" she interrupted. "What do you think about what I just said?"

"I *think*," I replied dramatically, "that Bergamot Station is the best-kept secret in all of Los Angeles." Bergamot Station is a huge cultural complex, home to several art galleries, located in the heart of Santa Monica. David and I had recently stumbled upon it, and I was still somewhat surprised I'd never known it was there. "Can you believe that place?" I continued. "It's like an art wonderland. Have you ever been?"

"Yes," she said, dryly, "along with everyone else on the Westside."

I playfully threw my hands in the air. "SEE?" I shook my head in astonishment. "This is my point! Just *look* at all the new things I'm discovering!" I leaned back triumphantly into the couch.

The therapist was exasperated. "This is *my* point," she said, softening her tone. "Don't misunderstand. I'm thrilled about all these new experiences you're having. But the root of it—the excitement, the exploration, the obsession with domesticity, the fantasy

homemaking—they sound like limerence, the first phase of love."
She shook her head sympathetically, and added, "Which, as you
know, doesn't last."

I looked down my nose at her. "Wow," I said with a sneer.

"Well, do you want me to be honest or not?" Dr. Carlin asked.

I rolled my eyes to signal reluctant compliance.

"Because I've been trying to talk to you about this for a while. You
had only just agreed to stop using your behavioral prescriptions when
David arrived," she explained, "so we weren't ever able to process
your experience with apathy and pressure without them. We weren't
able to help you find healthier ways of coping. And, to be quite honest, I'm concerned about it."

"Why?" I exclaimed happily. "This is what I've been trying to get
you to understand! The apathy is gone. So the pressure's gone, too.
It's like I've found a permanent prescription. I'm cured!" I announced
semi-sarcastically. "Cured by love."

"You mean by proxy," Dr. Carlin said.

"What does that mean?"

"That it's *not* permanent," Dr. Carlin insisted. "None of this is
permanent. Your apathy may be temporarily displaced but it *will* come
back, along with the pressure and most likely the anxiety. And when
it does, I want you to have a healthier way to deal with it." She sighed,
her face full of concern. "Sociopathy doesn't just disappear. You know
that. I'm only saying this because I want you to be prepared."

"I understand," I told her earnestly. "And I *am* prepared. I'm trying to be, anyway."

That surprised her. "What do you mean?"

It had occurred to me a few weeks earlier. I'd been sitting next to
the picture window in the living room, listening to music, waiting
for David to come home. It was the same window through which
I'd often watched the neighbors from Tarzana, making sure they'd
both left for work before I ventured into their home for my weekly

"prescription." I looked at the dark, empty house across the street. The couple had moved and it was for sale. *Would it still feel the same?* I wondered.

I didn't bother to close the door behind me when I left. From my living room, Miles Davis's *Volume 2* played, his trumpet wafting its way to my ears as I walked. I tapped my lock-picking kit against my thigh. The metal tools made satisfying clinks in my pocket. I'd never visited the house after dark, and the yard seemed oddly unfamiliar as I approached the back door. I twisted the knob and discovered it was unlocked. "So not technically *breaking* and entering," I whispered.

When I stepped into the kitchen, my muscle memory triggered, and I braced myself to meet my canine accomplice. But Samson was long gone. Moonlight poured through the windows and provided just enough illumination for me to navigate the vacant house. I walked into the living room and climbed the staircase to the second level, running my hand along the blank walls as I went. Then I followed the short hallway into what had been the main bedroom. From its window I could see my own house across the street. *If anyone saw me up here*, I thought, *they'd think I was a ghost*. Seen yet unseen. The best of both worlds.

I set my hands on the window frame and pushed my thumbs against the locks, gently lifting the pane. Canyon breezes filled the room along with the notes of woodwinds still blaring from my living room speakers. I felt everything and nothing at the same time. The effect was narcotic, and I slid down the wall, coming to rest beneath the open window. I leaned my head on the ledge.

"If this isn't heaven," I said aloud, "I don't know what is." I gazed at the shadows on the opposite wall and smiled. Being inside the house seemed different somehow, and it wasn't just the lack of furniture. *I* felt different. Something had changed and I liked it, though I couldn't put my finger on exactly what.

I recalled a favorite Radiohead song. "For a moment there," I sang softly, "I found myself." It was a verse from "Karma Police," slightly altered to suit my circumstances. As I sang my thoughts drifted to Dad's comment about being a sociopathic Buddhist. I looked around the bare room, amused. "How much karma would a visit like this cost?" It was a rhetorical question, but it got me thinking.

Being in this house isn't hurting anyone. And it doesn't feel "bad," I thought. *So who's to say that it is?* It was the same question I'd first asked myself in middle school. All these years later, I still didn't have an answer.

"Only now I don't care," I whispered.

I tilted my head lazily to the side and from the corner of the room a glimmer of metal caught my eye. I crawled across the floor to investigate. It was a Statue of Liberty keychain, or at least it *had* been. The chain was broken and the key ring was missing.

I picked up the statue and ran my thumb along the smooth base. "You're coming with me," I told her. Then I sat for a while in contented silence. A flash of headlights from the street below snapped me out of my reverie. I stood and took a long and satisfying inhale. Then I closed the bedroom window, trotted down the stairs, and left the house. Only this time I didn't bother with the back entrance. I exited through the front door, the provocative music from my living room still soft and distant but growing louder as it welcomed me home.

In bed that night, I told David about my visit to the house across the street and showed him the trinket I'd found inside.

"I think it should be our signal," I said.

"What do you mean?" he asked.

"Whenever I do something . . . unorthodox," I told him, choosing my words carefully, "I'll leave this on the table next to the front door. That way you'll know."

David pulled me close and said, "'Unorthodox'? Is *that* what we're calling it?" I giggled.

"Yeah," I said. "So this is our unorthodox statue. It's just like the Bat-Signal."

He shook his head. "It's nothing like the Bat-Signal."

I made a show of rolling my eyes. "Whatever. The point is: When you see it, you can ask me what I've done, and you have my word I'll be honest. Or if you don't want to know, I won't tell you. Whatever you want."

"What I *want*," David replied, "is to understand why you went over there." He sounded disappointed. "You said you haven't felt like doing anything bad lately. You said you hadn't been feeling the apathy since I got here."

"I was getting to that," I said, excited to explain. "Because you're right. Tonight, I wasn't apathetic at all. I went because I *wanted* to," I told him. "Isn't it wild?"

"Wild *how?*" He turned and pushed an elbow into the pillow, resting his head on his palm. "That's the part I don't get. You said you don't like feeling like you have to do stuff like that, that you were happy to finally just be normal. You've been telling me that was your wish practically since the day we met."

"Yes! And that's true!" I squeezed his arm affectionately. "That's what's so crazy about it." I gestured around the house. "Our whole life, everything we do together. It's been incredible. Living like this— with you—*feeling* like . . ." I started laughing. "That's the thing—just feeling. *Consistent* feeling. God, David," I said. "You can't imagine what it's like."

"Then why?" he asked gently. "I promise I'm not judging you. I'm just curious. If the only time you feel like you have to break the rules is when you *don't* feel, then why—if you've been having so much 'feeling' with me—did you break into that house tonight?"

"Because I didn't feel like I *had* to," I explained. "I felt like I *wanted* to. I wasn't chasing a feeling or trying to get ahead of my apathy or trying to prevent the pot from boiling over. And, like you said, I knew you wouldn't judge me."

I got up and sat cross-legged on the bed, my blood pumping with enthusiasm. "It's like without the anxiety of being 'outed,' there's me the sociopath," I said, putting one hand out to the side, "but now there's also me the normal person." I matched the gesture with the opposite hand. "It's like I found the missing piece or something. And now—boom!" I slapped my hands together.

"Boom *what?*" he asked.

I grimaced and shook my head. "That's the thing," I said. "I haven't worked that part out yet." David fell onto his back, shaking his head at the ceiling.

"All I know is the way I felt tonight, in that house, is the same way I felt in elementary school when I stabbed Syd. And when I locked the girls in the bathroom." I decided against telling him about the cat in Virginia.

David looked deeply concerned. "But how is that *good?*" he asked.

He listened patiently as I talked about the euphoric effect that violent acts had always produced, and my steadfast refusal to commit them as a result. "I've never found *anything* else that produces that same feeling." I paused. "Until tonight."

"So, what *is* that feeling?" David asked, sitting up. "Can you describe it to me?"

I allowed my gaze to disappear into the folds of the giant white comforter as I thought about how to explain it. "Surrender," I replied slowly. "Complete apathetic surrender. Like I don't care about anything but, more importantly, I don't care about not caring. And I'm in complete control."

"I still don't get how that's good," David replied.

"It's good because so much of my bad behavior has been the result of anxiety, stress about the fact that I *don't* feel. But tonight, none of that was at play." I smiled just thinking about it. "Tonight, I did something I knew was wrong because I wanted to. Not because pressure or stuck stress was forcing my hand, but simply because I could. I knew that I wouldn't have any guilt or fear or remorse or anything." I shrugged, then smiled. "And because I knew it would be fun.

"It's like I allowed myself to just enjoy being me," I continued. "And when I did, I got that euphoric feeling. A sensation of wholeness. Total exposure but with none of the stress." I let out a satisfied exhale. "It was like a feeling of 'this is me, this is who I am.' And I don't care who knows it, or what anyone thinks about it, and I don't feel the least bit bad about it." I could tell he was still struggling to understand. "I promise, it was a nice feeling."

"Okay," he said. "Look. In the grand scheme of things, what you did tonight wasn't that bad. I get it. Technically you shouldn't have been there, but whatever. My only issue is the *complete* absence of guilt. It's no big deal to not feel bad about going into an empty house. The problem is when you don't feel bad about *other* things . . . bigger things. I worry about it being a slippery slope for you."

I started to protest but he cut me off, saying, "I know you think it's pointless, honey, but it's not. Guilt is one of the things that holds people together, y'know? Society would fall apart if nobody ever felt bad about doing bad things." He paused, then added, "Guilt, for lack of a better word, is good."

"So you're Reverse Gordon Gekko," I deadpanned.

David laughed. "What do you expect after twelve years of Catholic school?"

I shot him a sly smile. "Well, maybe I could help you shed some of that schoolboy guilt," I said, crawling on top of him. I put my lips to his ear. "Sociopathy has its perks, you know," I whispered. "Your first lesson could start next door . . . with me."

"You wanna go over there *now*?"

"Why not? There's definitely nobody home . . ."

David grabbed my waist and flipped me over, pinning me to the bed. Then he kissed me, and we forgot all about the neighbors' house.

The next morning, I tossed the little statue into the drawer of my bedside table. I didn't think I'd be using it anytime soon. Despite my excursion across the street, I was no longer keen on finding opportunities for misadventure. But as it turned out, I didn't have to go looking. Opportunities came looking for me.

CHAPTER 15

Punk'd

"Here's the key," she said. "Will you go? Will you do it for me?"

Her name was Arianne and she was a producer for MTV. She was also a friend. It was the morning of an elaborate prank we were filming for *Punk'd*, a reality series on the network. *Punk'd*, wildly popular for a while, chronicled celebrities as they fell victim to carefully orchestrated practical jokes. An artist I represented for my father's company had been selected as an unwitting participant on the show, and Arianne, who was part of the production crew, was pulling out all the stops. Including a few surprises of her own.

We were standing next to our cars after our final planning session. Arianne had followed me to go over some last-minute details, none of which were related to the show.

"So?" she pressed. "Are you good with the side-plan?"

The "side-plan" (as she had coined it a few weeks earlier) was for me to sneak into her boyfriend's house to find out whether he was cheating on her. Her boyfriend, Jacob, was a cameraman for *Punk'd*. According to Arianne, one quick glimpse of his journal would reveal if he'd been unfaithful.

Initially I'd been up for it. Like my trip to the house across the street a few months earlier, I *wanted* to do it. Arianne, for her part, had made the whole thing out to be lighthearted and *Punk'd*-ish at first. But recently things had started to take a more obsessive turn. In the days leading up to the prank, the "side-plan" was all Arianne wanted to talk about. Jacob, she was convinced, was lying to and manipulating her. She was consumed with the idea that he had a "mystery mistress" and what "we" were going to do once we busted him.

The problem was, except for my participation in the cloak-and-dagger stuff, I didn't *want* anything to do with Arianne's love life. The whole affair seemed melodramatic and childish. I didn't feel like dealing with it. Plus, I was having relationship issues of my own.

Since my trip to the Tarzana house, I'd started to experience an emotional rift that was difficult for me to reconcile. On one hand I was blissfully happy. David had been living with me for nearly a year, and in that time, I couldn't have imagined a more perfect existence. I was content and in love and completely fulfilled. Our life together was everything I'd ever wanted.

The problem was that I was still a sociopath. Like Dr. Carlin had said, I hadn't dealt with the anxiety or compulsions that so often accompanied my apathy, I'd simply been given a reprieve. But this wasn't thanks to any psychological breakthrough. It was all borrowed, likely the result of my proximity to David. It was as if I'd been awarded emotion by osmosis, normality by surrogate, and self-acceptance by proxy. Being with David was like living a daydream. Not just figuratively, but literally. I'd visualized it ever since I was fourteen and our eyes met for the first time. I *knew*. But Dr. Carlin's warning about the pressure returning was never far from my thoughts, and I was afraid of messing things up.

"Tell me again," I told Arianne, "what you want me to do."

She pressed the key into my palm. "If you get there at two, nobody'll be home. Jacob has to be at work by one thirty, so the place will be empty." She took a deep breath. "All I need you to do is read his journal. It's in his bedside table." She stopped and looked to the sky, trying to keep tears from flowing. "He writes everything in his journal. And he never *ever* lets me read it."

"That's kind of the point of a journal," I said dispassionately. I turned the key over in my hand. "Arianne," I pushed back one last time, "are you sure you want me to do this? No joke, this seems insane. And that's *me* saying so."

I was certain she knew I was right. She was a savvy friend who knew all about my personality. I'd half expected her to come to her senses and scrap the whole mission. Instead, her face went white with fear.

"Please, Patric," she implored, her voice trembling. "I can't live like this. I can't eat. I can't sleep. I can't work. It's all I think about. I feel like I'm going crazy."

I watched my friend crying and felt what must have been a hint of compassion. I couldn't empathize with her, but I definitely understood what it was like to feel crazy. Something was nagging me, though.

I shook my head again. "But why *today*?" I asked. "Don't we have enough shit to do?"

The prank was scheduled to take place that afternoon in Holly-wood. It required last-minute preparations, and the two of us were already stretched to the limit in our efforts to get everything done in time. But Arianne wouldn't budge. "Because," she said, collecting herself, "he's gonna be on set from two 'til eight. And besides," she added, "he lives a block from the park. Even if it takes you twenty minutes, you should still be back in plenty of time."

Our production base camp was in Griffith Park, which was not far from the prank location. I couldn't be there for the actual gag without giving it away, so the plan was for me to watch remotely from a trailer in the parking lot.

"Fine," I said, giving in.

Arianne looked at me gratefully, her eyes puffy but now full of relief. "Thank you," she whispered.

"What's a sociopathic friend for?"

The rest of the day was a blur. Between preparations for the event and the production details, I hardly had time to breathe. When two o'clock rolled around, I was relieved to be alone and parked in front of Jacob's place. I got out of my car and headed for the house. As I approached, I saw an older man sitting on his porch a few doors down. He waved at me and a Ronald Reagan quote my grandfather always liked sprung to mind: "There's nothing better for the inside of a man than the outside of a horse."

I smiled and thought, *There's nothing better for the inside of a man than . . . the inside of another man's house.* I liked my version better.

My heels made sharp clicks as I crossed the porch. I scoffed at the Master Lock Light Duty Entrance Series doorknob protecting the house. *Pfft*, I thought. *I should have brought my kit.*

Inside I was surprised to discover the house was immaculate. The simple furniture was tastefully arranged. Bookcases framed one wall and every shelf was stocked with nonfiction, meticulously alphabetized by author. Several framed black-and-white photos of Arianne lined the hallway leading to his room. Her boyfriend was a lot more interesting than I'd imagined. *Who* is *this guy?* I wondered. It didn't take me long to find out.

The journal was where Arianne said it would be. I flipped to the back and started reading.

May 13:
Took Arianne to St. Nick's. She's always so cute when she drinks.

I flipped to the previous page:

May 10:
Fight with Arianne. She hates my job. I hate my job. Need to get home and check on Dad.

Suddenly I felt a strange sense of disquiet. I sat on the floor and jumped back to the first page. Then I started reading. By the time I was done it was after four. When I looked up, I was startled to see the room was covered in shadows. I looked down at the book as I contemplated its contents. Arianne had been wrong about Jacob. He wasn't cheating on her. He wasn't selfish or manipulative or lying about anything. If anything, he seemed like a soul searcher. His diary was filled with questions and pleas for help like letters to God.

I stood up and gritted my teeth. "I can't believe I did this," I said to the shadows. I felt off somehow. Heavy. I didn't like it one bit. On the opposite wall was a mirror, and I caught sight of my reflection.

"Fuck you," I hissed. I tossed the journal into the drawer but didn't close it. Instead I stomped out of the house and slammed the door behind me.

The short drive to Griffith Park did nothing to improve my mood. By the time I arrived it was four thirty, and I was nearly an hour late. I managed to take my seat in the production trailer just in time to watch as my client was expertly *Punk'd*.

When it was over, I congratulated the director on a job well done.

"Just another day at the office," he said. "You sticking around for the after-party? Your partner in crime is on her way back." Arianne had played a small role in the execution of the prank and hadn't left the set yet.

I shook my head. "I'm not feeling great," I told him. "I think I'll head out." It wasn't a lie. The thought of running into Arianne made me feel sick with rage, though I wasn't sure why. I was anxious to leave before she returned. The early evening air was cool against my face as I walked to my car. I called David, who, as usual, answered right away.

"Hey, gorgeous," he said. "How'd it go?"

I smiled, soothed by his deep voice. "Amazing," I said. "I can't wait to tell you about it."

"What's wrong?" he asked.

"Nothing. Everything went great," I answered evenly.

"Okay, well. I'm leaving work now," he said. "Wanna meet for an early dinner at Nozawa?"

"Race you there."

Sushi Nozawa was my favorite sushi spot in LA. But it wasn't the thought of faith-based sashimi that appealed to me that day. It was

David. I hadn't been able to shake the strange oppression I'd felt since leaving Jacob's. And as soon as I heard his voice, I knew why. David was my anchor. He was the person I loved the most. He was the one who kept me safe, even if it was mostly from my own dark side. And what had I done? I'd separated myself from him and drifted out to sea. Nothing I'd done that day felt good. None of it had triggered the psychological release that some part of me was still seeking. And it made me furious—not just angry but restless and desperate to swim back to my boyfriend and the normal life I'd managed to piece together with him.

I hung up and had just reached my car when I heard my name shouted from across the park. "Patric!" Arianne was yelling. She'd returned from the shoot and was heading my way.

I forced a thin smile. "Hey," I said. "Good prank."

"Right?" Arianne beamed. "I mean, we totally nailed it. He almost shit himself when we threatened to have him arrested. He had *no* idea what was happening."

I smiled in spite of myself. "It was amazing."

"Wait," said Arianne, when she realized I was getting ready to go. "You're not *leaving* are you?"

"Yeah," I said. "I'm meeting David at Nozawa."

"Well, hold on," she said, lowering her voice and looking around. "What happened?! Did you . . . *do* it?"

"Yup," I said curtly. "Read the whole thing."

"Aaaaand?" she pressed, oblivious to my change in tone.

"Good news," I said, trying to keep things light. "He's definitely not cheating on you."

"Really!?" Arianne grinned and put her hands on my shoulders, gently rocking me back and forth as if trying to shake me up to her level of revelry. "That's so great!" she said. "Right?"

I offered a compulsory nod. "He seems like a really good guy," I said. "You're lucky to have him. Speaking of which, David's waiting for me, so I really gotta go."

"No, hold *on*," insisted Arianne, her hands still on my shoulders. "The journal," she pressed. "What else did it say?"

I shrugged indifferently. "Not much."

"Not . . . *much?*" Arianne asked, dropping her hands.

"Yeah," I replied. "You asked me to find out if he's cheating on you. He's not. End of story."

Arianne looked shocked. "You're really not gonna tell me what else it said?"

"No."

At first, she was dumbfounded. Then she put her hands on her hips, her bratty side rearing its ugly head. "Well, I wanna know what's going on with him," she said, "and I think it's weird that you won't tell me."

I glared at her. "Well, *I* think it's weird that you asked me to read it to begin with," I said, surrendering any pretense of cordiality, "so if you wanna know what else it said, you can fucking break into his house and read it yourself."

"So . . . What?" Arianne snapped. "Now you're mad at me? I didn't do anything!"

"No, you had *me* do it," I said. "This whole thing was idiotic, and I'm pissed at myself for agreeing to it. So if I were you, I would back the *fuck* off."

She wasn't prepared for such a drastic rebuke. She looked around nervously and shifted her position. "I'm sorry," she whispered. "Just . . . don't yell at me."

"Look," I said. "It's been a long day. I just wanna get outta here." I opened the car door and got in. Arianne looked sad and confused. I was reluctant to leave any emotional loose ends, so I took a deep breath and forced a conciliatory tone. "I apologize for yelling at you," I offered. "Like I said, I'm just annoyed."

"That's what I don't get," she said, after a beat. "Why are you annoyed?"

"I already told you." I was exasperated now. "It was a shitty thing to do."

"What do you care?" Arianne asked. "You're a sociopath."

I stared up at her, rage quickly rising from the pit of my stomach. I sighed softly and dropped my head. Then I looked back up at her, her face barely visible, backlit by the sun. "Fuck you, Arianne," I said.

Her mouth dropped open. She took a step back in shock as I yanked my door shut. Then I shoved the key into the ignition and sped off.

CHAPTER 16

Abyss

The next day I told David what I'd done. Determined to keep my end of the bargain, I left the Statue of Liberty keychain on the table for him to see when he got home. To be honest, I'd hoped he wouldn't notice it. Or that if he did, he'd ignore it and we could go about our lives as if nothing "unorthodox" had happened. I was wrong on both counts.

"This is fucked up," he concluded. We were sitting across from each other in the living room. He looked at me as if my confession was weighing on his conscience instead of mine. "I'm serious, Patric," he said. "Do you feel bad about it at least?"

Cleckley's list. Number six. Lack of remorse or shame.

"Do you feel *anything*?" David pressed.

"I don't know," I said. "When I finished reading it, I definitely felt different. Not like I normally do when I've done something bad."

"What does *that* mean?" he asked.

I was annoyed. He knew exactly what I meant. We'd discussed this so many times. So why, once again, was he asking questions when he already knew the answer? I steadied my gaze and took a deep breath, trying hard not to betray my frustration.

"As I've said *before*," I began, my voice clipped but steady, "normally, I'd feel happy. Like, relieved." I tried to remember exactly how I felt after reading Jacob's journal. "But I didn't," I told him. "It was more of a negative feeling . . . heavy almost." Then I added, "I definitely wouldn't do it again."

He sighed. "Well. That's something at least," he said.

We sat for a few seconds, neither of us knowing what to say. Then he came over and sat next to me on the couch. He put his hand on the back of my neck and stroked it gently with his thumb.

"Listen," he said, "I love you. I love you so much sometimes I don't think my heart can take it. It's like you're part of me. Nothing you could ever do could change that, nothing."

I nodded, my teeth tugging one corner of my lower lip.

"It's just . . . It's hard for me to understand sometimes. How could you break into someone's house, read their *journal* . . . and then have dinner with me like nothing happened? That's what bothers me. Why didn't you tell me?"

"I'm telling you *now*." I shrugged and toyed with the fringe on one of the couch pillows. "And technically, I didn't *break* in," I offered. David glared at me.

"That's another story," he said. "What *you* did was bad enough. But Arianne . . . some 'friend' she is. Getting *you* to do her dirty work? What a shitty person."

I looked up at him thoughtfully. "No," I said. "I don't think she's a shitty person. She's just ruled by feeling."

"*Most* people are ruled by feeling, honey," he interrupted.

"I know. But people who can't control those feelings are dangerous. At least, they are to *me*."

"Okay," he said, pulling me close. "So maybe you need to be more careful with who you tell about your . . . condition." His tone felt patronizing, and I recoiled.

"Okay, *Dad*."

"Not cool," he snarled.

David had become increasingly wary of my father. He hated that I worked for Dad and wanted me to quit. His biggest concern was how often I was expected to attend meetings and late-night concerts for work, usually with men in the music industry. A recent dinner with an especially creepy (and successful) producer had left us both on edge.

"Sorry," I muttered.

"My point," David went on, "is that I think your diagnosis gets used against you. People know you'll bend the rules. That you can steal and lie and break into places, and do God knows what else without caring . . . it's attractive to assholes. It's like you have a super-power they can exploit."

"I don't see that," I said.

"That's because *you're* not an asshole," David explained. "But, trust me, most people are. You're . . . different. And that's appealing to people who either can't or won't do those things. They use you." He waited for me to understand, then added, "I think your dad uses you sometimes. I *know* Arianne did."

It was hard to argue. "You're right about Arianne," I said. "But I don't think Dad is like that."

We sat in silence for a minute. Finally David said, "Regardless, I don't think you should be so open about how you feel. Or don't feel. There's no upside." He sat up on the couch. "Think about your research," he said. "What have you told me a thousand times?"

I smirked. "That it's okay to lie if you plan to tell the truth eventually?"

He rolled his eyes. "That sociopaths don't always do the wrong thing. So why open yourself up to exploitation?" He shook his head. "You have a choice about whether you want to be a 'bad' sociopath . . . or a good one. And it's *your* choice, Patric. Not anyone else's."

The following week, I barged into Dr. Carlin's office.

"I did something last week and—before you say anything—I want you to know that I know it was wrong, and I won't do it again. But I didn't do it for the reasons I used to do stuff like that . . . This was different."

Dr. Carlin listened as I confessed to going into the house across the street months earlier. I told her about David and the keychain, too. Then I explained what had happened recently with Arianne and

David's reaction to it. When I was done, she was skeptical. "How is this any different?"

"Because I wanted to do it!" I exclaimed. "I made the choice. I admit it wasn't the best choice. But what's important is that I didn't feel *compelled* to do it. If anything—in the case of Arianne—I did it to help someone else."

The therapist sighed. She was clearly unimpressed. "But it was still wrong, Patric," she said. I nodded.

"No. I know," I said. "But my point is that without the feeling of compulsion—without the anxious reaction to the apathy that compels so much bad behavior—the *inherent* psychological traits of sociopathy aren't necessarily negative," I explained. "In fact, I think I remember having this exact conversation with Dr. Slack."

"Your psychology professor?"

"Yes," I said. "When I first started researching, I saw that most sociopathic traits are behavioral. Lying, stealing, manipulation, anti-social tendencies . . . that's all behavior."

"And?" Dr. Carlin pressed.

"And those behaviors are wrong, right? They're explicitly 'bad,'" I said, using air quotes. "There's no room for interpretation."

"Right."

"But the *psychological* characteristics of sociopathy are *not* good or bad," I continued. "Like, there's nothing 'wrong' with apathy. You can use that trait to make bad choices *or* good ones. And the more we can normalize things like that—the more that sociopaths can be educated to understand they're not 'wrong' or 'bad'—the less stress they're likely to have about it. Ergo, the less compelled they'll feel to act out *because* of it."

Dr. Carlin gestured for me to keep going.

"Look, sociopaths might not be able to do anything about their psychological makeup, but they can be educated to change their *behavior*. I realized it when David said it was like a superpower. Sociopaths are unique because, by default, we don't internalize things based on feelings or peer pressure. At least, I don't. I don't have that struggle."

"And David thinks this is a superpower?" she asked.

I leaned forward excitedly in my seat. "Well, it's definitely a strategic advantage. Think about it. So many people are ruled by emotion, dangerously so. Like Arianne. She's so full of emotion, right? She's so 'in love,' right? And what did she do? She had me break into her boyfriend's house." I rolled my eyes. "Jacob is the person Arianne claims to care about the most. Yet she completely violated his trust . . . because of her emotions."

"Yes, but emotion doesn't always cause people to do bad things, Patric."

"But a *lack* of emotion doesn't have to, either!" I said. "Don't you see? It's the opposite side of the coin. Normal people act out when their emotions become too stressful. Sociopaths act out when their lack of emotion becomes too stressful.

"You have to understand," I continued, "it's not so much that I'm flooded with emotions now that David is here. I mean, yes, I love him and that's all great, sure. But I don't think that's why the stress went away. My anxiety isn't gone because it's been replaced by love. It's gone because I feel *accepted*. David doesn't judge me when I don't care about things; he doesn't think it's weird when I get quiet. I don't have to constantly be on defense about my apathy, so the apathy itself has become less stressful."

I let this sink in. "Because the mainstream opinion is that not having feelings is 'bad,' sociopaths—from a very early age—are taught to hide or deny their apathy, lest they become outed as monsters. So the emotional void becomes a trigger for stress, for *anxiety*, which leads to destructive behavior. It's a vicious cycle.

"But if you can reframe that belief system," I continued, "if you can educate sociopaths to understand that their inherent traits are *not* bad, then you can replace that anxious reaction with acceptance and maybe reduce the bad behavior." I rocked my head from side to side. "Theoretically speaking."

"But normalizing antisocial behavior isn't good, Patric," she argued. "Or ethical. It's why I asked you to stop using your prescriptions. Because I wanted us to figure out a healthy coping strategy."

"I'm not talking about normalizing behaviors," I insisted. "I'm talking about normalizing psychological *traits*. I know that, for me, the more I understand my personality type—the less concerned I am about the apathy—the less I act out. Remember, apathy isn't the *cause* of sociopathy. It's just a symptom. I know because—even though I'm not acting out as much—I still *feel* like a sociopath."

"Now you've lost me," the therapist said.

"Even though I haven't felt compelled to act out in extreme ways lately," I said, "I'm still *me*. I still don't experience emotions the way you do. I'm still immune to shame and guilt."

"So you don't feel bad about reading Jacob's diary?"

"No. I'm only sorry that I let Arianne talk me into doing something I didn't want to do. I allowed myself to be used. *That's* why I got so angry. At myself, for making a bad choice."

"But you're always the one who makes the choice."

"Not really. Not any more than people with OCD are making a choice when they count things, or wash their hands, or do any of the things they feel like they 'have' to do."

I could tell she didn't believe me.

"This is what I'm trying to tell you!" I insisted. "So much of a sociopath's negative behavior is *compulsive*. It's driven by an anxious reaction to the pressure, by the urge to dispel the apathy. That's the way that it *feels*. But in the absence of that anxiety—sociopaths have a choice," I explained. "I went into the house across the street because I wanted to, because I *chose* it. And because anxiety wasn't the motivator, I was able to enjoy the experience."

"Okay. So let's get into *that*," she said.

I shook my head, grappling with the answer. "My entire life I thought I wanted to be like everybody else. I wanted to be normal. But I don't now. I *like* that I don't care what other people think. I *like* that I'm not weighed down by guilt like everyone else. If I'm being really honest," I said, "I even like the apathy sometimes. Feeling like nothing . . . It reminds me of the Great Blue Hole."

Dr. Carlin blinked. "The *what?*"

I smiled and told her, "The Great Blue Hole. It's this sinkhole off the coast of Belize. It's hundreds of feet deep, and all around it the water's light blue and crystal clear. But over it, where the seafloor drops out, the water's black." I looked out the window. "It's one of the only things that has ever truly petrified me," I said. "As a child, when I would see pictures of it, just the *thought* of swimming across it always made me want to . . ." My voice trailed off, and I felt a deep sense of stillness.

"Made you want to what?"

I frowned and looked her in the eye. "Hurt," I said.

She raised her eyebrows and waited for me to go on.

"My apathy always felt like an abyss, even before I realized it, even when I was a kid." I looked down and felt myself disappearing into the patterns of the carpet. "I think I was scared of it because I never knew what monsters would come out of that darkness."

"And now?" she asked.

I shrugged. "Well, now I've met the monsters." I smiled. "And I surrender."

The room was quiet enough to hear the clock ticking. Afternoon shadows made their way into the corners of the office and settled around me like old companions. That's when it hit me.

"This is how it should be," I said softly. "This," I repeated, "is how sociopaths *should* feel. This is the hope." I was starting to relax. "Sitting here, right now, and for maybe the first time since I was a kid, I *like* who I am. I'm at peace with *what* I am. And I'm starting to realize that the only thing I ever didn't like was what I was doing. I didn't like my behavior."

Dr. Carlin nodded.

"This is the other side of darkness. It's how all sociopaths should feel." I scowled. "And it's not fair that they can't."

"I don't understand," she said. "Why can't they?"

I shrugged. "Because there's no one around to explain it. The only ones talking are the *faux*ciopaths. The only people writing books are idiots with bullshit information," I complained. "I mean, how are real sociopaths supposed to figure things out?"

"Well, *you* seem to have figured it out," Dr. Carlin offered.

"I got lucky," I said with a sarcastic laugh. "The only reason I understand any of this is because I just happened to find a bunch of research inside a library." I looked out the window again as I settled back against the couch cushions.

"What about all the people who aren't so lucky?" I asked, lifting my hands weakly. "Where are the therapists for *them*? Where are the support groups for *them*?" I was exasperated. "Where are the books for *them*?"

Dr. Carlin waited a beat and then said, "So write one."

I looked at her like she was crazy.

"I've said this before, Patric. I think you have a real gift for psychology. I think you should look into graduate school." She studied my reaction. "And I think you should write a book."

I was stunned. "Who am I to write a book?"

"You're a well-adjusted sociopath, for starters." She laughed.

"Right," I said. "I'm a sociopath. Who the fuck's gonna believe anything I say?"

"*Other* sociopaths. Like you said: You can relate. You know what it's like to live with this. You've got a unique perspective because you can dissect it from both a personal *and* a professional point of view. Even if you don't have all the answers, you have the insight to understand other sociopaths and to help them just like you helped yourself."

I returned to my now-familiar view of the park.

"They say sociopaths are impulsive, irrational, incapable of introspection," she added. Then she shook her head. "Not from where I'm sitting. They say sociopaths can't love, but I've seen you love." She leaned forward to get my attention. "They say sociopaths are incapable of empathy."

I turned to look her in the eyes. "I'm not very good at it," I said quietly.

"Oh, yes, you are," she protested. "With *other* sociopaths." She leaned back and folded her arms. "Now tell me, who else can do that?"

I glanced at the clock. "Wow, look at that," I said, getting up from the couch. "Time's up."

She smiled and lifted her hands in resignation. "Just think about it," she said.

CHAPTER 17

Orion

I was at work a few weeks later going over expense reports with my father. The weather outside was uncharacteristically gloomy, and looking out the windows that framed his large corner office, I kept returning to my conversation with Dr. Carlin. Dad was squinting at his computer, battling with a spreadsheet, when I asked him, "What would you think about me going back to school?"

He looked puzzled.

"For psychology," I explained. "My therapist thinks I'd be good at it."

"That's a great idea," he said. "Really. I think it's long overdue."

"What is?"

"Finding something you're passionate about." Dad leaned forward. "What's David think?"

"Well, he loves the idea of me getting out of this job, that's for sure."

He tilted his head. "He doesn't really like me, does he?"

I shrugged. "He doesn't *not* like you," I said, tiptoeing around the question. "He just hates the music business."

"That's the problem with people like him," he said, waving a hand dismissively. "Everything's black and white. He doesn't get that the world is mostly gray."

I shifted in my seat, anxious to change the subject. "But that's why I love him so much," I said. "We balance each another."

Dad was silent.

"Anyway," I continued, "I could probably use a little structure, y'know? Going back to school would mean having a schedule, and a goal."

"Right up David's alley," Dad taunted. "I'm sure he's thrilled."

"Actually, he's *not*," I said.

"Really?" he replied. "That surprises me."

It had surprised me, too.

The evening after my session with Dr. Carlin, I'd been excited to tell David all about it. Admittedly, the whole idea of graduate school shocked me, and I wasn't entirely sure about it in the moment. By the time I got home, though, I was fully committed.

"So lemme get this straight," David said, after I told him. We'd just finished dinner and I could hear Keith Jarrett playing softly in the living room. "You're saying that in the time between leaving her office and getting home . . . you decided you wanted to get a graduate degree? In psychology?"

I grinned. "Yup."

"It's just weird timing," he said. "Most people don't go back to school on a whim."

"Most people aren't like me," I reminded him.

"True," he laughed. "It's just that *I've* been thinking it's time to start planning for the future," he said. "*Our* future."

When he saw I had no idea what he meant, he leaned close and whispered, "Like, kids?"

"*Kids?*" I asked, taken aback. "You want to start talking about kids? We're not even married."

"I know, but we're gonna get married. Someday." He smiled. "Right?"

I instinctively returned his smile. I knew I'd wanted to marry David from the second I laid eyes on him. To me it was always a fait accompli, never up for debate.

"Yes," I replied. "We know that."

"That's all I'm saying," he said. "We both want to get married. We both want to have kids. Maybe going back to school—right now—is a bit much."

"I don't think so," I said, frowning. "The way I see it, right now is the best time to go back to school. *Before* we get married. *Before* we have kids. Going back to school will only be harder if I wait."

He stood and took my hand. "Come with me," he said. He led me through the French doors that opened onto the back patio. "You see that?" he asked, pointing to the sky. "Those three stars in a line?"

I squinted as I followed his finger. "I think so, yeah."

"That's Orion. The hunter. The protector. My mom taught me about him when I was little," he said. "She knew all the Greek myths and their constellations. But he was her favorite."

I wondered where he was going with this. "That sounds nice," I replied quietly, recalling Kimi's go-to response.

He took a step back and held both of my hands in his. "I've been waiting for the right time to tell you this," he said, trying unsuccessfully to hide his excitement. "I got offered a job last week."

"You did?" I was excited for him. "Where?"

"It's a start-up in Santa Monica," he said. "They need a cofounder, someone who knows tech. And they've got money. A lot."

"David! That's great!" He looked nervous. "It *is*, right?"

"I think so, yeah," he said. "It's probably gonna be hard for a while, though. They want me to build a huge system. But when it's done it'll be awesome."

I tilted my head, confused.

"Patric," he said, "I love you. I want to marry you. I want to take care of you, forever." He pulled me into a hug. "You don't have to go back to school. You don't even have to work for your dad anymore. You can quit tomorrow if you want."

I shook my head, struggling with how to respond. "But I *don't* . . . want," I finally stammered, and pulled away. "Honey, please don't misunderstand. I think it's sweet that you want to take care of me. But you don't have to do that."

He gave me a lopsided grin. "I know I don't have to," he replied softly. "I *want* to. I want you to be free," he said. "Not just from work and bills . . . but from everything you've spent your whole life dealing with." He shook his head. "Think of how nice it would be to have a . . . normal life. The life you've always wanted." He kissed my hand. "The life *we've* always wanted."

His deep brown eyes were warm and inviting. It was a look I'd only ever gotten from him, a compassionate expression on the face of someone who knew all my darkest thoughts. David didn't kid himself about the battles that raged inside my head. He wasn't in denial about the atrocious things I was capable of doing. What's more, he accepted them. In that instant, I felt completely seen. It was as though he was speaking to my soul, saying things aloud I'd only ever whispered to myself for as long as I could remember. I wanted it, too, more than either of us could have possibly imagined. The idea of that type of freedom, of that type of life.

I swear to God that I tried.

For months, I strived to push all thoughts about school and sociopathy to the side. David started his new job soon afterward, and I continued working for my dad. Though I had to admit things between us were no longer the same. David had been right about the longer hours. From almost the day he started, he was rarely at home. He'd spend late nights—sometimes entire weekends—locked in his new office as he and his team prepared to launch their Web application. It was an extreme change to our lifestyle, and I wasn't prepared. But I tried to make the best of it. At least, I did at first.

For those first few months, I perfected the role of supportive partner. On nights when he worked late (which was the norm), I would make the long trek to the other side of town so we could have dinner together, homemade meals in tow. I kept my mouth shut when he'd head to the office on Saturday mornings. I tried not to get angry when he'd call at the last minute to cancel dinner plans. I kept my complaints and opinions to myself. But as time passed, I found it was harder to bite my lip.

"Are you fucking kidding me?" I said after David called one night to let me know—for the third time that week—that he wouldn't be home for dinner. "You're doing this *again*?"

"I'm sorry, honey," he replied. "I was literally walking out the door when Sam pulled me into a meeting."

Sam was David's boss and business partner. He was stiff and socially awkward, a real personality-minus. There were few people I liked less than Sam, and my disdain was steadily increasing.

I set the bowl of whipped cream I was whisking on the kitchen counter, its solid base making a loud thud. "Well, I just finished making dessert. Homemade Key lime pie. I had to go all the way downtown to find the right limes." I exhaled impatiently, my voice slightly softening. "Can't you just say we have plans? Can't you just say no? Just this once?"

"I would if I could," he said, and I could tell he was trying to rush me off the phone. "But Sam is freaking about this launch next week . . . Listen: It's just one more week," he added. "After that, things will go back to normal. I promise."

To his credit, things did return to normal the following week, and everything was wonderful again. He'd get home around six and we'd do things like have dinner and watch the news and be . . . normal. But "normal" never seemed to last. The following week he was back to working around the clock, this time for a "quarterly update" that needed to be ready by the end of the month. That was what I hated most about his job. There was never any finish line. He'd kill himself to wrap up some big project, only to immediately start a new one. Each time he'd insist that Sam promised *this* would be the "last time," but it never was. I tried to be supportive, but after a while, I started to get resentful.

This sucks, I said to myself.

I was home alone after another last-minute late-meeting phone call. The table was bathed in candlelight, but the roasted halibut I'd prepared was cold and the vegetables wilted. I picked up David's glass of wine and drained its contents. Then I walked into the living room. I turned the record player's volume rebelliously high and made my way to the window seat. I looked at the yard across the street, wishing the Tarzana house was still empty, or—at least—that its new owners hadn't been paranoid freaks who'd installed a bunch of security cameras.

Hypnotic notes of blues and bass filled the room, and I rested my head against the wall. I gazed into the kitchen at the pyramid of apples I'd perfectly assembled on a vintage cake stand. And I found myself thinking about the movie *Beaches*. In the film, Barbara Hershey's character (Hillary) has given up a law career to provide a cozy home for her successful husband. One morning, on his way out the door to work, the husband asks what she plans to do with her day.

"I'm going to buy a wrench," she tells him.

The husband thinks for a second and then says, "Super!"

Hillary offers a weak smile. In the dining area where the scene takes place, a plate of apples sits next to a pitcher of coffee. She takes one and sets it on top of her head, staring straight ahead as her husband leaves for work.

My eyes narrowed as I stared at my own apple tower. I rose from the bench and walked to the kitchen. There I plucked a ripe Granny Smith and leaned over the island counter. I took a bite of the apple and balanced it on top of my head.

"Maybe I should buy a wrench," I muttered. It sounded like a decent idea. One that wouldn't have been completely out of character. A large part of me wanted to run out and buy the wrench that instant. I could think of lots of ways I might use it. Most notably against the side of Sam's car, which I knew was parked alongside David's at the office.

Yet something told me that Hershey's character was not going wrench shopping because of some to-be-determined, enthrallingly antisocial task. She was doing it because she had nothing better to do. And I was furious that I could suddenly relate. David's claim that he wanted us to have a normal life was authentic, but his idea of normal wasn't the same as mine. He was working around the clock to achieve his goals. So why couldn't I do the same?

I tried talking to him about it, but he was always preoccupied with work. There was never a "good time" to talk. Anytime I tried to bring it up, he just became annoyed.

"Why the hell'd you do that?"

We were in his office having lunch a few days later, and I'd made the faux pas of mentioning that I'd just spent an hour on the phone with the UCLA psych department.

"Don't talk to me like that," I said, instantly frustrated by his snappish tone.

"I'm sorry," he apologized, his attitude softening. "I'm just stressed out. And I don't get it," he said. "Why were you calling them?"

"Because I wanted to see if Dr. Slack was still there," I continued, trying to get the conversation back on track. "And you know what? She is."

David didn't seem impressed. "So?"

"So I figured that I could go and ask her about graduate school. UCLA isn't the only one in town. If I'm gonna do this, I should apply to as many as I can, so I have some options."

"Options for what?" David asked, bewildered. I felt my anger rising.

"Stop it," I snapped.

"Stop what?!"

"Stop asking questions when you know the answer." I was now seriously pissed off. "You do it constantly and it's infuriating."

"Because what you're saying doesn't make sense!" he nearly shouted.

"It doesn't make sense *to you*, David. Because the only thing that 'makes sense' to you is me sitting at home being a happy little wife while you work all the time!"

He looked shocked. "You think that's what I want?"

"Isn't it?! You want me to quit my job. You clearly don't want me going back to school—"

"Because I'm trying to protect you!" David interrupted.

I was stunned. "Protect me?" I asked, finally. "From what?"

After a long pause, he replied, "I *know* what you used to do in college, the things you'd tell me about."

"Oh, come on," I replied, exasperated. "I was a completely different person then."

"I know," he replied. "But I hated hearing about you stealing cars and breaking into houses when I was three thousand miles away. Now I'm here. I can take care of you." He paused, then added, "It's why you leave me the keychain."

My eyes widened when I realized how much he'd misunderstood everything. "Oh, David, no," I said, desperate to clarify. "I leave it because I want to be close to you. I want you to know what I do because I want to be honest with you about everything, *all* the time, just like I promised. Not because I need you to 'protect me.'"

He wouldn't look at me.

"Hey," I said gently, walking around to his side of the desk. "I'm serious. I'm your partner, not some insane person you have to look out for." I held his face in my hands, looking him deeply in the eyes. "I mean it. I would never want you to feel like you're responsible for the things I do. I'm sorry if I ever made you feel that way."

"No, *I'm* sorry. I'm just in a really shitty mood right now," he admitted. He pointed at the flat-screen monitors on his desk. "Sam's all over me about this new fucking program, and I need to get it finished." He sighed and said, "Of course I support you going back to school." He offered one of his irresistible lopsided grins. "Can't we please just talk about it later?"

I frowned. "You said you'll be here all night."

"Right. Crap. I'm sorry." He shrugged. "Tomorrow night. Or maybe this weekend?"

"Sure," I said softly. The phone rang, and he picked up. I kissed the top of his head and stood there awkwardly for a few seconds. Then I picked up my purse and left.

An hour later I was behind the wheel of my car, my thoughts a jumbled maze as I headed home. It was late afternoon, the worst time to be caught in LA traffic. As I inched along, I thought about our conversation and why the idea of school seemed so scary to him. Part of me got it.

It is sort of nuts, I mused. *I'm not even a good student.*

All the same, I'd spent years chasing down information about sociopathy and psychology on my own. Going to graduate school seemed like a natural progression. Challenging, but doable. Deep down, I knew I'd be good at it.

I crossed the 405 out of Brentwood and decided to avoid the freeway. Instead, I continued toward Westwood, deep in thought. When I got to Hilgard, I stopped at the red light and rested my head against the seat, lost in nostalgia. I knew the intersection well, probably better than any other in town. Hilgard Avenue was, after all, my first LA address. I looked down the street to where my dorm had been. A lot had changed since I'd arrived. The street was bigger than I'd remembered. The entire campus, in fact, seemed to have exploded in development. But some things remained the same.

Tightening my grip on the steering wheel, I suddenly yanked it to turn off Sunset onto my old street. Large gold letters gleamed from the rock wall that framed the north side of the campus. *UCLA*. The wide street was empty and welcoming, and I felt an unexpected rush of freedom. A hundred yards down was a side road that I still remembered well. I turned sharply onto the narrow path and maneuvered my car toward the nearby parking structure. This, I knew, was the one closest to the psychology department.

Thirty minutes, I thought, as I pulled into a parking spot. *The building closes in thirty minutes. That's plenty of time to see if Dr. Slack can meet with me.*

When I got out of the car, the early evening air put me at ease. I glanced up and instinctively looked for Orion. I smiled to myself. This, I already knew, was the right decision. *My* decision . . . one that would change the course of my life. I headed for the psychology building, envisioning a plan.

"I'm going to get my PhD," I decided. "And I'm going to specialize in sociopathy."

Impulsive or not, the trajectory of my future had become clear. I was already gone.

PART III

CHAPTER 18

Rebel Tell

A year and a half later I stood in the living room of a dilapidated cottage off Mulholland Drive. There was a hole in the roof through which I could see the faint outline of a crescent moon against the bright California sky.

The house wasn't far from the campus where I'd recently started the second year of my graduate program at a private school in West LA. It was rare for me to take a break in those days, let alone kill time in a stranger's house. A full course load, combined with the long hours I spent still working as a music manager, typically consumed most days and left little time for "unorthodox" errands. But that afternoon I'd made an exception. And I had company.

A new friend stood by my side. Her name was Everly. The lead singer of a band I'd recently signed to my management roster, Everly was my favorite client. She was a prolific songwriter and talented singer with a style that was a cross between Mazzy Star and Courtney Love. What's more, she'd just released a demo that had several major labels buzzing. In preparation to showcase her live performance, the singer and I had been spending a lot of time together and I, for once, was grateful for the company.

David was still working nonstop. His company was no longer a start-up. It had blossomed into a successful firm that was planning to go public. For more than a year he'd been working practically around the clock in preparation for the initial public offering, a move that was all but guaranteed to solidify his financial future and allow him real freedom in his career.

Vocationally speaking, the two of us weren't just surviving. We were thriving. But it had come at a steep price. Between school and work, David and I had become passing ships in a passive-aggressive ocean. We hardly spent any time together and when we did, we bickered. Even after living with me for years, he couldn't wrap his head around the idea that his "dream girl" was a socio-path. He didn't get that it had nothing to do with being a good person or a bad person. It was a personality type, its traits simply a part of my psychological fabric. I started to get the sense that his acceptance of me had stopped being unconditional. He approached my sociopathy like it was a series of choices, and ones he had no problem cherry-picking.

David, I noticed, was quick to vocalize his disapproval of socio-pathic behaviors he didn't like. Yet he was happy to co-opt elements of my personality type when it suited his purpose. For example, he didn't seem to mind when I surreptitiously punished those I felt had wronged him. And he had no problem breaking into empty houses together to have sex. It was like I wasn't allowed to be a sociopath without his per-mission, and the hypocrisy was frustrating. It was the same hypocrisy I saw repeatedly in society when it came to people like me.

Ever since discussing it with Dr. Carlin, I couldn't stop thinking about how my traits were only ever seen in a negative light. This per-spective seemed shortsighted to me. Certainly, some of them could be used destructively. But—like any other trait—they could also be used *con*structively. For example, my reduced capacity for emotion made me far more capable of pragmatic decision-making than, say, David, whose surplus of emotion made him more prone to people pleasing. As far as my lack of guilt, I felt fortunate to have been spared such a burden.

The more time I spent studying psychology, the more convinced I was that guilt was a state of mind designed to oppress, not set free. It seemed to me that people didn't have to think for themselves as long as they had guilt doing it for them. And, while the research on sociopathy was sparse, there was no shortage of resources on the harmful effects of shame and guilt. From emotional reactions such as low self-esteem and a propensity toward anxiety and depression, to physical ones like increased sympathetic nervous system activity—including problems with sleep and digestion—the negative aspects of guilt and shame seemed to far outweigh the positive. And my new friend agreed.

Everly was no stranger to the by-products of guilt. Despite being the lead singer of an up-and-coming rock band, she often let the opinions of others (and an overwhelming drive to be "good") undermine her success. I was stunned by this. By all accounts she was a good person, a great person. Yet she was constantly having to fight off feelings of contrition. In a lot of ways, she and David were similar. They were both exceptionally kind, compassionate, and loving. Both possessed an abundance of generosity and emotional fluency—which I considered the ability I most lacked—to connect and communicate through feelings. Both were highly intelligent and fiercely talented. But they were also ironically hobbled by what seemed to me an almost compulsive sense of morality. Everly was fascinated that I'd never experienced anything like it.

"Do you know how rare that is?" she once asked me. "Most people spend their entire lives trying to rid themselves of guilt and shame bullshit. I know I do," she confessed. "You're like a unicorn." Everly's appreciation of my sociopathic traits made me feel seen, in a good way. Whereas David now seemed obsessed with getting me to express emotion and evolve some semblance of shame and guilt, Everly embraced me the way I was. As a result, I found it easier to embrace myself.

"Being friends with you is like taking a guilt immunity pill," she said, looking around the abandoned house. "Seriously, do you think I've ever broken into a house before? No way. I can't do things like this. But I can do it when you do it." Then she added, "I love riding your dark coattails."

I smiled and shifted my gaze to an ancient grand piano sitting in one corner of the ramshackle living room. The weather-beaten wood was blanketed with leaves and water stains, but otherwise it was remarkably intact. I took a seat on the bench and pushed down on the keys. To my surprise, the strings were in tune. I glanced at Everly, who was wandering around the ground floor. "So do you like it?" I asked. "I think I want to buy it."

"Is it for sale?" she asked.

"Not yet," I replied. "But it will be."

"I think it's magical." Everly lifted her foot forward, cautiously inspecting a pile of junk on the floor. "How'd you even find it?"

"Oh, I've had my eye on it for years," I said. "It's the place I've told you about, where the little old man and woman live. The ones who are always outside."

Her head snapped up in surprise. "*This* is that house?"

"Yes!" I nodded enthusiastically. "Isn't it amazing?"

"Yeah." She laughed, looking around. "An amazing disaster!"

She had a point. The house *was* a disaster. Not only was there the large hole in the ceiling, but there were vines growing through broken windows, the kitchen looked as though it hadn't been touched since the 1940s, and there was no telling when the electricity had last been working.

"How do you know it's going on the market?"

I'd found out a few days earlier. It had been weeks—months even—since I'd seen the old man and his wife tending to the garden out front. After doing some snooping, I'd learned their fate. "The old man got hit by a car. He was riding his bike to the Glen Centre to get water."

Everly's jaw dropped. "So he's *dead*!?"

"Oh, no," I reassured her. "They're both fine. They just had to take him to the hospital. The thing is, when the police came to tell his wife"—I stopped and looked around—"they found out they'd been living like this." I waved my hand at all the junk and disrepair. "Apparently they were removed from the house."

Everly grew somber. "That's so sad."

I shrugged. "At least they're in a place with electricity and running water. The city is gonna sell the house on their behalf. It's part of a conservatorship or something."

Everly looked around again, her expression softening. "Wow," she said. "Can you imagine living here? Like this?"

"I actually kind of love it," I said. I walked over to the giant staircase opposite the piano and took a seat on a crumbling step.

"You would," she replied with a laugh.

"I mean, yes, it's old and it needs a lot of work," I continued. "But it's got such cool energy. It reminds me of Miss Havisham's house."

"From *Great Expectations?*" she asked, eyeing me dubiously. "The decaying old mansion that goes to shambles after she gets left at the altar?"

I shot her a smug glance. "Yes. The one Estella would have remodeled after Pip said he needed to live on the Westside." Everly nodded sympathetically.

David and I had been having a similar argument for months. The house on Coldwater, he'd decided, was no longer where we should live. He wanted a new place closer to his job. I'd reluctantly agreed, but I loved my house and wasn't wild about moving. Especially because of *his* job. The prospect of buying the Mulholland cottage, however, had shifted my perspective. The whole idea sounded like a creative adventure.

Everly grinned and walked across the room to lean against the piano. "This is why I love you," she said. "Only *you* would like a house like this. Only *you* would have the balls to buy it." She grimaced as she looked around. "I'd be way too nervous. All I'd be thinking about is *Money Pit*," she added. I had to admit I'd thought of the Tom Hanks movie, too.

"That house ended up being a masterpiece," I reminded her.

"That's my point," Everly said. "You have no doubts because you're fearless."

"What can I say? There are perks to being a sociopath."

"Speaking of which," Everly said, changing the subject. "I need to borrow some of that fearlessness for the show tonight."

The "show" was a kickoff performance for a weekly residency Everly's band had been offered at the legendary Roxy Theatre. Wanting to capitalize on the excitement surrounding her demo, I had invited several of the major labels to attend.

My phone started buzzing and I looked to see a text from David.

Good luck tonight, my love. I can't wait to see you!!

I smiled. David didn't love that I still worked for my dad, so I really appreciated that he was so supportive and coming to the show.

I texted: *Thank you, baby. I'm so excited!*

"Is that David?" Everly asked. "He's coming tonight, right?"

"Of course," I said, putting my phone away. "He just has to come straight from work."

She shook her head. "Your boyfriend works more than anyone I've ever met," she said. "Seriously, if Ben spent as much time at work as David, I'd be showing up at his office like Glenn Close in *Fatal Attraction.*"

Ben was Everly's boyfriend and a member of her band. He was also her self-appointed "business manager." He was harmless enough, but there were certain things about him that annoyed me. For one thing, I didn't like that he made jokes at her expense, often in front of his "friends," a revolving crew of wannabe insiders. He strongly resisted any attempt I made to showcase Everly as an independent artist, and he never seemed to pay attention to her unless it had something to do with the band.

I rolled my eyes at the thought of *anyone* giving a shit where Ben was, an expression that Everly misinterpreted as disapproval.

"Don't judge me!" She laughed. "You know how jealous I get. I *wish* I could be more like you." She wrapped her arms around my neck. "My feisty little kitten!"

"Stop it," I said, struggling to get away. Everly knew how much I hated hugs.

"I can teach *you* a thing or two," she said. "Things like love and affection!" She planted an exaggerated kiss on my cheek. "Symmetrical symbiosis!" she shouted. "Put us together and we're the perfect person!"

I broke free, laughing. "That's enough education for today." I glanced at my watch. "Anyway, we have to get going. Sound check is in thirty minutes."

"Yes!" replied Everly, her blue eyes sparkling. "Let's go play a rock show."

Later that night I sat backstage in the Roxy dressing room looking over the guest list. Though not social by nature, I found my role as manager of a rock band a counterintuitive match for my personality. There was never any standing around for me at Everly's shows, never an opportunity for someone to approach me or start a lengthy conversation. Except for the brief interactions I had with people I'd invited from the music business, I kept my eyes down and my hands busy. I never so much as stopped to get a drink while I was working one of Everly's performances. Not, that is, until about twenty minutes before the show. That's when I would disappear upstairs to collapse on one of the couches for a quick pre-set catnap.

The small dressing room space was filled with people that night. I tossed the list aside and rested my head against the arm of a couch, my eyes growing heavy from the soft hum of hushed conversation.

"Hey," said Tony, nudging me with his toe. I opened my eyes and smiled at the band's road manager, who never ceased to make me laugh with his quick wit and endearing grin. "You gonna sleep through the show?"

"No way," Everly said playfully, winking at me. "Patric just likes to hide."

"Rest in peace."

The door to the dressing room flew open. "I'm here!" announced a short, obnoxious man. "Now the show can start." Dale was one of Ben's industry buddies. Though precisely *what* industry, I'd yet to discern. He was a casserole of douche energy, a walking, talking amalgam of every Los Angeles cliché. I couldn't stand having to deal with him.

"Sorry I'm late," he told us, tugging conspicuously at his nose. "It took me a fucking hour to find a place to park. I ended up leaving my car halfway up Wetherly."

"*Wetherly?*" Ben yelped. "It's residential parking only up there. You're gonna get a ticket!"

"Patric," he whined, clearly aggravated that I hadn't somehow predicted the unfolding scenario. "Can you please get Dale a parking pass?"

"Of course," I said, rising from the couch. "Gimme your keys and I'll handle it. What kind of car?"

Dale shot me a smug glance and tilted his head forward. He was wearing a baseball cap emblazoned with a shiny metallic Z. He pointed to it and raised his eyebrows, waiting for me to respond. I shook my head to indicate I didn't recognize the symbol. "I have no idea what that is."

"It's a Z," Dale replied, incredulous. "A *Nissan* Z?"

"Oh, just give Patric your keys," Everly said. "We don't want you getting a ticket."

Dale smirked at her, reached into his pocket, and pulled out a set of keys. There was a large silver Z on the ring, and he dangled it in front of me like a dime-store hypnotist. I did my best not to laugh. Instead, I calmly reached to take the keys. But just before I could, he snapped the ring out of my reach.

"Not a chance, doll," he said, tossing them onto a nearby coffee table. "No one touches the Z." He paused. "But I *will* take a drink," he said.

Everly recoiled. "Dale," she said, dropping any pretense of kindness. "Patric isn't a waitress."

Realizing he'd overplayed his hand, Dale put his hands in front of his mouth, eyes wide with false regret. "Oh my God! I'm *so* sorry!"

"It's *fine*," Ben barked. Then he muttered, "That's what she's here for."

"I actually don't mind," I said to Everly. This was true. I would have done just about anything to leave the room.

I felt my phone buzz in my pocket. "Besides, David's calling," I said, after glancing at the screen. "He's probably outside. I'm gonna go grab him."

"And a Jack and Diet for Dale!" Ben shouted as I left.

I ran down the back stairs and made a beeline for the entrance while my phone continued vibrating in my pocket. "Hey," I said when I answered, "I'm on my way." I could hear David's voice, but through the crush of the crowd I couldn't make out a word he said. "I'm walking out the door right now."

I stepped outside and scanned the sea of faces looking for him, but he was nowhere to be seen. *That's weird*, I thought. I looked down at my phone and saw I had a text message.

Stuck at work. I'm so, so sorry, honey! I promise I'll make it up to you. Be good!!!!!!!!

I inhaled sharply. The message was nothing new. I'd probably received dozens of texts just like it over the last few months. But that night, something about it seemed particularly infuriating. I squeezed the phone, my fingertips growing white with anger as I spun on my heel and walked back inside.

After the show I returned to the dressing room to congratulate my friend. "You were awesome," I said.

Everly beamed at me, her face still flush with adrenaline. "I feel like celebrating!" she said excitedly, grabbing my hand. "Let's go to Dorian's."

Her bandmate Dorian's cliffside house was almost walking distance from the Roxy. Normally I would have wasted little time heading over to what had become a frequent postshow gathering spot. But all I wanted to do was go home. I shook my head and looked down, trying to conceal my disappointment. "I'm actually gonna head out," I said.

Everly looked at me sadly, her perceptive gaze boring into my psyche. "He didn't come, did he?"

"It's fine," I said flatly.

She shook her head. "That sucks," she said. "I mean, you know how much I love David. But not showing up tonight? Not showing up *any* night? That's fucked up." She grabbed my hand. "Come over," she pleaded. "We can drink wine and go night-swimming in the sky."

The thought of Dorian's hilltop infinity pool made me smile. "I guess I could come for a little bit," I said, relenting.

Everly grinned. "Yay!" she exclaimed. "Follow me and Tony." The singer kissed me on the cheek. "I'm gonna change real quick." She disappeared into the bathroom. "Dale rode with Ben. Will you grab his keys?" Everly called.

Rolling my eyes, I turned to get the wretched keys from the coffee table but was interrupted by a burst of air. I spotted an open window in the corner of the room. It was the Santa Ana winds blowing through the second story with the force of a medieval army. I went to the window and pushed my head through the narrow frame, watching as the raucous breeze fiercely lashed through the alley below. I stared in awe at the hills above Sunset Plaza. The wind was an invisible assailant, jostling everything in its path. And then, just as quickly as it arrived, it disappeared . . . as if pausing to catch its breath. Resting my head against the windowpane, I basked in the fleeting stillness. I knew the winds would return any second. Like the break between a set of waves, their absence was only temporary. As I waited, a gust of cool air hit my cheek. I reached my hand outside and noticed that the temperature had dropped ever so slightly. Fall had officially arrived.

"Witching weather," I said with a smile.

A flash caught my eye, and I looked down to see the reflection of the moon gazing up at me from a puddle. I cocked my head, thinking it was odd to be looking down at the moon. And not just any moon, but a Cheshire moon, the same one I'd seen through the roof earlier that day. My expression darkened as I thought about David's text message. *Be good*, I thought bitterly. *What the fuck is that supposed to mean?* I shook my head. Why did he get to tell me how to behave? And why was it okay for him to break his promises? Or stay out late working every night? How come he didn't have to sacrifice his house? Or work hard to "be good"?

Outside the wind howled again. As I stared with envy at the chaos left in its invisible wake, a delightful idea began to take shape. I looked at the keys. The silver Z, though still obnoxious, now represented infinite possibilities, an opportunity to rebel against my boyfriend and get a much-needed dose of oblivion.

"Hey, E," I called. "I'm gonna hit In-N-Out. You want anything?"

Everly briefly considered her options. "Double-double with cheese, animal style," she yelled back, "with two fries and a chocolate shake."

"See you at the house," I replied.

The walk only took a minute. I turned the keys over in my palm, then paused at the base of the street to look up the hill. I had no idea what a "Z" looked like. I pressed the key fob and waited for the car to make its introduction.

"Nice to meet you," I whispered.

The breeze whistled its approval as I approached the sports car and opened the door. I relaxed in the driver's seat and rested my head against the headrest. The car, like so many before it, felt like a sort of decompression chamber. Only now, instead of pushing against the sensation of apathy, I was excited to welcome it.

It was an odd feeling. Sitting there, I was anything but safe. If anything, I was flirting with disaster, about to embark on an adventure that was both illegal and risky.

Poor judgment and failure to learn by experience, I thought. Number eight on Cleckley's list. From where I was sitting, it appeared to be true. But I didn't care.

Something about this joyride was different. It felt like a new kind of freedom—a widening gyre from which I had a higher, more informed perspective. This was an evolved sense of liberation: the kind that came from understanding myself and following my own instincts, instead of having to placate someone else. I might have been up to my same old tricks, but this time I wasn't pacifying myself or trying to avoid boiling over. I wasn't even doing it because I simply wanted to break some rules. I was doing it for a very specific reason: to rebel.

Despite the glorious honeymoon period we'd enjoyed, my relationship with David was becoming stifling. I loved him intensely, but it was all too much. The pressure of feeling like I had to conform to his ideals and expectations filled me with anger. And not just any anger, but a familiar type of rage. It was a sharp spear of fury that had been forged in my childhood, the scars from which I'd spent most of my adult life trying to ignore.

Since the day David came to town, I'd been working to keep myself contained. Restrained. To be the good little girl he wanted. And that was fine. But this was so much better.

"Be good," I scoffed again, as I put the key into the ignition. "Where's the fun in that?"

I shoved the gearshift into drive and hit the gas. The car made a satisfying whine as I gunned it down the hill. I knew precisely what David would say if he knew what I was up to.

You don't have to do this.

But that was the problem. Because there—with the city streets at my mercy—I didn't feel the way I had all the times before. David was right. I didn't have to do it.

I couldn't *wait* to do it.

CHAPTER 19

Anonymous

A few weeks later I was sitting at work when an email appeared in my inbox. It read:

> dear patric,
>
> its a shame I never got to meet you but i have heard a lot about you from your daddy. now, let me tell you who i am. I am one of seversl of your dads "girls" that comes to the office "after hours" for some after-hours fun. i have photos of your dad with myself and other girls and these pics would damage his reputation and end your career. your father promised to take care of me and make me a star, well thats not happening soooo, heres the deal: i want $50,000 placed in a package and taken to the Holiday Inn on Highland next to to the Best Western. when i have the package, a friend of mine will be fed exing an envelope to your office addressed to you with the pics.
>
> if you tell anyone or go to the cops, i will hurt you. i know where you live. i will hunt your down like an animal and leave a nice scar on that pretty face. your boyfriend wont want an ugly girl, dont you think? The decision is up to you!!!!!!

I squinted at the screen. It had been written anonymously, but I had a sneaking suspicion who'd sent it. Her name was Ginny Krusi. The mother of a spectacularly talented singer/songwriter named

Oliver, Ginny had a well-earned reputation for being unhinged. I'd witnessed this firsthand as a member of her son's management team. This woman gave new meaning to the word "entitled."

As far as Ginny was concerned, Oliver's success was the financial win *she* deserved. Like most "momagers" I'd come across, Ginny had an insatiable thirst for money she didn't earn. Having one offspring meal-ticket wasn't enough. So she'd recently set her sights on her youngest child, Liam. Unfortunately, Liam had nowhere near the same level of talent as his brother. Ginny insisted, though, begging my father to sign Liam as a client and "make him a star."

To his credit, my father did everything he could, hiring vocal coaches and guitar teachers, media trainers and stylists. He went above and beyond to help. But Liam failed to impress. He was sweet, and his vocal skills were undeniably strong. The issue was he didn't seem to *want* to be a singer. After months of record label rejections, Dad finally had to break the bad news.

"I'm sorry," he'd said to Liam and his mother. "But we've tried everything we can for right now. Let's give it a shot in another couple of years." Dad had kept it positive, but there was no mistaking the message: Liam was not going to follow in his brother's footsteps, not anytime soon. They shook hands and parted ways. That's when Ginny Krusi went off the rails.

Within days we started getting threatening phone calls. Ginny would call the management offices at all hours in various states of outraged entitlement. She'd always ask for my father, but when she couldn't get him on the phone, she was just as happy to direct her aggression at me.

"You listen to me, little girl," she'd said one afternoon. "You *owe* me. I quit my job to support Liam's career. So *you* need to tell your daddy to give me an advance on his advance."

I handled these calls with placatory indifference. "Totally," I'd say, in my most pacifying tone. "I'll have him reach out the second he gets back to the office." Then I'd hang up and forget the call ever happened. After a few weeks of this, Ginny realized that her tactics weren't getting her anywhere. She started upping the ante by appearing in person. At first, these visits were startling but not overtly menacing. Over time, though, they became more disturbing. She showed up several times each week, harassing our receptionist and demanding to be "taken seriously."

Following a dramatic visit during which she brandished a baseball bat, Dad decided he'd had enough. He alerted his attorneys, who called Ginny and threatened legal action, and we finally stopped hearing from her. That is, until I got the email.

Reading the message again, I could almost smell Ginny's foul breath as she finger-pecked her keyboard. I thought it had to be her. But to be certain, I decided to enlist the help of a professional.

I contacted Anthony "Tony" Pacenti, a private investigator who'd done some freelance work for my father. Known as the "detective to the stars," Tony's tactics were discreet, if not always legal. So when he called me a few weeks later, I wasted little time heading to his office.

"It's Krusi, all right," Tony said. "I traced it to a Kinko's near her place." He handed me a black-and-white photo of Ginny hunched over a keyboard. "You said you got another email last night, right?"

Indeed I had. Since her first demand had gone unanswered, Ginny had continued sending messages, each one increasing in specifics and threat level. "Yeah," I replied, taking out my laptop. I opened my mailbox. "It came in at eight oh six."

Tony nodded. "Then I caught her red-handed. This is the IP address of that email," he said, pointing to a window on my screen. He took out a notepad with numbers written on it. "And this is the IP address of that computer." The numbers matched. "Look at the time stamp," he added. "This photo was taken at seven forty. She was probably in the middle of writing it."

I studied the photograph. The proof of Ginny's desperation made me smile slightly. "Thanks, Tony," I said, looking up. "This is exactly what I needed."

Ginny lived in a small run-down townhome located in one of the many sleepy suburbs of Los Angeles. My trips there began shortly after I met with Tony. Like Ginny's visits to *my* office, they started out fairly innocuous. The first time, I didn't even get out of my car. I just sat in front of her building, the satisfaction of hidden proximity filling me with a familiar sense of serenity. In a lot of ways, the experience was like sneaking out my bedroom window to observe neighbors during their nightly rituals. Except Ginny was no neighbor. And my interests were no longer those of an innocent spectator. This was different. At Ginny's I felt a sort of desire, a longing for wickedness I wasn't entirely sure I wanted to contain. And I *liked* it.

For almost a month, all I did was case the place. With David working on yet another project that kept him at the office until after midnight for weeks at a time, I had a relentless string of evenings where I could slip away unnoticed. I tried to keep things level. Sort of. But the intensity of my craving eventually became too much to resist. Perhaps inevitably, I allowed myself to inch closer.

One night, I parked my car in a space labeled VISITOR and cut across some grass toward her building. The community was in obvious need of repairs. Burnt-out streetlamps and narrow footpaths rendered me nearly invisible as I made my way to Ginny's unit. I ran my fingers along the high wooden fence that bordered her yard. Then I paused for a second and peered through the slats. The yard was empty and—save for the lights from her living room—dark.

I hoisted myself up and over the fence, landing with an awkward thud on the grass. Sliding glass doors extended the width of the building and may as well have been a movie screen for the view they provided of the interior. Secure in the assumption that her yard was private, Ginny made no use of the tacky blinds that hung open to either side. She lived her life as if no one was watching. Except *I* was watching. And the timing was perfect.

My life, in that moment, wasn't going particularly well. In addition to being blackmailed, my boyfriend was hardly speaking to me. David hadn't taken kindly to my joyride in Dale's Z, leaving me wondering whether our keychain confessionals were really such a good idea.

"You stole a fucking *car?*" David couldn't believe it. "Why?"

It was the day after Everly's concert and we were in the living room talking about my most recent transgression. He paced angrily, the miniature Statue of Liberty swinging from his fingers like a metronome. I kept my eyes on it, wishing it would put us both to sleep.

I shrugged. "Because I felt like it."

He glared at me. "But you *knew* it was wrong."

"Yes, I knew it was wrong. But I didn't *care*. Don't you get it? I have to *want* to make the right choice, to follow the rules. And what do I get in return? Nothing. That's what."

This had been on my mind since Everly had described our friendship as a "symmetrical symbiosis." As easily as she adopted certain "dark" traits of mine, I borrowed various "light" traits of hers. The result was a psychological cross-pollination that benefited us both. We supported one another. But whereas my friendship with Everly was based on equal give-and-take, my relationship with David was not.

"What the fuck does *that* mean?" he snapped.

"I don't think you realize how often you come to me for advice. How often you're okay with my sociopathic behavior when it suits you," I responded. "And I don't mind! I like seeing you explore that side of yourself. I love sharing myself with you. But I don't feel like you do the same for me. Ever since you moved here, I've busted my ass to be a good partner for you—to *understand* you. And not only are you not showing up for me, but you're borrowing my ego-strength while at the same time telling me I have to be a good girl. It's fucking bullshit."

"I'm not the one boosting cars, Patric."

"Neither was *I* until last night. And I did it because I wanted to rebel—against *you*. I knew you'd be pissed and we'd fight and . . . maybe hash things out."

"So this is *my* fault?!"

I clenched my fists and closed my eyes. The French doors were open to the backyard, and the smell of firewood drifted in from a neighbor's chimney. God! How I wished I could be lighting a fire, with jazz on the stereo and a glass of wine in my hand. How I wished I could be sitting at the picture window, happily waiting for David to return. Instead, I felt trapped in my own home and was fighting the urge to beat the shit out of him.

"No," I managed to reply evenly. "But I think the balance of our relationship is skewed." I pointed to the figurine he still held. "For one thing, I don't think that's a good idea anymore."

His fingers instinctively closed around the statue. "What? Why not?"

"Because it's dumb!" I told him. "Why should I have to confess anything to you? You're my boyfriend, not my priest." I reached forward and took his hands. "You're the man I love," I insisted. "I want you to accept me like I accept you. I want us to be partners. *Equal* partners."

He looked confused, but I could tell he was trying. "I want that, too," he said.

So, we agreed. We would do our best to support each other. We'd work harder to communicate. But nothing seemed to change. If anything, David threw himself even deeper into his work. Any attempt to draw him into my world was met with consternation, if not outright anger. I knew I was partially to blame. Being in a relationship with me was no picnic. But I felt like David used that to his advantage. After all—*I* was the sociopath, so he never had to take responsibility for any of *his* behavior. He hid his flaws behind mine, and there was nothing I could do about it. It was like being on the guillotine and waiting for the blade to fall.

Our relationship was in a state of suspended animation, and I had

nowhere to go. My own home—the only true refuge I'd ever had—
was now my least favorite place to be. Everywhere I looked, I was
reminded of happier times. I was haunted by memories and photo-
graphs of a "normal" life that seemed to be slipping through my fingers. If anything, being in my house was annoying. Claustrophobic.
So I set my sights on Ginny's. Her tiny world was the perfect environment for my expanding restlessness. If David no longer accepted me,
I reasoned, then I didn't need to play by his rules. I could embrace my
full self. In a way, I felt like a tiger that had escaped the zoo. I wasn't
hungry, per se, but I was excited to finally get to hunt. And I wasn't
the only one.

In recent weeks, Ginny had grown desperate in her attempts to
extort money from me. At first it was a steady barrage of emails. But
when I didn't reply to those, she started making threatening phone
calls. Day after day and night after night, the screen on my phone
would announce messages from an "unknown" caller. Her increasingly irrational voicemails left little to the imagination. Ginny's calls
were like a gift from the abyss, risk-free meat on which my dark side
could feed. The woman's deranged warnings, however baleful, were
no match for the strength of my indifference. With every "anonymous" email and "unknown" phone call, she was triggering an ava-
lanche of sociopathic provocations. The strongest of these was her
depiction of my father as something other than an honorable man. I
wasn't sure how to handle it.

On one hand, I knew my father had a well-earned reputation for
being a "ladies' man." Only this had never bothered me. Maybe it
should have, given the toll his wandering eye had taken on my mother.
Except he—like so many men in his cohort—did a phenomenal job
of normalizing it. "I'm a desperado, kid," he liked to say, "just like
the song."

But even I had to admit there was something occasionally off about
his extracurricular activities. It was never anything blatant, just a subtle awareness that things weren't quite right, a puzzle with one missing
piece. Like the night we were having dinner and a woman—thinking

we were on a date—followed me into the bathroom and cautioned me to "watch out." Or the time I was cleaning the attic and stumbled across a stack of pictures of him with dozens of different young women in various stages of undress.

That was what really troubled me about Ginny's email. Like any good con, the information was just accurate enough to seem credible. I knew Dad often stayed late at the office, for example. More than once, I'd driven by the building after midnight and seen his car there. And the description of the pictures Ginny claimed to possess were similar to the ones I'd found in the attic. The problem was that I couldn't decide if any of it was *bad*. Ginny hadn't accused my father of doing anything illegal. Her only grievance was that he hadn't made her a "star." The photos she claimed to have were meant to embarrass, not incarcerate him. So did it matter if he was going to the office late at night for some "after-hours fun"?

I was in a tricky spot. I knew better than anyone that I wasn't the best person to judge good behavior from bad, especially when it came to others. Dr. Carlin had confirmed this during one of our first sessions.

"You have what is called a high tolerance for pathology," she said.

When I asked her what that was, she explained, "It means you have a high fear threshold. People and circumstances that most everyone else recognize as dangerous or problematic will not always register that way for you. Your judgment is skewed to perceive potentially threatening situations as nonthreatening. It's quite common among sociopaths." I remembered the man with the kittens.

Was that happening now? Were my father's relationships with women atypical? Had my "high tolerance for pathology" blinded me once again to what everyone else could see was "dangerous or problematic"?

I didn't know what was going on and, worse, I didn't have anyone to ask. David had made his feelings clear. Obviously, I couldn't confide in my father. Everly was technically a client, so she was off-limits.

Even my own therapist was a no-go. I knew Dr. Carlin wouldn't be okay with me stalking Ginny. It would mean I had broken our agreement.

"This is why I wanted to process things in therapy years ago," I imagined her telling me. "So you'd be prepared when your destructive urges returned. For *any* reason." And she would be right. What's more, she would likely want to contact the authorities. It's what any rational person would do. But I didn't want to tell the police . . . or anyone else for that matter.

Bringing Ginny's threats to light would neutralize the outlet I'd found for my darkness, and I wasn't quite ready to surrender that. Why send her to prison when it was much more gratifying to deal with her myself? I was uncaged, in a way. So I decided to make the most of it.

It was a weeknight, and I was standing in Ginny's backyard, watching her through the windows. By my standards, I was in a great mood. Harlowe was in town, and I'd spent much of the afternoon hanging out with her and Everly at the abandoned house off Mulholland, the vacant dwelling providing a temporary break from my frustrations at home.

The trip to Ginny's was a last-minute decision. I'd dropped Harlowe at Dad's after dinner and was heading home to an empty house—I knew David wouldn't be home for hours—when I realized: *I don't feel like it.*

For the first time in a long time, I was relaxed. I was in the mood to be mischievous, not depressed. I figured a trip to Ginny's would be the perfect way to end the day. I took the freeway to the suburbs, where the shadows of her little yard enveloped me like a warm bath. The night air was crisp as I stood under a tree in the corner, well-hidden behind its thick trunk as Ginny paced in her living room. It was clear she was agitated about something.

My long detour was playing out better than I'd thought. Catching Ginny in a foul mood was a bonus. I *liked* seeing Ginny upset. I *wanted* her to be miserable, even if I wasn't directly responsible for her misery. After about a half hour, though, I got bored. I was about to leave when my phone buzzed. I looked at the screen.

Unknown Caller

I couldn't believe it. I looked up to see what Ginny was doing. She was standing in front of her bedroom window, a phone against her ear. I covered my mouth with one hand to control myself as I answered.

"Hello?" I said softly, disguising my voice with a Southern accent.

I changed the tone of my voice every now and then to throw Ginny off-balance. It always pissed her off, and that night was no exception. I grinned as I watched, her expression switching to confusion as she double-checked to make sure she'd dialed the correct number.

"Hello?" I said again, antagonistically.

"Oh," Ginny said, after a beat. "Is this *Harlowe?*"

The blood drained from my face at the mention of my sister's name.

"I *heard* you were in town," she said. "Can you give your big sister a message for me?" Her voice was raspy and malevolent. "Tell her she needs to pay her bills. Or else I'm going to find you and hurt you, Harlowe. Even if I have to fly all the way to *Florida.*"

I hung up. When Ginny heard a dial tone, she looked at the receiver smugly before returning it to its cradle. Every muscle in my body grew still as a long-lost memory rose to the forefront of my consciousness.

My grandparents' farm in Mississippi had a stable where they kept horses. Harlowe and I loved to visit it when we were kids; we did so on every trip there. Most of the horses were gentle, barn-broken, and easy to ride. But there was one that wasn't. Charlotte was a giant black mare with a ruthless disposition and an unkempt mane that hung halfway to the ground. She was notoriously unpredictable and willful, so much so that she was never allowed out of the barn when we were there. But I'll never forget the sound she made when she wanted to protest her confinement. At first it was isolated, one sharp kick to the door of her stable as she watched the other horses being led out to pasture. BOOM.

"Charlotte!" my grandfather would shout. "Don't you start!" Then he'd look to my sister and me. "Just ignore her," he'd whisper. But Charlotte wouldn't be ignored. Over and over she'd kick, her objections forceful and rhythmic. The planks would shudder from the power of her hoof. BOOM. BOOM.

I remember looking up at that horse, her black eyes boring dispassionately into mine as she displayed her will. BOOM. BOOM. BOOM. Only her top half was visible, and I saw no movement in that torso. The force of her kicks seemed to have no impact on her upper body, which was stoic and methodical as she continued her controlled protest.

With the phone still in my hand, I realized I had my own thunder building deep inside. It was barely noticeable at first, buried as it was under a few years of discipline and control and therapy and hope. But it had started to grow. BOOM. BOOM. BOOM. BOOM.

A clattering of venetian blinds snapped me back to the present, and I saw Ginny step onto the patio for a cigarette. It wasn't the first time this had happened. She was a chronic smoker and frequently wandered outside during my visits, lost in her cognitive dissonance as I stood nearby, watching. For the most part, I enjoyed these one-sided interactions. The experience was the closest I could get to actual invisibility, providing extra jolts of excitement as she would sometimes look straight at me and have no clue I was there. But that night, something was different. I stared at Ginny as she sucked contentedly on her menthol light. The look on her face made it clear she was no longer agitated. She seemed almost giddy, and I knew why.

It's because you threatened my sister, I thought. *Or at least, you* think *you did, you fucking bitch.*

Ginny extinguished her cigarette in a nearby planter. Then she did something she'd never done. She stepped into the yard. I watched as she began to meander mindlessly, each step drawing her closer to the spot under the tree where I stood watching. Waiting.

With the fortitude of my discipline only slightly stronger than the pull of my darkness, a sociopathic battle of wills was playing out only steps from where Ginny strolled, blissfully ignorant. The heightened risk produced acute satisfaction. God, I loved how it made me feel. Power and strength and nothingness and acceptance all rolled into one. *She'd never see it coming*, I thought with a smile.

Every muscle in my body braced for movement as I considered my options. She was only a yard or so away now. All I needed was for her to take one more step. One more step, and my dark side could take the lead. One more step, and I wouldn't even need to move out of the shadows for the force of my darkness to flex its strength. I couldn't wait for the high, for the *release*.

Ginny stopped. It seemed she'd made up her mind to stand there forever. But then, finally, she lifted her foot to move toward my tree. I took a slow inhale as I prepared to make my move. That's when the front door slammed. Ginny and I whirled around to look at the house. "Hello?" she called out.

There was no reply. We both stood still, our eyes on the entrance to the living room. A young boy appeared.

"Hey, Mom," Liam said. He stood in the doorway while Ginny returned to the patio.

"How was the movie?" asked Ginny.

The boy shrugged. "Stupid."

Ginny embraced him. "Are you hungry?" she asked, planting a kiss on his cheek. "You wanna order pizza?"

Liam smiled. "Extra cheese?"

Ginny nodded. "You got it."

She put her arm around her son, and the two of them walked inside. I watched, my dark side shrinking further into the shadows with their every step. For a second I was frozen. I stood there, disabled by my spinning psyche but also unable to stop watching the scene unfolding: a mother and her son turning on the television and setting up a coffee table for late-night pizza.

The juxtaposition was paralyzing. I might have stayed there all night. But then Ginny did something else she'd never done before. Turning to face the yard, she reached to the side and tugged on the cord to close the blinds. Like a moviegoer who had stayed too long, I stood awkwardly in the corner of the yard, watching the vertical slats as they slid slowly sideways and pitched the entire space into darkness.

CHAPTER 20

Smoke and Mirrors

It was safe to say things weren't going well. My personal life was a wreck. David and I were hardly talking. My extracurricular activities were highly questionable. And I was seriously starting to wonder whether I should commit myself to a mental institution.

It had been weeks since I'd seen Dr. Carlin. Between work, school, and my frequent escapes to Ginny's backyard, I hardly had time to eat, much less drive back and forth to the other side of town for therapy. This was irrelevant, though, because as my sociopathic behavior reared its head, my choice to remain distant from her was less about logistics and more about self-preservation. That most of my free time was playing out like a test of the Tarasoff rule meant that my therapist was no longer an acceptable confidant.

I was on my own.

The buttons made sharp clicks as my fingers flew over the keyboard. It was the morning after that visit to Ginny's house and—instead of working—I was at my desk googling "modern asylums." My actions the previous night had left me rattled. What had started out as a harmless stretch of sociopathic muscle had transformed into something I wasn't sure I could control. I was unsettled by how quickly my intentions had shifted from disciplined deviance to near ferocity. In the light of day, it became clear: I needed serious professional help. And I was willing to do just about anything to get it.

"Anorexia," I read, "bipolar, depression." My eyes scanned the list of disorders treated by a prestigious northern California wellness center. I frowned at the options as I scrolled through the list. "Schizo-affective disorder, schizophrenia, social anxiety disorder, Tourette's syndrome."

"Fuck," I muttered, disappointed by the absence of sociopathy among the options. Just like the dictionaries.

I scratched another name off the spreadsheet I'd printed. It was number thirty-three on my list. In the several hours since I'd started, my search for professional intervention hadn't produced a single viable option. None of the psychiatric services listed on any of the mental institution websites offered any treatment related to sociopathy. None of the people at the various places I'd called could even point me in the right direction. Sociopathy was "clinically obsolete," one woman had explained. Schizophrenia, she'd unhelpfully suggested, was remarkably popular.

"Are you hearing voices?" the woman had asked. And I'd said "no" before I'd had the time to properly consider it.

"Absence of delusions and other signs of irrational thinking" was number two on Cleckley's list. Sociopaths, the psychologist had theorized, don't suffer from signs of psychosis the way that schizophrenics do. As a result, they're capable of logical reasoning and are believed to have control over much of their antisocial behavior. In other words, sociopaths are tempted to do violent things because they think they want to, not because they hear voices that compel them.

"Patric," my assistant's voice crackled over the intercom, "your dad wants to see you."

I look a deep breath and rose from my desk.

Maybe I should pretend to be schizophrenic, I thought, as I walked down the hall. After all, I *was* hearing voices. My own. And they were encouraging me to do terrible things to Ginny Krusi.

"Hey," Dad said, when I shuffled into his office. "I need you to check on the Hudson demo." The Hudson demo was a collection of songs by a pop group we represented. Dad had been waiting for weeks for it to be completed. It was in the final stages of production at a recording studio in Hollywood.

I didn't acknowledge him because I was still thinking about what I'd have to do to pull off a convincing schizophrenic impression.

"Patric," Dad said. "Are you listening to me?"

"Yeah," I answered. "Sorry, I'm just confused. Are you sure it's done?"

"No," he snapped, "but I need it to *get* done. I'm meeting with three labels next week. So, if I have to send you to the studio every goddamned day to nag them about it, then that's what I'm gonna do."

It was a quick drive to the studio. I waved at the receptionist in the lobby and strolled down the long main hallway in search of the Hudson team. I'd been fond of recording studios ever since I was a child and Dad would take me with him for work. They resembled artistic caves to me, always dark, always cold, always filled with music. You never knew what you might find.

After a few minutes of searching for them, I spotted a producer I recognized. He was leaning against an open studio door, facing me as he stood casually inside the frame, talking to someone I couldn't see.

"Hey, Patric," he said, as I approached. "What's up?"

"Hey, Neil," I replied with a smile. "You haven't seen Bill around, have you?" I asked, referring to the head producer. "I'm trying to track down a demo."

Just then another man peeked out from inside the studio. An acoustic guitar hung from a thick strap strung across his shoulder and I recognized him at once, even though he was taller than I thought he'd be.

"Hi," he said.

"Oh, I'm sorry," Neil said. "Do you guys know each other?"

The guy shook his head. He stepped self-assuredly into the hallway, extending his hand. And I laughed. I'd never quite gotten used to being introduced to someone whose identity was obvious. Despite growing up around the entertainment business and spending much of my adult life working in close proximity to all sorts of successful artists, the ritual of the introduction—as if the name of the person standing in front of me wasn't laughably plain—had always struck me as funny. I decided to say exactly that to the man with the guitar.

"I never thought about that," he said, grinning. "So, how about this," he offered, his eyes sparkling mischievously. "Pretend I'm not me." He extended his other hand and said, "The name's Max. Max Magus."

"Nice," I said, playing along. "Like a Batman villain with a hint of porn."

"Your turn," he said.

"I'm Patric," I said.

He nodded an approval. "So, tell me, Patric, do you know any good places to eat around here?"

I nodded. "Yes."

"Well, what do you say about lunch?"

I shook my head, simultaneously impressed and put off by his confidence. "Thanks for the invitation," I said, smiling, "but my boyfriend frowns on me going on lunch dates with strange men."

"Oh, great boyfriend placement," he replied, not missing a beat. "You see what she did there, Neil?" he asked. "She let me know she's taken, and so smoothly. But the joke's on you," he said, "for I, too, have a significant other."

"How nice for her!" I said, laughing.

"So how about it?" he asked. "Now that you know I'm not hitting on you, it's perfectly innocent. Besides, I'm starving, and Neil refuses to come with me."

"I'm in the middle of mixing *your* album," grumbled Neil. Max waved his hand dismissively.

"I can't," I said. "I'm working, too. I'm only here to find a demo."

"Mike!" Max shouted suddenly.

Another man appeared in the doorway. "What's up, boss?"

"I need you to track down a demo." Max looked at me expectantly.

I sighed, feigning exasperation. "It's the band Hudson," I said, smiling apologetically at Mike. "Bill Gross is the producer."

Mike picked up the phone. "One second. I'll call the engineer."

"Looks like you're out of excuses."

"I really have to get back to work," I said.

"Me, too," he pressed.

"But if you feel like waiting around for me to drop off the demo," I gave in, "there's a place near my office called the Smoke House."

When I got to the Smoke House, Max was already there. He was waiting for me in a crescent-shaped booth. "Took you long enough," he said.

I'd almost decided not to go. Having lunch with someone I'd just met was atypical for me. Having lunch with *anyone*, really. But after a morning of asylum-seeking, a spontaneous lunch with a prominent stranger sounded like a decent way to spend the afternoon. It sure beat any distraction measures I'd been using lately. And the Smoke House provided the perfect backdrop. Its dark wood interior and high-backed booths always made me feel like I was disconnected from the world and my problems—if only temporarily. As soon as I sat down, Max asked, "How'd you find this place?"

"It's one of the oldest restaurants in the city," I told him. "It's also one of my favorites, tied with Jar. And James Beach. El Coyote. Giorgio Baldi. I could go on."

"You sound like a foodie," he said. "So, tell me. If you could go to any restaurant in the world right now, which would it be?"

"Per Se," I replied without hesitation. "In New York. I've never been, but it's number one on my culinary bucket list."

"Then you have good taste," Max humblebragged.

I smiled and leaned back against the warm leather booth, taking stock of my lunch date. He was fun. I already felt like I was having a conversation with an old friend, someone effortlessly engaging and uninterested in mindless chitchat.

After the waiter brought us our drinks, Max asked me, "Do you ever feel like you're crazy?" I was briefly thrown by the question, and I got the feeling that was the point, as if he was trying to get me off-balance. It was a tactic I used with people, too. I smiled, pleasantly surprised, and said, "Yes, actually."

He lowered his voice and leaned slightly forward. "No, but I mean like *really* crazy. Like, right now I feel totally sane. But then I'll think back on something I did, say, a few months ago that was totally fucking *in*sane. Only, at the time I did it, it seemed like a completely logical decision."

"You're worried you have a false sense of self-awareness," I offered.

"Yes," he replied, impressed that I understood so quickly.

"Like you can't trust yourself to know, at any given time, what is and isn't sane behavior."

"Christ," he said, running a hand through his thick dark hair. *"Yes."*

"I do feel like that," I told him. "In fact, I spent most of the morning searching for a mental asylum so I could have myself committed."

I relished the words as they left my mouth. It was nice to simply speak the truth. Max's reaction—good or bad—meant nothing. With nothing to lose, I'd decided to just be myself. I didn't know how long the freedom would last, but I intended to enjoy it.

Max was looking at me as if he couldn't decide whether to take me seriously. I found the list of wellness centers in my purse and placed it on the table. "I'm a sociopath," I disclosed. "I was diagnosed a few years ago, and I've been trying to get treatment ever since."

He took a deep breath and leaned back in his seat. "What does that mean exactly?"

He listened as I outlined my struggles with sociopathy and frustration that there wasn't more clinical information or any treatment options. "I was seeing a therapist for a while, and she was great. She wasn't a specialist, though, and that's what I think I need." I paused, then confessed, "'Cause I've been having some problems lately."

"Problems like what?" Max asked, fully absorbed.

"Impulse control, for one. There's a woman who's been trying to extort me for a few months," I explained. "And last night things . . . escalated."

"Escalated . . . *how?*"

I shrugged. "I almost jumped her in her backyard."

He did a spit take and grabbed a napkin.

"The good news," I went on, "is that when I woke up this morning, I knew I needed to take some preventive measures. But I haven't had any luck finding someone who can help me." I frowned. "Sociopathy isn't considered a 'treatable disorder.' I'm actually working on my doctorate in psychology just so I can learn more about it."

"Wait," Max said, wiping his chin. "I thought you were a manager."

"I am. I do both."

"Quite the double life," he said with admiration. "So who is this person?"

"What person?"

"The extorter!"

"Oh," I said. "It's Oliver Krusi's mom."

He craned his neck at me, his eyes bulging. "Oliver Krusi," he repeated. "The *singer*?!"

"Yeah."

"My manager just pitched me on working with him," he said.

"Well, unless you're cool with losing most of your valuables, I wouldn't invite his mom to the writing session." I took a sip. "Though I'm not one to pass judgment."

"Wait," he said, shaking his head. "Go back. Why is Oliver's mom blackmailing you?"

I rubbed my eyes. "She says she has compromising pictures of my dad, and if I don't leave fifty thousand dollars in cash at the Holiday Inn on Highland, she's gonna go to the press with them. And cut my face open. Or maybe cut my face open and then go to the press. I can't remember."

My words hung briefly in the air and then we both started laughing, struck by the absurdity of the situation, which, for the first time, had become hilarious to me.

"Okay, hold on," he said, catching his breath. "Your dad's a manager, too, right?"

I nodded.

Max dropped his voice, conspiratorially. "So, you think she really has pictures?"

"Probably," I said, then sighed with relief. Again, it was refreshing to be honest, as if a thousand-pound weight had been removed from my shoulders. "Although I'm not sure it matters. That's part of my problem. I can never tell when something bad is *bad*."

"Yeah, but you must have known what *she* was doing was bad," Max observed. "Otherwise, you wouldn't have wanted to punish her."

"That's the thing," I replied. "I don't think it was about punishment at all."

I recounted my multiple trips to Ginny's backyard and the sense of release I experienced afterward. "I wasn't going over there because of what she did," I admitted. "I did it because the opportunity presented itself." I fell silent as an ancient memory drifted across my consciousness. "Just like Kiki," I murmured.

Max cocked an eyebrow.

Kiki was my mother's cat. A house cat from birth, she spent her entire life indoors . . . until the day I let her out. "It was a true accident," I told him. "I opened the door and she just bolted. She'd been hiding behind the couch, I guess, waiting for the chance. And the second she got it, she was gone. After about an hour, though, she came back. I found her on the porch, lounging in the sun." I rested my head against the booth as I continued my stroll down memory lane.

"Mom never knew, but every afternoon after that, I'd sit outside after school and leave the front door open so Kiki could come out. Sometimes she'd lie next to me. Sometimes she'd roam around the yard. But she never ran away again."

"She knew what was good for her," Max replied.

I smiled. "It's true. Kiki didn't want to be an outdoor cat. She just needed to make the choice for herself." I thought about it. "Don't misunderstand. My mom's protective instincts were right, but her strategy was wrong. Mom wanted to keep Kiki contained." That's when it clicked. "Like David," I said.

Max blinked in confusion.

"My boyfriend," I clarified. "He doesn't like that I'm a sociopath," I said bluntly. "He doesn't like that I don't feel things the way he does, the way everybody else does. He used to. I think. But now it scares him. I think he's afraid that if I get out of the house, I'll never come back. Y'know, metaphorically speaking."

Max tilted his head as puzzlement and delight spread across his face. "Are you for real?" he asked. "Like, are you a real person or am I just having the best fucking dream of my life?"

I chuckled at his bravado. I could tell he was flirting, but I wasn't bothered. I sort of liked it. It was nice to be accepted for who I was. Rewarded, even. And anyway, it was harmless.

I smiled. "I might have to get back to you on that."

"How long have you been together?" Max asked.

"A few years."

"That's a long time," he said.

"I know," I said. "But that's why I jumped at the chance to go to Ginny's. I think some part of me was like, 'It's only a matter of time before David and I stop fighting, and I decide to be good again. I may as well go for it while I can.'"

"But is that what you want?" he asked provocatively. "To be *good*?"

I sighed and looked up at the ceiling. "What I want is to be better," I said, my voice betraying a hint of exhaustion. "Different."

He looked shocked. "Why?"

"Because I'm not *well*." I laughed. "Didn't you hear what I said? I almost assaulted someone last night."

"But you didn't," he countered. "I don't know. I think it's interesting. And the fact that you're so open about it." He shook his head and took a long sip of his drink. "I wouldn't change a fucking thing."

I shifted slightly in my seat. It was another bold statement, one that resonated more than I was ready to admit. I forced an inquisitive expression, eager to change the topic.

"So what about you?" I asked. "What's your vice?"

"Flattery, probably," he answered, after a beat. "Attention, validation." He shrugged. "Not very original, I'll admit. That's the thing about this business, though," he said. "The addiction feeds the addiction."

"It must be such a crazy existence."

"What do you mean?"

"Everyone's attracted to fame," I said. "It's all very alluring. But at the same time, it's terrifying." I shuddered, thinking about the lack of invisibility. "I'd kill myself if everywhere I went, people knew who I was."

"Instead of killing other people, you mean?" he quipped.

I laughed.

"On that note," he replied, signaling for the waiter, "I say we get another round."

I considered objecting, but then thought, *Why not?* It wasn't like I had anything better to do.

The waiter approached our table. Martini for me. Whiskey for him. Max waited for him to leave, then said, "It's my problem with everything, actually. Sometimes I'm comfortable with success. Sometimes I hate it. Sometimes I want the girl. Sometimes I want her to disappear."

"That's totally normal," I told him. "You get that, right? It's a boundary issue."

"What do you mean?"

"People who don't have access to conventional boundaries are always looking for new ways to set them. Just like me."

Max looked down his nose at me. "So you're saying I'm a latent sociopath?"

"No. You need too much validation." Then I had an idea. "Though I bet I could conduct a study on sociopathy and the negative effects of fame."

"Huh?"

I leaned back, deep in thought. "Sociopaths don't recognize natural boundaries," I said, mostly to myself, "and they aren't easily socialized as children. So they don't live by the same social rules as everyone else." I redirected my attention to Max. "But that's the same thing that happens to famous people, isn't it? The more they achieve, the fewer boundaries they have. They don't have to play by the rules, so they start acting destructively to find a new normal, to find new boundaries. They start *acting* like sociopaths." I realized I was rambling. "I'm sort of a psychology nerd," I said with a shrug. "Sorry."

"I thought you didn't feel remorse," he joked.

"I said it doesn't come naturally. But I can fake it pretty good." I flashed a wide grin.

"I'm starting to pick up on that. But you still haven't answered my question." He rested his elbow on the table and dropped his cheek against his palm. "I asked you if you were real. You said you'd get back to me."

"Oh." I chuckled. "How about you decide?"

He stared at me intently. "I say you're real."

"Great."

"So, how long would you say we have?"

I shot him a playfully disapproving glance, his question intentionally vague but bold. Still, harmless.

"Now that we know you're real, I mean," he said. "How long you think before you check yourself into an asylum?"

I sighed and looked to the ceiling again. "Who knows? I have to find one that will take me first."

"Well . . . Do you think you'll be around tomorrow night?" he asked.

"Most likely. Why?"

"Some friends of mine are playing the Hollywood Bowl. You can be my guest." Max grinned. "Along with your boyfriend, of course."

Later that night I sat in the living room waiting for David to get home. I'd poured two glasses of wine and, as I relaxed on the window bench overlooking the street, I couldn't help but bask in the contentment brought on by my lunch with Max. I'd started out the day despondent, resigned to the idea of committing myself to a mental institution. But now, incredibly, I felt clear. I hadn't been looking for one, but Max had turned out to be an exceptional acceptance surrogate. Hanging out with him had been fun. Unexpected. For the first time in months, I finally had the chance to just be myself, the way I *liked* myself. And I was hoping to keep that momentum going with David.

The air was cool, and I had the French doors open to the backyard. A burning log in the fireplace crackled, jazz floated from the speakers, and I thought I might explode in relief. Twenty-four hours earlier, I'd stood beneath a canopy of tree branches, inches away from making a huge mistake. But now I couldn't imagine doing anything of the sort. The desire to go to Ginny's house—to do anything destructive, in fact—was as distant to me as a Louisiana Baptist hymn, like something vaguely remembered from my youth.

I leaned my head against the picture window. A soft glow illuminated the canyon road below. I saw the glint of David's headlights and scrambled out of my seat. I closed the shutters, rushed to turn off the stereo, and picked up the other glass of wine as I hurried to the front door. I had planned to meet him in the driveway. I'd wanted to hand him a glass of wine the second he stepped out of his car to give him a warm welcome home. But in my haste, I'd forgotten to set down my own glass. Now, with both hands full, I didn't have any way to open the door. I bent at the waist in an attempt to twist the doorknob with my shoulder. But I couldn't get it opened before David's silhouette appeared in the frosted window of the door panel.

"Patric?" he asked through the door. "What the *hell* are you doing?"

I giggled and straightened up as he pushed the door open. "I was gonna meet you outside," I explained, "except I didn't have any hands."

He laughed and closed the door. "Well, this is nice," he said, happily accepting the wine. "Why are you still up? It's almost midnight."

I wrapped my arm around his neck and pulled him into a long kiss. "I know," I said. "I figured you might be hungry."

"Mmmm . . . I am starving," he said.

"There's chicken potpie in the oven."

He smiled. "That's not what I meant."

Hours later, the two of us lay in bed. He patiently listened as I rattled off the details of my afternoon. He nodded as I told him about my trip to the studio and my serendipitous introduction to the curious musician.

"So . . . like, the two of you are friends now?" he asked.

"I wouldn't go that far," I said, laughing. "But he invited us to a show at the Bowl." I shook my head. "Isn't that awesome?"

"Well, I don't love you getting randomly drunk with the guy in the middle of the afternoon."

"Oh, live a little." I nudged him. "Besides, it wasn't like that."

"Uh-huh," he said. "So, what was it like?"

I tried to find a way to explain it. "Today—hanging out with this stranger—I could just be myself. It didn't matter who he was. He could have been a talking robot for all I cared. It was just nice to talk to someone about my diagnosis and say the word 'sociopath' without it being a bad thing."

"You *told* him that?" David asked, astonished. "Why?"

"Because it's who I am, honey. It's my life," I told him. "And it was fun! That's why I was in such a good mood all day. It was . . . liberating. Liberating to feel *accepted*."

"I accept you," David replied quietly.

"Not always," I replied in kind.

He cocked an eyebrow. "What an exciting life he must have," he mused, changing the subject.

I looked at him in horror. "Are you kidding? All he does is write, record, tour. Write, record, tour. Where's the normalcy? Where's the *life*?" I shook my head. "Do you think any of those people—artists, I mean—get to have normal relationships or normal lives? Just think of how transient their existence must be. It's like the second someone decides to be an artist, successful or not, they stop evolving with the rest of society. They're trapped in a state of suspended impermanence."

David smiled. "I guess I never thought of it that way. But I do adore how you thoroughly analyze everyone you meet."

"Because it's fascinating to me! That's what I love about school. I never knew any of this stuff before, all this people stuff. The only thing I ever researched before was sociopathy. But now I'm learning about *all* the different personality types. *All* the different ways people cope with their psychological shortcomings. It's like I can't get enough." I locked eyes with him. "People are fucking amazing, you know?"

He offered a faint grin and pushed a lock of hair across my forehead. "I'm proud of you," he said. "The work you do on yourself, getting a PhD . . . It's amazing." He paused. "I think *you* are amazing."

I smiled and pushed back against the faint tug of responsibility. I was quite aware that I hadn't truly been keeping my end of our bargain. I hadn't told him about Ginny, or my visits to her condo, or that I'd spent the morning looking for a mental institution. But I also knew it wasn't safe. Not yet, anyway. And certainly not in that moment, with everything so relaxed and wonderful.

"So what about tomorrow?" I asked eagerly. "Can you come home first and we'll go together? Or you wanna just meet me at the Bowl?"

He made a pained face. "Oh, honey," he said. "I can't go *tomorrow* night. It's the company dinner, remember?"

"Dammit," I muttered. "I forgot." I leaned back against him and sighed. "Never mind, then," I said. "I'll just meet you at the restaurant."

I could feel him shaking his head. "Honey, no," he said. "It's a fucking work party with the most boring people on Earth. Escape while you can."

I settled against his chest, my body surrendering to exhaustion. "Well, when you put it *that* way," I replied.

"Just be good," he said drowsily.

CHAPTER 21

Exposition

A month later, I sat in Max's dining room, with a bunch of his friends, having dinner. In the short time since our chance encounter at the studio, our friendship had grown by leaps and bounds. And I liked it. I enjoyed having another friend who liked me for me. The acceptance made me feel stable. It was a welcome relief.

Despite the break in the clouds a few weeks before, things with David had continued to deteriorate. I found myself inventing reasons to argue with him, and then using his angry reactions to justify disappearing. The night I finally confessed to the trips I'd been making to Ginny's house, for instance, he practically lost his mind.

"What the *fuck*, Patric?" he said. "You've been going to her *house*?"

It was a hopeless dynamic that reminded me of my childhood. Once again, I regretted my decision to be honest. "What does it matter?" I snapped back, pissed at him for judging me. "It's not like I did anything violent." (Barely.) "It's not like I lost control." (Sort of.)

Talking to David about my dark desires was pointless. It only ever ended with him trying to suppress or negate them. Talking about them with Max, on the other hand, was fun.

I relaxed against a plush cushion and watched with amusement as Max rose from his chair. "Everyone raise a glass," he told us. "I'd like to propose a toast to a very special person." He winked in my direction. "A complete lunatic who just happened to get her very first research grant this afternoon!" He grinned when I winced at being in the spotlight.

"To Patric!" Max announced. "May her psychological discoveries bring us all closer to sanity."

I smiled and rolled my eyes at him over the rim of my glass.

When everyone settled back into their seats, the woman next to me, an actress named Michelle, asked, "So, what is it you're researching?"

"Sociopaths," I told her. "I'm studying the relationship between sociopathy and anxiety."

Her expression switched from detached curiosity to wholehearted interest. From the corner of my eye, I could see Max grinning. He loved watching these conversations play out.

"Wait," interrupted the brunette seated at his side. "Aren't sociopaths, like, evil? They're the ones who have no feelings—like Ted Bundy and stuff—right?"

"Not exactly," I said. "They aren't really evil. They just *feel* differently than most people."

"Is that the difference between a sociopath and a psychopath?" asked Tim, a guy seated across from me. He, too, was a musician, and one of Max's oldest friends.

"It's a tricky question," I answered, "because they're grouped together, along with antisocial personality disorder."

I paused to think of an easy way to summarize it. "It comes down to diagnostics. People with antisocial personality disorder are assessed using criteria in the *Diagnostic and Statistical Manual of Mental Disorders*. It's like the Bible of the psychological field. But psychopaths and sociopaths *can't* be diagnosed that way. There's a special test just for them."

"Why do they get their own test?" he asked.

"Because they measure different things," I said. "Being diagnosed as antisocial doesn't automatically make you a psychopath or sociopath. And vice versa."

"Then why are they all grouped together?" asked Michelle.

"Because they're varying *types* of the same disorder. It's sort of like different shades of the same color," I explained.

"So, then what's the difference between a sociopath and a psychopath?" Tim pressed.

"Well, there isn't one right now," I replied. "Not clinically speaking, anyway. But I think there should be. There's lots of research indicating that those on the extreme end of the spectrum are physically *incapable* of learning the social emotions, like shame or remorse," I told him. "I consider them 'true psychopaths,' the ones biologically blocked from progressing through the normal stages of emotional development. It's like the wiring in their brain is off. They never learn from consequences or punishment."

"But aren't sociopaths like that, too?" Max's manager, Brian, asked me.

"No," I said. "That's why I think they should be separate. There are lots of people who score way higher than most on the psychopath test, but fall just below the threshold. They're physically capable of learning social emotions; they just need to be taught differently. *Those*, I believe, are the true *sociopaths*. And I think most of them probably fall somewhere on a spectrum."

Max's brunette was wide-eyed. "I had an ex like that," she said breathlessly. He lifted her hand and kissed it affectionately.

"Okay," Michelle said, "but what's that have to do with anxiety?"

"Well, that's what I want to know," I said. I told them about Cleckley's psychopathy checklist and how there were traits on it that I thought were questionable.

"Take number three: absence of nervousness or psychoneurotic manifestations," I explained. "That's saying sociopaths don't experience nervousness and don't get worried or stressed. And while I agree with the nervousness part, I don't believe sociopaths are immune to anxiety. In fact, I think it's the thing that really sets them apart from psychopaths."

Michelle shook her head and reached for her wine. "So fascinating," she said. "What got you interested in all this?"

"Wait!" Max interrupted. "Can I tell them?"

I grinned coyly and said, "Yes."

"Patric here," he declared with a dramatic flourish, "is a bona fide sociopath." He flashed a proud smile and leaned back in his chair.

"It's true," I admitted. "I was diagnosed a few years ago. I've tried to get treatment, but there's no 'official' treatment for sociopathy. So, I figured I'd go back to school to try to find one." I paused. "Instead of sitting around and waiting for my bad behavior to get worse." Michelle's eyes widened.

"On that note," Max said, getting up and heading for the kitchen. "Anyone need anything?" he called over his shoulder.

I felt my phone buzz and saw I had a text message.

On my way home. Will you be there?

David was leaving town early the next morning for work, and I wanted to see him before he left. Business trips had become a more frequent part of his job. As his company expanded, he would some-times spend a week or more setting up computer systems in different parts of the country.

I frowned when I read his note and felt a twinge of sadness. I knew he was trying. Over the course of my life, he'd probably tried harder than anyone. Thinking about that made me uneasy. Suddenly I was eager to get home to be with him. I excused myself from the table, grabbed my glass, and walked quickly into the kitchen.

"Hey," I said to Max, who was opening another bottle of wine. "I gotta go. David's on his way home."

"Bummer." He frowned. "He's leaving tomorrow, right?"

"Yeah," I said. "It's a short trip, though. Just a week."

Max nodded and put the opened wine bottle on the counter. "Any plans while he's gone?"

"Not really."

Max cocked his head. "Then let's have dinner at Per Se Thursday night. It'll have to be on the late side. How's eight thirty?"

It dawned on me that he was serious. "What are you up to?" I asked.

"I gotta do a press thing," he said. "The label's flying me to JFK at the crack of dawn. Come with me. We'll land around three. I'll be done in an hour and then we can do whatever we want. Fly back after dinner."

I laughed. "And what am I supposed to tell David?" I asked, crossing my arms. "That I'm just gonna pop over to New York while he's out of town?"

"Why not? It's not a date. It's just two friends flying off on a whimsical adventure," Max insisted. "He won't care."

I stared down my nose at him. "He would *absolutely* care."

Max shrugged. "Then don't tell him," he said with a grin.

Stifling a smile, I looked away. "You're a bad influence."

It was true. Unlike David, who always wanted me to suppress my sociopathic traits, Max had been pushing me to embrace them since the day we met. We shared a rapport that was easy and natural, if not altogether healthy. I knew it. I also knew that hanging out with Max wasn't the wisest choice. He was like a recreational drug that made me feel invincible and strong. My saving grace was that I could only take so much. Being high on Max simply wasn't something I could do all the time, nor was it what I *wanted*. He was too flamboyant for me, and his access to nearly unlimited resources made him a frequent magnet for chaos. I, on the other hand, preferred discipline. So I was mindful of the dosing.

I gave him a friendly peck on the cheek. "I'll think about it," I said.

"That's a terrible idea!" he yelled, as I walked out the door.

Thursday morning, I woke to my phone buzzing with texts. I squinted at the screen and saw one was from Max, a photo of his shoes kicked up against the window of a jet cabin.

Loser

I smirked and scrolled to the next message. It was from David.

I know you're probably sleeping, but I just wanted you to know how much I love you. There's no one in the world who drives me crazier than you do. But there's also no one else I'd rather be with. I love you so much, Patric.

I sighed as I closed the screen and leaned back against the headboard. I was glad I'd decided not to accept Max's invitation. Though it hadn't been easy. The musician knew just how to appeal to my dark side. When it came to the New York trip, I had no problem with his mental gymnastics. It wasn't wrong to take an impulsive trip with a *friend*. Max and I weren't going to do anything illegal or embark on some illicit affair. Dinner in Manhattan would have been decadent and fun. The only issue, as far as I was concerned, was that David wouldn't have liked it.

It wasn't fair. Why should I have to abstain from doing something fun simply because someone else felt it was wrong? Why was I constantly expected to abide by a set of emotional rules to which I couldn't relate? Why couldn't it be the other way around for once? When was someone going to relate to *me*?

God! It would have been so easy to get on that plane. I could have jetted off and back, and David never would have known. What's more, I wouldn't have felt bad about it. But something held me back. The morning David left, I'd become aware of a heaviness in my chest. It was barely noticeable at first, but the longer I contemplated a quick trip to Per Se with Max, the heavier the sensation became. Was this *guilt*?

I knew it wasn't. I'd witnessed guilt enough in other people, especially David. As the firstborn son of Catholic parents, he was often guilted into doing things against his will.

"This makes no sense," I'd said to him once, watching him pack for a trip home. "You say you hate going to your uncle's for Christmas. You tell me he's an asshole, and every year he picks a fight with your mom. Everyone always ends up crying. So, why are you going? I just don't get it."

He stopped packing and glanced at me affectionately. "I know you don't get it," he said. "And you're lucky."

Now, lying in bed, semi-wishing I was on a plane flying across the country, I understood what he meant. I hadn't decided to stay home because going would have made me feel guilty. I'd rejected Max's invitation because I chose my relationship with David. But in doing so I felt hobbled. I felt weak. It made me think of the second *Superman* movie, when he has to surrender his powers to be with Lois Lane. I wondered if something similar was happening to me. *Is this what I have to do to be with David?* I thought. Ignore my sociopathic "superpowers" and live like a normal person? Always make sensible choices? *Well, fuck* that, I thought. I'd file this one under "Better in Theory."

Frustrated, I got out of bed and headed for the bathroom. I didn't like the way that I felt, not one bit, and I hoped a shower would wash it off. I turned the knob all the way to hot, and as scalding ribbons of water hit my scalp I willed myself to stabilize, but the discomfort continued to rise.

I felt so conflicted. On one hand, I knew that I wanted to spend the rest of my life with David. I'd always sensed a sort of preternatural connection with him, like we were destined to be together. On good days we fit together perfectly. He excelled at so many of the things that I didn't. And I excelled at so many of the things *he* didn't. Things we were both good at, we were good at together. And things we were both bad at, we were bad at together. On good days, we were *connected*. Which is what made the bad days so bad. Bad days were when I wouldn't tell him the truth, when we were so *dis*connected that nothing seemed to work at all. Every conversation was an argument, every word misinterpreted. On bad days I felt lost. Adrift. Those were the days I questioned the point of trying to evolve at all.

I took a deep breath, turned off the water, and grabbed a towel. "But today is going to be a good day," I said to myself.

Still, I couldn't totally shake the claustrophobic sensation. It was nothing pronounced, merely a shift in my perception. And yet, however slight, it was jarring. Like the movement of a broken electrical toy that was long presumed dead.

Stuck stress.

Dr. Carlin was right. My feelings for David could never be a permanent solution. I'd been using him. Without even realizing it, I'd been coasting off my love for him for as long as I could to avoid having to deal with my problems. But now that the cracks in our relationship were becoming impossible to ignore, the cycle of apathy and pressure had returned. Only now, I had no way to handle it. I was out of practice. I didn't know what to do, and the pressure—that compulsive urge to act out—was once again starting to rise.

CHAPTER 22

Company

The bathroom floor seemed like the safest place to be. Sitting there, I felt less like a doctoral student with years of psychological research under her belt, and more like the person I'd been when I first got to LA. It was as if, psychologically speaking, I'd been transported back in time. *But I haven't gone back in time*, I reminded myself. I took a deep breath and tried to focus. *This is simply an old response to a familiar pattern*, I thought. *I just need to change it.*

My legs ached as I rose from the cold tile. I pushed open the door and instinctively shielded my eyes from the sun, which fell across my bedroom floor in giant bright beams. Pulling a robe across my shoulders, I walked to my bookcase and pulled a text off the shelf. *Overcoming Destructive Beliefs, Feelings, and Behaviors: New Directions for Rational Emotive Behavior Therapy*. We'd covered it in my first clinical psych class. Rational emotive behavioral therapy (REBT), developed by Columbia University psychologist Albert Ellis, is a treatment designed to help people recognize irrational and destructive beliefs, feelings, and behaviors and restructure them. The key component of REBT is the ABC Model. When examining behavioral choices, the model asks an individual to identify three things: the "activating event" (A), the "belief system" related to that event (B), and the "consequence" that results from that belief (C).

I decided to apply the ABC Model to myself. Obviously, the stuck stress I'd experienced earlier that morning was the "activating event." The conviction that I needed to act out to combat that anxiety was my decades-old "belief system" related to that event. And the "consequence" of that belief system would be the destructive behavior I would then commit.

I may have been a novice at therapeutic intervention, but this model seemed like a workable solution for identifying—and thus preventing—my malevolent urges. It all boiled down to mindfulness.

The destructive methods I'd always used as a "prescription" for my apathy were remarkably effective, and a powerful testament to the subconscious mind. The urge to act out (which I *now* understood was a counterbalance to apathy) had started when I was a kid. That was decades before I learned what was going on behind the psychological scenes. It was something I did out of instinct, not any conscious awareness. So it stood to reason: If I could drag these psychological processes out of the darkness and into my conscious mind, if I could make myself become mindful of the interaction between my anxious reaction to apathy and my belief that I had to do something destructive to make it go away, could I change my belief system? Could I alter the behavior?

I snapped the book shut, a sudden burst of determination bringing everything into sharp focus. "Fuck it," I said out loud. "If I can't find a professional to treat me, I'll just become one and treat myself."

A month later, I started a new semester at school. In addition to a fresh chapter in my academic career, it was also the start of another calendar year. Inside the classroom, a windowless lecture hall that provided idyllic insulation against the drizzly Los Angeles winter, I tapped a pencil against my desk. As a third-year doctoral student, it was time for me to select a topic for my dissertation. Though I'd long assumed that sociopathy would be my general subject, I hadn't decided which aspect of the disorder I wanted to research. Not, that is, until I realized what should have been obvious all along. On my desk was an application for doctoral candidacy. The words DISSERTATION TITLE were printed next to a long, vacant line. I lifted my pencil and wrote,

"Sociopathy: Its Relationship to Anxiety and Response to Treatment Intervention." I sat back in my chair and exhaled.

When I went to the library a few days later, I brought all of my old research with me. I revisited many of the papers I'd discovered during my years of independent study and came across some new ones. What I found gave me hope.

Dr. Ben Karpman—one of the first physicians to receive credit for distinguishing between primary psychopathy (i.e., true psychopathy) and secondary psychopathy (i.e., true *socio*pathy)—argued that the antisocial behavior demonstrated by sociopaths is often the result of stress. Karpman theorized that, though they may share the same symptoms as primary psychopaths, secondary psychopaths are not hardwired to pursue an antisocial lifestyle and may be responsive to treatment. He was optimistic about his findings related to this secondary category because he believed they comprised the greatest number of people commonly included in the group of psychopathy.

I found another study by Dr. Lykken, who shared Karpman's stance on sociopathy. Like Karpman, Lykken's findings indicated that addressing anxiety could reduce the destructive traits of secondary sociopaths. He stressed the importance of socialization (the process through which a person's core values and belief systems are programmed to align with the rest of society) in early childhood development.

My favorite researcher, Linda Mealey, furthered this theory by hypothesizing that sociopathy was the product of biological and environmental pressures, which lead those affected to deliberately pursue manipulative and predatory social interactions. As I had explained to Dr. Carlin, Mealey described sociopaths as psychologically disadvantaged people who use cheating tactics to make the best of their bad situation. Hers was the theory that most closely aligned with my experience.

Based on this research, I decided to focus my dissertation on treatment plans designed to address anxiety. With the stuck stress at the forefront of my consciousness, I resisted the urge to return to my old "prescriptions." Instead, I doubled down at school. I rearranged my schedule to accommodate a full roster of classes. I signed up for every course I could manage, from sociology to psychopharmacology. Then I buried my nose in research whenever possible. It wasn't easy. There were only so many hours in a day. And I still had other responsibilities to manage.

In addition to school, I was also still working as a music manager. Juggling these conflicting pursuits was extremely difficult. Each required tremendous amounts of energy yet demanded very distinct skill sets. I knew that eventually I would arrive at a tipping point. I couldn't continue to do both, particularly when my academic and professional careers were pulling me in such different directions.

Working as a manager let me use my sociopathic traits with aplomb. Even though it hadn't been my goal, and ironically *because* of my personality type, I'd managed to excel at it, successfully carving a niche for myself in the music industry. Being a good talent manger required moral flexibility, which I had in spades. The entertainment world offered a relatively safe environment for me to flex my sociopathic muscles, and I was reluctant to abandon it. But the side I was determined to nurture and grow—my "good side"—was strengthened by things like graduate school and my relationship with David, which I was determined to save. The more time I spent at school, the more I understood that so many of the fights we had were related to aspects of my personality type that I didn't know how to change.

I wanted to show him my research. If we could discuss things in scientific terms instead of emotional ones, maybe he'd see that my issues had nothing to do with him. Maybe I could get him to stop wanting to change me. But with both of us working around the clock, we rarely had time for dinners together—much less deep discussions about sociopathy.

And then, of course, there was Max.

Despite my heavy course load, my self-directed, intensive research, my full-time job, and the fact that I shared a home with my boyfriend (however fraught our relationship), my friendship with the musician had only grown. The strength of our platonic connection wasn't something I'd anticipated, and I didn't always enjoy it. Indeed, I was often frustrated by the ease with which I could be sucked into Max's orbit. When it came to distraction techniques, he was incorrigible and masterful, frequently showing up at my office after hours and unannounced when he knew I was trying to study.

"Stop it!" I said, shoving his hand away from my screen. "Seriously. I need fifteen more minutes."

I'd stayed late at the office to study for an exam, something I did often in those days. Studying at home never worked. There was always something to clean or cook or play or organize. But my office was like a sensory deprivation chamber. At least, it *was* . . . before Max started dropping by.

"But I'm leaving tomorrow," he whined. "You won't see me for months." Max and his band were going on tour through several cities across North and South America and parts of Europe to promote his latest album.

My phone rang and caller ID showed his manager's number. "What the hell?" I asked. "Why is Brian calling me?" It wasn't unusual for me to hear from Max's management team when they couldn't find him. He shrugged, and I gave him a look of resigned annoyance as I reluctantly answered.

"Hello?"

"Hey, Patric. I need to go over travel details for the tour and haven't been able to reach my elusive client. If you see him, could you have him call me?"

"I'd love to." I hung up and glared at Max.

"Respond to your manager so he can finalize the travel stuff," I ordered. "Why the fuck is he bugging me anyway? I'm not responsible for you."

Max snorted and stood up to lean against the edge of my desk. He started rearranging my collection of decorative pens, something he knew I found infuriating. "Maybe he's afraid I'm gonna find a *new* manager," he whispered provocatively.

"Not interested," I replied sharply.

It wasn't the first time he'd mentioned it, and my terse response—like so many things regarding Max—didn't convey the whole story. The truth was that I had no desire to be his manager. As it was, my relationship with Max gave me the one thing I'd always wanted: social impunity. His rejection of boundaries and my ethical elasticity combined to create a perfect storm of inspired chaos that was both exhilarating and combustible. But I knew I could only push the limits so far. My love for David meant my time with Max was always going to be finite. I liked it that way. It felt safe. Contained.

I slapped his hand to stop him from playing with my pens. He responded by stretching his arms. "Come with me," he crooned playfully, "and you'll be . . . in a world of pure imagination . . ."

"Jesus," I muttered in mock horror.

Max crossed his arms. "Come *on*," he said impatiently. "You can study tomorrow."

I slapped my laptop shut. "Fine," I said, collecting my books and pretending to be exasperated. "You win." I exhaled. "What is it you'd like to do?"

His expression switched to glee. "Anything," he said. "Everything! Let's go on an adventure. The sky's the limit. Stretch your sociopathic mind."

"Well," I began slowly, "we could go somewhere *really* expensive for dinner, and you could pay for it."

"Orrrrr," Max carried on, ignoring my suggestion. "We could grab something quick downtown and then go explore the Cecil."

"The Cecil" was a notoriously macabre LA landmark, an infamous hotel known primarily for its association with suicides and violent crime.

"*That's* your idea of stretching the sociopathic mind?" I replied, unimpressed. "Maybe we should swing by the Galleria on the way there. You can buy some combat boots and a Jack Daniel's T-shirt."

"Well, what's *your* idea?"

"I don't have any ideas!" I laughed. "My plan was to study all night, remember?"

My phone rang, and I shot Max another aggressive glance. "Did you respond to Brian?" I asked. "Seriously. If he's going to call me all night, I'm going to tell him he has to split your commission."

"Fine by me," Max grumbled.

I saw *Unknown Caller* and let out a sigh. It had to be Ginny again.

"What's up?" Max asked, reacting to my shift in mood.

I shook my head in resigned disgust. "Oliver Krusi's mom."

"It's *her?*" he asked, his curiosity piqued.

"Yeah. She backed off for a while, but just started up again. Whatever." I ran my hand through my hair. "I should probably go to the police at this point. How about it?" I asked, forcing a thin smile. "Feel like a trip to the LAPD?"

His eyes widened as he tried to decide if I was sincere.

"I'm dead serious," I replied.

He grinned, a devilish look spreading across his face. "Actually," he said, "I have a better idea."

I pulled my car into a visitor spot at Ginny's housing complex. Max sat in the passenger seat, giddy with excitement.

"Okay," I said, getting serious. "This is your last chance. Are you *sure* you want to do this?"

He rolled his eyes while opening his door. Without waiting for me, he took off across the parking lot. I got out and stood next to my car, arms folded on the roof. He stopped to glance back at me. "You coming?" he asked.

I smiled smugly. "That depends," I said. "Is your plan to go to Ginny's, or did you have another stop you wanna make?" I pointed to the other side of the lot. "Because she lives *that* way."

Max bit his lip to suppress a grin as he scurried back.

When we reached her yard, I ran my hand along the exterior wall as my feet crunched on the gravel. It had been a while since my last visit. I wasn't sure how I'd react to being there. But now that we'd arrived, I was relieved to find I was pleasantly elated. Allowing Max to participate introduced a playful energy into the typically toxic errand. And when we got to the back of her property, I realized how much easier it would be to hop the fence with an accomplice. I quietly explained the yard's layout to Max.

"So, I'll lift you over," he whispered.

I turned toward the fence and motioned off a short count to three. Max made a cradle with his hands, and I stepped into it with one foot. He lifted me, but before I'd started to jump. This resulted in a half-lift that threw us both off-balance. I managed to get one ankle over the slats, the other half of my body hanging limp against the back side of the fence as Max did his best to support my weight.

"How the fuck," he managed to whisper through silent hysterics, "have you ever broken into *anything*? You have the coordination of a baby giraffe."

I took several slow breaths, forcing myself to stop laughing. "Shut the fuck up and push!"

Max did as he was told, shoving me up and over the fence. I landed with a quiet thud next to the tree and directed my attention to the back patio. I looked at the sliding doors and noticed, with relief, that the blinds were open. So were the ones in Ginny's bedroom. As usual, all the lights were on. After checking to make sure the coast was clear, I signaled for Max. He cleared the fence in one swift movement, smirking with pride.

"In case you were wondering," he quipped, "that's how it's done."

"Practicing your Grammy speech?" I smiled sarcastically. "In case *you* were wondering, I wouldn't stand where everyone can see you."

Max lowered his head and hurried to join me under the tree, the canopy of branches concealing us. He stood close behind me, our eyes fixed on the back of the house.

"So, now what?" he whispered.

"Now, we wait."

We stood there in darkness, an occasional breeze rustling the leaves. After a few minutes of window-watching, I caught sight of Ginny walking into the living room. I heard Max take a sharp inhale when she stepped into the light, her frame in full view from our position in the backyard.

"Is that *her*?" Max asked. "She looks so . . ." His voice trailed off.

"Pathetic?" I offered.

"Yeah."

It was true. Though it hadn't ever registered with me, Ginny did seem sad wandering around her little condo. She didn't look like an enemy deserving of vitriol . . . or anything, really. We watched as she puttered around and then moved into the bedroom. We could see her rummaging through drawers. "She's looking for cigarettes," I whispered.

Sure enough, a few seconds later she walked back into the living room and toward the sliding doors. With a pack of menthols and a lighter in hand, she stepped out onto the patio. No longer separated by physical barriers, I experienced a tidal wave of anticipation, which provided an unexpected kick of additional psychological release. I exhaled, content. *This is what I want*, I thought, *a treatment plan that makes me feel like* this.

I looked at Max. He was decidedly *not* content. His eyes were locked on Ginny and his jawline was sharp. Every muscle in his body was tense but still. Ginny sucked distractedly on her cigarette. I watched as the smoke made hazy circles in the air and was reminded of the blue caterpillar from *Alice in Wonderland*. I leaned forward to tell this to Max, but he held up his hand to shush me. He continued to stare.

Ginny stretched her arms over her head. She took a few steps toward the planter she used as an ashtray. Savoring another long drag on her cigarette, she turned her head lazily in the direction of the tree. I held my breath. This was usually my favorite part: She would look right at me but have no idea I was there. I braced myself for the rush of feeling that typically followed this sensation of invisibility. Only I didn't get it. When she shifted her gaze, Max deftly leaned to the side, completely blocking me from her line of sight.

For a moment I was immobilized; the intensity of being in Max's shadow made me feel both defended and defenseless. He was protecting me. His instinct to safeguard me against what he perceived as the threat of exposure was incredibly self-sacrificing. It should have made me feel safe or, at the very least, grateful. Instead, I grew uneasy. A creeping discomfort swept over me as I tried to identify what was happening. It reminded me of when he'd invited me to New York. I was edgy and disoriented and didn't know why.

What the fuck? I thought.

Desperate to stabilize, I took some deep breaths. After several excruciating seconds, Ginny finished her butt and tossed it into the planter. She returned to the house, then we heard the sliding glass door make a definitive *click*.

I turned to Max and said, "We're leaving."

It was late and we were in my office parking lot, where he'd left his car. Except once I'd parked, he'd shown no inclination to leave.

"That was unbelievable," he said. "I've never felt anything like that. Not even onstage. It was like every part of me was pulsing." He looked at me and asked, "Is that how *you* feel? Is that why you go there?"

I sighed. "Sort of."

"Well, I *get* it." He looked at me expectantly. "So, what happens now?"

"What happens now is I go to the police," I said. "I mean, it's time. I should have done it months ago . . . instead of using her as a sociopathic pressure valve."

"What does that mean?" he asked.

I took a deep breath and for the first time explained to him the specifics of my lifelong struggles. He listened attentively as I told him about my battles with the pressure and how I learned young that destructive measures yielded the swiftest relief. I recounted my visits to Ginny's backyard, but this time I elaborated on the bliss they brought me. And that going to the police meant surrendering that supply. "That's what I mean when I say it's time," I said. "I know turning her in is the right thing to do. But that's the problem. I always know it. I just don't *feel* it."

I smiled weakly and shifted my gaze to Max. I was certain he'd agree. It had always been this way. My mother, my father, my therapist, my boyfriend—everyone in whom I had ever confided about my dark side had always said the same thing—the *right* thing. But he wasn't like everyone else.

"Fuck the police," he said, shaking his head. "What are they gonna do?"

I stared at him, flabbergasted.

"I mean it," he went on. "They're not gonna do shit. She'll probably get off with a warning, if that." He turned to look directly at me. "You know that, right?"

"But . . ." I stammered, trying to get my bearings. "Haven't you been listening? This isn't about her. It's about *me*. It's not safe for *me* to have this random person out there as a convenient bull's-eye. It's like an alcoholic keeping a bottle of liquor in the house 'just in case.'"

"I want to *understand* my urges instead of reacting to them," I continued. "And these past few months I've been working on that." I stopped for a minute and toyed with some elastic hair bands wrapped around my gear shifter. "But now, I don't know," I said. "I need to fucking *deal* with the situation, that's for sure. I need to deal with *her*."

Max thought for a moment, staring through the windshield. "I agree," he said finally. "I think you *should* deal with her. But on your terms." Then he added, "And I'll help."

I groaned, angry with myself. "It was stupid to take you there," I said.

"Why?" he argued. "Because now I've seen her? Now I get it?"

"Get what, exactly?" I snapped. "What it's like to feel like you have to stalk and hunt people? I almost attacked her last time, or did you forget?" I shook my head and said, "That asshole got *lucky*."

"That asshole had it coming!" he replied. "She deserves it!"

"They *all* deserve it," I explained, frustrated. "Don't you see? I'm not an idiot. I choose people like her specifically *because* they deserve it, because they do things I can use to justify my behavior. But it's not good," I told him. "Not feeling guilty, my missing emotions . . . none of that shit is any fucking *good*."

"You're wrong," Max insisted. "Those things you're talking about are *strengths*, Patric. You shouldn't be trying to dull your personality type. You should be trying to sharpen it." It was exactly the opposite of what David would have said. "Correct me if I'm wrong," he continued, "but *she* started this. And *she's* the one keeping it going, not you." He paused. "Fuck, even I wanna kill this bitch."

I dropped my head back against the seat and gazed at the ceiling. "I don't want to kill her," I said.

"I know," he replied, "but even if you did, it wouldn't make you 'bad.'" He paused. "I envy you. Do you know how much I'd give to not care what other people think? To be able to live even one day without the constant need for approval? I think *most* people would love to be like that."

"That's because you can only see one side of it," I said. "You don't know the whole story."

"And *you* do?" Max asked. "You've spent your whole life trying to suppress who you are. It's like saying you know what it's like to drive a Ferrari when you've never taken it out of the garage." He looked into my eyes. "I'm telling you, Patric, you need to embrace that shit because it's fucking amazing. I would love it if I were you," he said. "I *do* love it."

I broke his gaze and looked out at the empty street, unsure of how to respond.

Max cocked his head. "Just so we're clear, I'm not saying I'm *in* love with you."

"Oh, yeah?" I chuckled. "Because if I did kill her, you'd definitely be considered an accessory. You'd be tied to me for life whether you love me or not."

He smiled. "I can think of worse things. But, like you said, you don't wanna kill her. That's why I'm saying: There are things you can do besides go to the police." He caught himself and corrected, "Things *we* could do."

I stared down my nose at him. *"We?"*

"Hell yeah," he said. "I'm invested now." He paused. "You've been recording her calls, right?" I could see the gears turning. "We could start calling her late at night and play them back to her. We could blackmail her ass right back . . . and that's just an appetizer."

I grinned in spite of myself and told him, "You need to go home."

"Admit it," he said, smiling mischievously. "It's fun to have a co-conspirator."

I looked at him, and for a second I was floating across the surface of the Great Blue Hole, my fingers skimming the water, baiting the monsters to come play. I smiled faintly. "Go," I said again, this time more forcefully.

He nodded and took a sharp inhale through his nose. "You better text me while I'm gone," he said. Then, without another word, he left.

CHAPTER 23

Transparency

I didn't sleep that night. I just lay in bed staring at the ceiling until eventually soft beams of sunlight illuminated the corners of the room. I braced myself, anticipating David's alarm clock. When it erupted, I shut my eyes and pretended to be asleep when he got out of bed. Minutes passed like hours as he took a shower, got dressed, kissed me on the cheek, and headed for work. I waited until his car was clear of the driveway, then jumped up, threw on some clothes, and drove to Everly's house. She pushed a cup of coffee into my hand as I stepped across the threshold.

"Thank you," I said, my voice gravelly from exhaustion.

She led me into the living room. Logs were already crackling in the fireplace. She pulled me down next to her on the couch and rested an elbow on one of the cushions, her eyes full of concern.

"It's just us," she said. "Ben's at the studio all day. So, tell me. What the hell is going on?"

I took a deep breath and started talking. I described the struggles I'd been having with David and my frustrations with him. I told her about how the pressure had returned, and what I'd been studying in school about my own personality. And, finally, I revealed the details of my complicated relationship with Max, the situation with Ginny, and the events of the previous night. Everly listened as I confessed to every thought, impulse, and behavior. When I was done, she settled back into the couch.

"Jesus, Patric," she said.

"I just don't understand what the fuck is happening," I lamented. "I honestly feel like I'm losing my mind."

"Well, one thing's for sure," Everly said. "Ginny Krusi is a fucking cunt."

The comment caught me off guard, and I started to laugh.

Then she hit me with, "And you have feelings for Max." It sounded so odd to hear someone else refer to him as Max, a bright spatter of dishonesty on an otherwise pristine confessional canvas. His real name was the one detail I'd omitted.

"Well, yeah," I said with a deliberate shrug. "He's my friend."

"Don't play dumb. All this time you're spending with him . . . the fact that you never told me about him . . . even the way you describe meeting him. You *like* him," she said. "I'm not judging you," she added. "But what you're describing, that's what attraction *feels* like. That's what love feels like."

"I know what love feels like, Everly," I replied, a bit too sharply. "That's not what this is."

"Then what *is* it?"

"I don't know," I admitted. "That's what I'm trying to tell you, I don't process certain emotions the same way as everyone else." I rested my head against the couch. "Even if I comprehend that an emotion is occurring, it doesn't always land the same way with me. I might intellectually register it, but I don't internalize the feeling and *that's* the problem. That's always been the problem." I shrugged. "But in this case, it's the solution. I don't have to internalize a feeling to cut it off. I can shut down my emotions whenever I want. What do I care?"

"Because that's not what you want," she answered patiently. "You *want* to feel things. I know you try." She looked at me sympathetically. "But you can't pick and choose." She flipped my hand and lifted it like a scale. "When the basic feelings get stronger," she said, lifting my other hand, "the complex ones do, too."

"But my feelings for Max aren't complex." I paused, then added, "It's sort of like you and tennis."

Everly raised her eyes dubiously.

"You love to play tennis," I explained, "but your boyfriend doesn't. So, do you quit playing? No! You just play with someone else."

"Except this isn't fucking tennis," she snapped. "Do me a favor," she said, grabbing my phone. "Show me a picture of Max."

"No," I said.

"Why not?" she demanded. "I mean, do you want to have a real conversation about this or not? Because we both know goddamn well 'Max' isn't his real name. This whole situation is sketchy, *at best*. And you know it."

"Wow," I said, crossing my arms. "My entire life I've been told I should feel bad because I *don't* feel things. And now you're telling me I should feel bad because I *do*?" I huffed. "Fuck that noise."

"I'm not telling you how you *should* feel," Everly explained, ignoring my attempted deflection. "I'm telling you what you *do* feel. And that, my love, is probably why you're also now feeling the claustrophobic stress. Because you feel trapped. Trapped by feeling."

"I'm just tired," I admitted, my shoulders slumping. "I love David more than anyone, more than I could ever love anyone. But you need to understand"—I looked at Everly—"at the *most*, my capacity for love is a fraction of David's. But he expects me to match him *all* the time. And when I can't, he takes it personally, as if I'm intentionally choosing not to love him the same way he loves me." I shook my head. "So, I find myself pretending to have feelings I don't have, but actually *do* have, just not at the level he wants." I sighed. "It's maddening."

"Then why don't you *talk* to him about it?" she asked. "Why can't you tell him what you just told me? All relationships are hard some—"

"Not the one I have with you," I interrupted. "Not the one I have with Max, either. He doesn't care if I'm affectionate or emotional. He doesn't care, period. That's why we have fun. There's never any pressure. There's never any stress. He just gets me."

"I think you mean he just gets *off* on you," she countered. "But whatever. You know that Max—whoever he is—isn't the answer. He's just a new prescription. And that's fine. You can get high on your new prescription. You can run away with your little distraction.

You can do whatever you want for as long as you want. Just remember, your problems will still be there when you're done." She waved a finger at me. "And not just your problems with David, either."

"What's that supposed to mean?"

"Who are you, Patric?" Everly asked. "I know who you are with me. I know who you are with David. I know who you *say* you are with this other guy. But who are you when no one else is around?"

A log in the fireplace crackled and popped. I stared at the wood; the flames devouring it hypnotized me. I thought again of *Alice in Wonderland*. "Who *are* you?" the Cheshire Cat liked to taunt.

"I don't know," I said.

"Oh, I think you do," she insisted. "I think you know *exactly* who you are. The problem is you're not allowing yourself to be that person, that *whole* person. I don't think you ever have. So, how is David—or anyone—ever supposed to accept you when you haven't fully accepted yourself?"

I stared at the fire. Everly followed my gaze. "Bottom line," she said, "you have to stop living this double life. You're miserable. And you're miserable because you're never being *Patric*. You have to learn to just be *you. All* the time. With *everyone*."

"And then what?" I asked.

Everly smiled and nudged me affectionately with her foot. "What do you care?"

Later that night I sat across from David at the dining room table. By all accounts it had been a lovely evening. I'd gotten home in time to make dinner, and David—who'd recently finished a big project—was in an excellent mood. At least, he was at first.

"I've decided to include my sociopathic diagnosis in my dissertation defense," I announced over dessert.

He stopped mid-chew and had the audacity to look confused. "Huh?"

"Going forward I want to be *more* transparent about the fact that

I'm a sociopath," I explained. "It makes no sense to hide it. Especially if I ever want to be an advocate for other people like me." I paused to let my excitement sink in. "I think it could be the start of something really cool."

He shook his head and swallowed hard. "So now you want to tell *everyone?*"

I sighed. It was a rehash of a fight we'd been having for years. He was uncomfortable with my desire to "lean in" to my personality type. Not only did he reject my decision to disclose my diagnosis in my dissertation, but now he refused to even discuss it. The conversation only lasted a few minutes before he got angry and stormed off to the bedroom.

I gazed at the taper candles that glowed from the center of the table. Bright orange flickers cast soothing dark shadows against the wall. *Everly was right*, I thought. I loved David, but I was done coasting with him. I wanted our relationship to work, to be a genuine partnership. It was time for me to be myself. And it felt good to feel free.

I watched the candles for a few more seconds before reluctantly blowing them out. I cleared the table and went about cleaning up. I took my time loading the dishwasher. I carefully wiped down the island and the countertops. Only then did I turn off the lights and make my way to the bedroom.

The door was closed. I opened it slowly and saw that David was already in bed. "Honey," I said calmly, "I love you. But what happened just now is precisely *why* I want to be more open about who I am."

He turned his head so he was looking up at the ceiling. "What do you mean?" he asked with a heavy sigh.

"You refuse to talk about the fact that I'm a sociopath. I can't even bring it up without you getting mad. And I get it," I said. "You don't want me to be a sociopath because sociopaths have a reputation for being horrible. And you don't want to see those parts of me."

He pushed himself up against the pillows. "I *don't* see those parts of you," he insisted. "I mean, I've seen you do bad things, but I don't think *you're* bad, Patric. Tell me you know that."

"I *do* know that," I replied. "And I can't tell you how much I appreciate hearing those things. I can't tell how much *your* perception of me as something other than a 'bad girl' has shaped my awareness of myself. You've changed my life." I smiled weakly. "But not everybody has a person like you in their life, honey. Not everyone has a David. And I want to help people who aren't as lucky as me."

He thought about this. "I hear you," he finally said. "And I get it. Of course, I think trying to help people is admirable. I really do. But how's that gonna work if you're telling everyone that you're a sociopath?" he asked. "The second you say that no one's going to hear anything else you have to say. Every data point will be scrutinized. Every story you tell will be questioned. Sociopaths aren't historically seen as reliable sources, let alone doctors." He paused. "They're just gonna hate you."

"Who cares?" I answered. "At the end of the day, the only thing I can do is tell the truth. How people choose to accept the truth is out of my control. Other sociopaths aren't going to hate me. They're going to see themselves. Finally."

He was quiet for a few seconds. "I don't know about this, honey," he eventually said. I shook my head.

"That's the thing," I told him. "You don't have to know. It doesn't matter whether you agree with me. It's *my* decision, David." I folded my hands in my lap. "And I've made it."

I could see the compassion draining from his face even as the words were leaving my mouth. "So how I feel doesn't matter," he said, shaking his head.

I frowned, disappointed. We'd come so close.

He pursed his lips. "Why are we even together?" he asked rhetorically.

"You tell *me*," I said softly.

David's eyes widened and he nearly shouted, "I don't know! It's not like we even see each other anymore. I'm working my ass off, and it's like it's for nothing. We can't even have one fucking dinner without fighting about the same shit." He exhaled forcefully. "Why can't we have *normal* problems, you know? Like a normal fucking couple!"

"*Normal?*" Now I was furious and struggling not to scream. "Where'd you get that idea? Was it when we met? When I was stealing maps and hiding in a basement? Or all the times on the phone, when I was telling you I thought I might be a sociopath?" I held out my hands in feigned curiosity. "Maybe it was the GODDAMN KEY-CHAIN I FOUND IN THE HOUSE ACROSS THE STREET TO LET YOU KNOW WHEN I'M DOING FUCKED-UP SHIT!" I pointed a finger at David. "No," I said sharply. "You knew *exactly* who I was when you got here. You knew I was a FAR FUCKING CRY from normal. It's just that once you got me, you decided you didn't want me!"

"That's not true!" he pleaded. "I just want the *real* you. I want you to be who I know you are, on the *inside*." He shook his head sadly. "I know she's in there. I know it, Patric."

I stared at the floor. "Oh my God," I said. "David. I'm not doing this with you anymore." I put a hand on my chest. "For the last time. There's only *one* me. *This* is who I am. And I can't keep suppressing it because you don't like it." I shook my head helplessly. "I can't change my personality, David. But *you* can choose the way you react to me. And if you don't get it—or can't or won't—then I don't know what to tell you. I'm done. I don't care anymore."

"You've made that pretty fucking clear," he grumbled.

I didn't know what to say. I *did* care about David. I cared about him more than I'd ever cared about anything or anyone. But if he didn't know that . . . If he still couldn't understand that . . .

"Maybe you're right," he said, his tone much quieter. "Maybe we shouldn't do this anymore."

I looked him in the eyes. He was so sad and angry. I slowly shook my head, confused. "I never said that."

He scowled. "You may as well have."

"But I didn't," I replied evenly. "So, if that's how *you* feel—if *you* think we shouldn't be together—then you need to say it. You need to own your feelings instead of projecting them on me."

"Fine," he said. "That's the way I *feel*. I *feel* like I don't matter. I *feel* like you don't care." Then he looked me in the eyes, furious. "Am I wrong?"

It was one last prompt, one last cue for me to intervene and resolve things, like I always did. One last passive-aggressive demand for me to make him feel better, to tell him everything was going to be okay, that I would change, that we could work it out. But I didn't feel the slightest bit tempted to acquiesce. So I just sat there. It felt good to feel impervious.

David, apparently frustrated when I didn't respond, blinked away his tears and fumed in silence. He leaned over and snapped off his bedside lamp, plunging the room into darkness. With an audible exhale, he rolled aggressively onto his side. Then he yanked the comforter across his shoulder. All the while, I stared blankly at the wall in front of me.

After a few seconds, I got up. I changed my clothes, brushed my teeth, and got into bed. I gazed at the ceiling, the deafening silence inside the house wrapping me in its embrace. I had a feeling that I should have been sad, except I wasn't. In fact, I was relaxed.

It felt good to feel nothing.

CHAPTER 24

Killer Queen

David moved out that weekend. I hated watching him pack. I knew I should have been upset. And I *was* upset. I just couldn't connect to the feeling. It was like chewing something I couldn't taste, which only added to my frustration.

"Are you sure this is what you want?" he asked, after putting the last of his things into his car.

"No."

He looked crushed. It reminded me of the first time we'd broken up, when we were teenagers.

"I love you, Patric," he said. He put his hands on my hips and pressed his forehead to mine, and for a second I thought I might cry. But I didn't. The sensation appeared and vanished before I could experience it, as it had countless times before. Eventually, David got into his car and drove away.

Standing there, watching him go, I knew the time had come. If anything was ever going to make me feel, watching David leave should do it. *It's now or never*, I thought. I planted my feet, willing myself to burst into tears. I stood in the driveway for twenty minutes before giving up. There was no emotion waiting in the wings for the right moment to surge. I felt the way I usually did. Ambivalent. I turned around and headed back to the house.

I closed the door behind me and welcomed the stillness of my now empty home. It was heavy, like a weighted blanket, and I was tired. I sat on the couch and stared at the floor until my eyelids relaxed. I thought of the hidden-image posters they used to have at the mall, stereograms. God, those posters irritated me. No matter how hard I tried, I could never adjust my gaze to reveal the tiger, or the rose. Time and again, I saw nothing but a meaningless mosaic of shapes.

The reverse was happening now. As I stared at the patternless wooden planks, I felt detached from my thoughts. I allowed them to float as my internal and external climates aligned. Instead of being annoyed at my inability to see something hidden, I let myself accept that there was nothing there to see at all.

Who are you, Patric? my disconnected mind wondered. I still wasn't sure. But I *was* sure I was done looking to others for the answer. Whether it was the longing for like-minded buddies or relationships with good people I could use as tethers to a "normal" existence or surrogates I could use for my own self-acceptance, I'd always naively assumed my "sociopath to enlightenment" would be a journey I wouldn't make alone. But now that I *was* alone, I realized what should have been obvious all along.

"I don't care."

I didn't care that there was no one else like me in my life. I didn't care that I was alone.

While everyone else spent their lives trying to avoid sociopaths, I'd always hoped to find them. While other kids in school were playing sports, I was breaking into homes. While other girls were playing house and dreaming about the day they'd hear those "three little words," I'd traveled a different path. I, too, wanted to embrace "three little words." It's just that mine were slightly different.

"I don't care!"

I was in the administration office at school a month later, reviewing PhD requirements with my supervisor. I'd noticed a "clinical" requirement in the graduation paperwork a few days before and had called the office for details. Dr. Robert Hernandez, the head of my department, had explained that—in addition to my coursework and dissertation—I needed to log five hundred hours as an intern to earn my PhD. In other words, I had to "train" as a therapist for five hundred unpaid hours. I wasn't happy about it.

"Come on, Patric," he cajoled. Dr. Hernandez was an easygoing clinician with a dry sense of humor. He'd taught my psychoanalysis class and we'd always gotten along. "Think of it as an exciting learning experience."

"Except, I don't *want* to learn," I said, crossing my arms. "I'd rather open a vein than listen to a bunch of Beverly Hills–adjacents whine about their first-world problems. No joke. I'll bleed out right here."

The doctor struggled not to laugh. "Then please go into the hallway first," he said, "because there's nothing we can do about it. It's required. You can get the hours at any accredited practice you choose. But if I were you, I'd just go down the street."

I stared at him blankly.

"The counseling center," he explained, as if I didn't understand.

"I know what 'down the street' is," I replied, before switching tactics. "I'm sorry. Did you forget? I'm a diagnosed sociopath," I explained. "You guys shouldn't be letting people like me work as therapists . . . not for normal people anyway."

"Why not?" he asked. "You've said it a dozen times—you want to help people, right?"

"I want to help *sociopaths*," I clarified. "Ideally, from a distance."

"Look on the bright side. Half the battle in clinical training is helping trainees compartmentalize their *own* emotional attachments," he continued, clearly enjoying himself. "But you don't have any!"

"I'm glad you find this so entertaining," I told him, collecting my bag from beneath my chair. "For the record, I take zero responsibility here. Whatever happens, it's on you." I turned and headed for the door.

Later that night I called David to rant. We'd been talking a lot since we broke up—more than we had the last few years. Our physical separation, jarring at first, had led to a deeper sort of connection. Strange as it was, I felt as though we were actually getting to know each other for the first time. His moving out, in a sense, had been liberating for both of us. Because we were separated, it was hard for him to feel responsible for my actions. As a result, he was able to talk to me as the person I was—instead of the person he wanted me to be. Conversely, after years of hiding aspects of myself from him, I wanted to tell him things again. It was nice.

"It's psychological malpractice!" I said, pouring myself some bourbon. "He knows I'm a sociopath, but he doesn't care! He's just going to sic me on unwitting victims."

"I think it'll be good for you," David said. "Though anything is better than the fucking music business."

"Except that ideally a therapist should *care* about the lives of her patients, don't you think?"

"Oh, please. You're interested in other people's lives more than anyone I know. Captain Apathy, my ass."

I laughed. "It's fun talking to you," I said. I meant it.

Spending hours on the phone with David again was like making a new friend. I started wondering if perhaps we'd made a mistake when he came to LA, moving in together so quickly. Overly dependent on the bond we'd forged as kids, we'd missed out on the opportunity to forge a new one as adults. I asked David if he agreed.

"You're probably right," he said. "I wish we could just start over, y'know? Blank slate. Like, I wish I could just meet you in a bar."

I smiled. "Like, for the first time?"

"Yeah," he said. "I swear, if I just saw you out sipping a martini"—I heard him take a deep breath—"I'd walk over and say, 'Hi. My name's David. I work in IT and I'm a Cancer.'"

"Right. And I'd say, 'I'm Patric. I work in the music business and I'm a sociopath.'"

He laughed. "So, I take it you haven't told Everly yet?"

I sighed. "No."

But the time had come. After nearly a year of playing weekly concerts at the Roxy, Everly's residency was coming to an end. Though dejected, nobody had been surprised. Music had always been a hobby for most of them, something they did during breaks from their actual careers. But that wasn't the case for Everly.

She was the real deal, and what she needed was a real manager, someone who could showcase her talent and help her do what she should have done from the start: Ditch the band and present herself as a solo artist. The time had come for me to admit I wasn't that someone. The truth was that I no longer wanted to be a manager. Not for my best friend. Not for anyone. After years of straddling the fence, I'd decided to quit. Unfortunately, I hadn't figured out how to break the news to Everly.

David was right. The music business, lucrative and sensational, was not a healthy environment for someone like me. From boozy lunches to creative accounting, there was something lawless about the entertainment industry. Left unchecked, there was no telling where I might end up or what unhealthy prescriptions I might find. Psychology, on the other hand, was more meaningful. The science of sociopathy mattered, not just to me, but to everyone *like* me. Karmically speaking, it was a net positive instead of a net negative. The more time I spent at the counseling center, the more obvious this became.

The Aloe Center offered psychological services to people who either didn't have insurance or couldn't afford to pay out of pocket for what was often expensive one-on-one therapy. In many cases, sessions were free. As a result, the patient population was extremely diverse, both in demographic and psychological terms. We got everyone from impoverished veterans struggling with PTSD to affluent victims of domestic violence who didn't want to be seen going to therapy anywhere near their Beverly Hills addresses. Interns like me were essentially thrown into the deep end of the pool in what was a crash course in treatment for every issue imaginable.

Just a few weeks into my residency, I started to see a pattern. As the newest intern, I had the lowest rank on the case-assignment totem pole, which meant I often got the patients nobody else wanted. This included people labeled with "excessive comorbidities"—that is, several overlapping symptoms that made diagnosis difficult. These were the patients who didn't fit neatly into any diagnostic box. The formula at the counseling center was straightforward: assess, diagnose, treat, repeat. The patients whose symptoms didn't lend themselves to a clear and specific diagnosis filtered down to me. Right off the bat, I started seeing personality traits I recognized. Although they were reluctant to speak candidly at first, many of them eventually admitted to feelings of "emotional emptiness" and a drive to do "bad things." They spoke of deviant behavior and a pointed inability to connect with guilt. These patients described acts of violence and difficulty with impulse control. They admitted to deceit for the sake of blending in. They recounted story after story of attempts to quell their emotional numbness through pain and destructive acts. They spoke of dark secrets and compulsive behavior. Even though some confessed to multiple crimes, none had criminal records. Some were married with kids. Most had college degrees. All were living a lie.

These patients exhibited many of the same traits from Cleckley's checklist that I did. They struggled with remorse. They felt disconnected from their emotions. They found peace in chaos. They found pleasure in confrontation. Yet in spite of their darkness, these patients described intense feelings of love and affection. They were able to grasp the concept of empathy and could express compassion. They could talk openly with me about their desire to understand themselves and to stop the cycle of their negative behavior. They demonstrated acts of kindness and a willingness to cooperate. They were friendly. They gave to charities. They were conscientious. They were self-aware. And they were terrified.

Most of these patients were no stranger to the word "sociopath." They, too, had seen themselves in the pop-culture depictions of the term and were scared of what they saw. They were afraid they were monsters. They were worried time was running out. Many of them had visited multiple therapists before, only to leave feeling helpless and alone, just as I had done. They, too, were struggling with harmful compulsions that were often becoming harder to control. What these people needed was someone who could empathize, a person who could listen without judgment. What they needed was help. What they needed was hope. What they needed was an advocate. What they got, was me.

"Patric," the receptionist buzzed into my office. "Your four o'clock just canceled."

I was sitting in my chair, staring at the ceiling. My "four o'clock" was Teri. She had been the first of my clients to describe what she called her "forces of bad." Affluent and intelligent, she struggled with apathy and violent fantasies. She started coming to the counseling center when she'd noticed an uptick in her destructive behavior. Her primary target was parking enforcement officers. These public servants were the perfect outlets for her ire. Being ticketed for a minor infraction—for which she was always admittedly guilty—would send her into a cold rage. She'd spend hours obsessed with meter maids, male or female, even stalking them on their rounds and following them home. After almost getting caught hurling a brick at the cruiser window of one of her "adversaries," Teri decided she wanted to get help. She was assigned to me purely by chance.

I looked at the clock and sighed. It was out of character for her to miss a session. I dialed her number.

"Why did you cancel?" I asked when she answered.

"I overslept," she said, although she sounded wide awake. "Sorry. After I got home from the gym, I crashed on the couch."

"So, you're at home?"

"Yup."

"Then send me a photo of your living room."

This request was highly unorthodox. My job as a therapist was to observe and assess *in session*. Asking a patient to send me proof of their physical location was inappropriate, especially for an inexperienced therapist. Had my supervisor known, he would have been upset. But he didn't know. And I didn't care.

"Teri?" I said when she didn't respond. "Would you like to tell me where you really are?"

"No," she replied. "But I'm leaving."

"Great," I said. "We can talk while you drive."

An hour later, I hung up and leaned back in my chair. *Parking cops, sleep well tonight*, I thought contentedly. The late-afternoon sun was casting long shadows around my office, and I sighed happily. Teri had been my last appointment, and I was glad to be done for the day.

I wonder what would happen if I stayed here one night? I thought. The idea was wildly tempting. *It's not exactly a suite at the* Ambassador, I thought with a grin. But it could be interesting.

My phone buzzed and I saw a text from Max.

   Knock, knock

He had been back in LA for a few weeks, though it hardly seemed like we'd spent any time apart. In fact, we'd been texting almost non-stop since he left. It was a form of communication I perceived as simultaneously liberating and circumscribed. I'd spend hours exchanging messages with him about everything from my attempts at psychotherapy to his various love interests. It allowed for the type of one-sided engagement I preferred. I enjoyed the company of someone who didn't want to change me or marry me or think about "the future" or anything more complicated than the next chord progression.

But since he'd come back to town, the dynamic had shifted. We'd been hanging out more often, and I didn't know how I felt about it. Prior to separating from David, I knew exactly where Max fit in my life, precisely how to dose my prescription. I had a boyfriend, and it wasn't Max. But now things were different. Our relationship was difficult to define. The lines had become blurred. Perhaps they'd always been blurred. Once again, I couldn't tell.

My office door cracked open, and Max stuck his head inside. "Knock, knock," he said.

"Jesus!" I exclaimed. The therapists' offices were only accessible through multiple locked doors. "How'd you get back here?"

"The chick in front buzzed me through." He took a seat on the couch in front of me.

"I'm sure she did," I replied dryly.

"So, what's up?" he asked. "Where are we going?"

We'd planned to meet for drinks after work. But I didn't really feel like drinking. I wrinkled my nose at him. "I don't know," I said. "I'm not in a bar-ish mood."

"My house, then," he responded, too quickly. "It's perfect, actually. I have a track I want to play for you in the music room." A windowless cave, Max's "music room" was an ad hoc studio featuring an impressive collection of musical instruments and memorabilia. It was impossible to step inside the music room and not instantly lose track of time, an asset he frequently used to his advantage.

"Hostage theater," I said with a smirk. It was how I described the often captive-like experience of being forced to listen to new music. It had always been my least favorite part of being a manager.

"Fuck off!" he replied, laughing.

"I swear to God, all you artists are the same," I griped. "It doesn't matter whether you've sold one song or ten million. When a musician wants to play you something, it's like being held at gunpoint.

"Lucky for me, though," I noted, "I don't have to do that anymore. I'm no longer a manager, remember?"

Unlike David, Max vehemently disagreed with my decision to quit. He flashed a sneer. "Not true," he reminded me. "Isn't your friend's last show tomorrow night?"

I nodded reluctantly. Everly's final Roxy appearance would mark the official end of her tenure with the band. It was bittersweet, because even though I was ready to get out of the music business once and for all, I still wasn't sure how Everly was going to feel about it.

"Yeah," I replied.

"So then, technically, you're still a music manager. Not that it matters, though. I'm not interested in your *professional* opinion." He grinned triumphantly and rose from the couch. "So come on," he said. "You can follow me."

I looked out the window of my office and as I did, my eyes fell on the mountains that framed the north side of Beverly Hills. I had an idea.

"Actually," I said, "you can follow me."

I sat on the piano bench at the small cottage near Mulholland Drive, looking at the sunset sky through the hole in the roof. A sign in the front yard declared that the property was now officially for sale. I heard footsteps from above and looked to see Max bounding down the staircase. "This place is wild," he said. "Have you been upstairs?"

Max didn't wait for me to answer but took a seat uncomfortably close to me on the bench. He said, "You better make sure this thing is included in the price." I got up and began to wander the living room as he lifted the piano's lid and fiddled with the keys. "Have you made an offer?"

I shook my head. "Not yet."

"Well, you better hurry," he replied, "or I might beat you to it." He played a few chords.

"Must be nice not having any material restrictions," I quipped.

"Must be nice not having any moral ones," he clapped back.

I rolled my eyes and sank into a dilapidated love seat in the corner. "You want a cozy house with a white picket fence now. Is that it?"

He winked. "I'd be willing to share."

I nodded noncommittally and felt my lids grow heavy, the bluesy notes he was playing making me feel slightly inebriated.

"Don't go falling asleep on me," he called out.

"Can't help it," I murmured.

At this, he changed course and began pounding out the energetic chorus to Freddie Mercury's "Killer Queen."

I laughed. "I love that song."

"Not surprised."

He continued plinking away at the piano. Softening the cadence, he seemed almost exploratory as he bounced from key to key. Finally, he landed on a mid-tempo melody. After a few seconds of trying to place the notes, I cocked my head. "This is new," I observed. "What is it?"

Instead of answering, he started to sing. The melodic rhythm was a perfect contrast to the lyrics, which were prosaic and sharp. It was a love letter to a sociopath. To me. I waited for him to finish.

"What do you think?" he asked, after a beat.

I shook my head slowly, doing little to hide my discomfort. "It's different," I offered. "It doesn't sound like you, like something you'd write. It's more . . . on the nose."

He smiled and swiveled sideways on the bench to face me. "What can I say?" he replied. "Maybe I'm evolving."

I fixed my gaze on one of the floorboards. The wood was cracked, and a spider made its way in and around a space closest to the center. I watched as it disappeared for good beneath the darkness. I sighed in admiration. *I wish I was a spider*, I thought.

After an awkward silence Max got up and crossed to where I was sitting. He bent down and took one of my hands to lift me out of my seat. Pulling me toward him, he rested his palm against my waist and pushed his cheek to mine. Outside, I could hear wind start to whistle as we began to sway from side to side. I wanted to scream. But I didn't.

Instead, I rested my forehead against his shoulder in resignation, trying to savor a final few seconds of a friendship that, deep down, I had always known was doomed. "Why?" I asked finally. "Why did you play me that song?" I already knew the answer.

"Because I love you," he said.

There they were. Those three little words. God, how much simpler my life would have been had they ever been the same as mine.

I knew what being with Max would be like. It would be fun. Fun and imaginative and reckless and extreme and unchecked and inculpable. I'd never have to work a day in my life if I spent it with Max—literally or figuratively. I could disappear into the existence my dark side preferred. Indeed, she was tugging at me now, practically salivating from the egocentric jugular Max had exposed. *Do it*, she urged. *Bleed him. Use him.* I thought about how easy it would be to take Max's three little words and use them to conceal my own.

There was no trepidation in his voice when he'd said it. Only confidence. He turned his face to mine, his lips grazing my temple. I lifted my chin to look at him. Staring into his eyes, I was reminded once again of the Great Blue Hole. And when he kissed me, I found myself wanting to sink.

The taste of Max—an aching mix of salt and licorice and whiskey—was everything my shadow self had convinced me I'd always wanted. An alluring abyss. Freedom and pardons and spoils, oh my! For just a second, I felt unsteady from the combustible chemistry we undeniably shared.

Max lifted his hands to either side of my face. I squeezed my eyes tightly shut. *God*, I thought. *Why can't this be enough?*

Life with a guy like him was the path of least resistance. Max did not delight in virtue but rejoiced in darkness. And there, in that darkness, I knew I could hide from the truth. The truth was that I *did* love Max, but not in any healthy way. Not in any way that was good. With him I could stay just the way I was. I would never be judged for being bad or encouraged to evolve. But I didn't want a relationship like that. What I wanted was a true partnership. Beautiful, cooperative, challenging, additive. It's what I wanted with David. It's all I'd ever wanted, period. But if I couldn't have what I wanted with the man I wanted . . .

I placed a hand on his chest and shoved myself gently away. "No," I said.

He was confused at first. He looked to the side and clenched his jaw, silent for several seconds. "Why?" he demanded.

"Because I don't want this."

"Bull*shit*," he barked. "If you didn't want it, we wouldn't be here!"

He was angry. For a moment, I could almost see my apathy expanding to envelop the house; my lack of emotion swallowing and negating his rage.

"What did you think?" I snapped, matching his temper. "That you were gonna write me a song, tell me you love me, and we'd live happily ever after?"

"Maybe I did!" he shouted. "What's wrong with that?"

"What's wrong is that I don't love you like that. I don't love anyone like that, remember?"

"Yeah, I remember," he shot back. "It's my favorite thing about you."

There it was. Max, I knew, wasn't in love with me. He was in love with the fact that he thought I *couldn't* love, not really. Not normally. Max knew I'd never judge him or be jealous or clingy. I wouldn't care if he was gone for months at a time. That made me safe. To him, I was a promise he didn't have to keep. And to me, he was a hiding place I didn't have to leave. A dark and murky cave where time didn't pass and consequences didn't matter. As long as I had Max, I could stay in the shadows. I could keep finding new prescriptions and stand still but pretend I was moving.

"Come *on*," I pleaded. "Don't make me the bad guy for telling the truth. You know as well as I do. This"—I waved my arm vaguely around the space between us—"only works because we're *friends*."

"Friends?" Max replied with a snort. "That's cute."

"Don't be a dick," I said. "We've always been friends."

Max went to the piano and slammed the lid closed. Then he turned to face me. "Trips to abandoned houses," he said, in a voice thick with sarcasm. "Late-night visits to strangers' backyards, sociopathic confessionals. Tell me," he mocked, "is that the kind of stuff you do with *friends*?"

I nodded. It was, actually.

He jabbed a finger at me and spat, "Then it's no wonder you don't have any."

He glared at me for a moment. Then he spun on his heel and left.

He threw open the door and marched to his car, nearly tripping on something in the grass. It was the wooden chair where the old man used to sit, keeping his wife company outside. The coffee cup next to it was sun-bleached and broken.

I waited until he'd driven away and then quietly closed the door. After a few seconds I climbed the stairs and walked into the main bedroom. A four-poster bed was pushed up against the far wall and I collapsed on it. Above the headboard was a window that looked out over the street. I stared through the muslin curtains for a while, watching passersby in secret. Then I went to sleep.

CHAPTER 25

Rorschach

I woke to my phone buzzing against the floorboards. I blinked several times to focus on the foreign walls surrounding me. For a moment, I reveled in having no idea where I was. Then I remembered everything. My phone buzzed again. I sighed and rolled across the mattress. Decades-old springs groaned in protest as I bent over the edge. I clicked "Answer" without looking at the screen and pressed the phone to my ear. "What time is it?" I asked.

"It's showtime!" Everly sang. "Can you believe it? My *last* Roxy show. I'm freaking out. What time you think you'll come over? I know we usually do afternoon, but today you should come earlier." She paused. "Like, now."

I put my hand over my eyes and cursed the morning sun, which had already flooded the little white room.

"I can't," I said, annoyed at myself for sleeping so late. "I have a shift at the counseling center and then I'm driving to the show with Dad." Everly moaned. "Don't worry," I told her. "I'll have plenty of time to get to the Roxy before things get nuts."

"Fine, but you're coming to Dorian's after," she said. "No excuses."

I agreed and hung up, rolled onto my stomach, and looked out the window. A woman was walking a dog down Benedict Canyon, and I enjoyed knowing she couldn't see me. Alone in a stranger's bed, my existence unknown to the world outside, I felt more at home than I had in a while. I loved being hidden, and—with Max's parting words ringing in my ears—I was starting to think it was probably for the best. "It *is* no wonder I don't have any friends," I said.

He was right. The things I liked to do, my reluctance to share, my aversion to affection—none of those things were relationship-friendly. Not in the traditional sense, anyway. I loved people. I truly did. But the way I loved was different than most. And, if I was being honest, not all that compatible. I didn't need to get love in order to give love. I never had. I preferred my affections to be anonymous. Independent. Not because I didn't care, but because I cared *differently*. I knew it better than anyone: The most palatable version of me was one seen from a distance.

I lay there a bit longer, soaking up the silence, contentedly cocooned in my apathy. Then I got up and headed to the closet. "No sense going all the way back home," I said to the empty house as I opened the door. A shoe rack hung inside and gently clattered as it swung. The clothes were mostly menswear. Pushing hanger after hanger aside, I'd all but resigned myself to work slacks and an old button-down. But then I spied the dress. It was a simple A-line with a drop waist and a lace collar. I smiled sadly as I ran my thumb across the neckline and imagined the old woman who used to live there. *She must have looked pretty in this*, I thought.

I turned my attention to the shoe rack. Eyeing a perfect set of leather pumps, I frowned in dismay. My feet, I knew, were far too big. So I settled on a slightly oversized pair of men's oxfords and bulky socks. I took my time getting dressed. When I was done, I looked in the mirror. Standing there in the old dress, with its floral pattern and vintage silhouette, I resembled a 1950s housewife more than I did a twenty-first-century sociopath.

Invisible. My favorite thing to be. But invisibility was a double-edged sword. *It's one thing to wear a disguise I create*, I thought, smoothing the pleats of the dress, *and something else to be assigned a costume.*

I'd seen it happening even with those who knew about my diagnosis. Uneasy with aspects of my personality they either couldn't or didn't want to see, people tended to "dress me up," usually with their own ideas of how a sociopath should feel, or behave, or react. The result was a kind of deception-by-proxy. People invented a version of me for themselves, and then blamed me when their invention fell apart. It was unsettling and destabilizing.

I walked slowly down the stairs. In the living room, sunlight pooled like a waterfall from the hole in the ceiling. My eyes fell on the piano and my thoughts darkened. The truth was that I was better off alone. Not because I disliked people or companionship, but because I found it nearly impossible to prevent myself from becoming who they thought I was. Unable to connect through traditional means, I'd learned long ago that my personality type could function like a mirror. I also knew that, by using it to my advantage, I could offer people what they'd always wanted. What better place to hide than in plain sight? People were so enchanted by my reflection of their interests that they hardly noticed when I sang off-key. Or laughed too loud. Or cried too little. Or stared without blinking.

Superficial charm, I thought. It was number one on Cleckley's list and considered the primary trait of the "classic" sociopath, evidence of a glib, insincere interpersonal style. That was accurate. What nobody seemed to get, however, was that this wasn't the offshoot of some voluntary deal with the devil. It was a coping mechanism born of necessity. I rarely used charm as a trick. Like others in my cohort, I imagined, I used it to hide, to conceal my sociopathy, spurred by the need to survive. Not because *I* was afraid, but because I knew others were. And what people fear, they eliminate. *Or cultivate*, I thought.

My phone buzzed again, and I braced myself for a message from Max. But when I looked at the screen, I saw a note from my father.

Pick you up at 9.

The sight of his text put me at ease. My father would know what to do. His endless patience and judgment-free style had always been a blessing. He had a unique ability to level with me and remain objective. He couldn't relate, per se, but he could reason. And that's what I needed: a person who could reason, free from passion. Free from emotion. Free from agenda.

I sat on my front porch after an uneventful day at the counseling center. Dad was on the way, but I was restless. I counted bricks on the porch as the minutes ticked by until, finally, headlights illuminated the front yard. I jumped up to meet him in the driveway.

"Sorry I'm late," he said when I opened the car door. I nodded as I slid into the passenger seat and rested my head against the window. Dad eyed me curiously. "Everything okay?"

He'd barely backed into the street before I was talking. As usual, nothing was off the table with him. I started by explaining that I'd decided to quit the music industry. The words tumbled out of my mouth as I confessed to the dangers I saw in remaining in that line of work. I told him what I was learning at school and the counseling center and my hope that, however unorthodox, I might actually be able to help people.

"I know it sounds crazy, Dad, but working there, it doesn't matter that I'm a sociopath. Hell, it might even be an advantage." I tugged thoughtfully on my seat belt. "With my patients, there's no expectation for me to feel or relate or connect or even talk. I don't have to do anything but observe." A good analogy hit me. "It's like the psychological equivalent of breaking and entering. Except instead of wandering around people's houses, I'm wandering around people's minds."

He said little but listened intently. When I finished, he took a deep breath. "Okay," he began, "let's start with work. I understand your concerns, Patric. I really do." He paused. "But quitting your job is a big deal. It's irresponsible."

I disagreed. "What's irresponsible is me staying somewhere I know is unhealthy for me," I said. "You need to understand: Having me in a business like this is like letting the fox guard the henhouse. The temptations are endless, and my self-control is mediocre *at best*." I considered how to phrase my next revelation.

"Do you remember Ginny Krusi?"

Dad was silent as I relayed the story of her antics. I told him about her blackmail emails and phone calls, sparing no details. I confessed to my trips to her backyard, my urges of violence, and the reasoning behind my reluctance to turn her in.

"I know what I've been doing is reckless," I concluded, exhaling with relief, "which is why I've made up my mind to go the police."

Dad momentarily appeared ill but eventually he responded. "Patric," he said quietly, his voice strained, "how long has this been going on?"

"About a year."

He shook his head, trying to get his bearings. Then he wearily rubbed a hand across his eyes, like he used to do in San Francisco. Whenever he did it, I always sensed there was something I was supposed to understand. But even now, I never knew what it was.

"Dad," I said evenly. "Take a deep breath. It's okay."

"*Okay?*" he yelped, looking at me like I was crazy. "How can you say that when you've been dealing with this woman, this . . ." His voice trailed off. I shook my head in consolation.

"Sociopath?" I laughed.

"That's not what I was going to say," Dad snapped.

"Why not?" I asked, gently accusatory. "Isn't that what sociopaths are? People who use others with no concept of consequence or compassion?"

He shifted uncomfortably in his seat. "That's not what you are," he said.

"Are you sure?" I asked. "Because after what I just told you, it sure sounds like it." I crossed my arms. "See? This is the problem. I don't know who I am any more than *you* do."

He frowned and took his eyes off the road for a moment to look at me. "No, Patric," he said, his voice level. "That's not true." He shook his head sadly, but with love. "I see you, honey," he continued. "And you are strong, and smart, and loyal. But most of all, you are brave."

I shrugged. "It's easy to be brave when you don't care about anything."

"Y'know what else is easy, I'd imagine?" he argued. "Doing the wrong thing all the time. Taking the path of least resistance. But that's not what you do." He reached over to squeeze my hand. "From where I stand, you've always taken the path of *most* resistance. And it can be a hard path, honey. I know. That's why I'm telling you, you are not alone." He shook his head. "As long as I live, Patric, you will never be invisible to me." He turned to look at me again. "Between the two of us, I promise we will always figure it out."

For just a moment, I knew what gratitude felt like. Who was I to have been blessed with such an ally? Who was I to have been blessed with anything?

"I love you, Dad," I said, my voice small.

"I love you, too." He smiled as he squeezed my fingers again, then put his hand back on the steering wheel. "That's why I'm going with you when you go to the police."

I frowned, then rejected the offer. "That's . . . unnecessary," I said. "I don't think you should get involved at all."

He looked at me askance. "You're not gonna tell them about the stuff *you* did, are you?"

"No," I said, scoffing. "Why would I incriminate myself?"

"Well, that's what *I* was thinking. I mean it's obvious this woman is crazy, right? *You're* the victim here." He waited for a beat too long before adding, "So maybe you're right. Maybe we just keep my name out of it completely."

My eyes fixed on the dashboard. The texture of the leather reminded me of a Rothko painting I'd always liked.

"What do you mean?" I heard myself asking him.

"Well, you're the one she's blackmailing," Dad said, now sounding concerned. "Involving me is just gonna complicate things, y'know what I mean?"

"No," I ventured, more directly.

He sighed. I could tell he was annoyed by my response, hoping I'd make the connection myself. "I just think it's better to tell them *you're* the one she has pictures of," he said. "I mean, that makes more sense, right? Why would she try to blackmail *you* with pictures of *me*?"

The air in the car felt thin. My heartbeat slowed as my gaze took me deeper into the folds of the leather. "I don't know," I replied carefully. "But that's what she did."

"Right," he said, his tone overly casual. "But if you say the photos she *claims* to have are of you, then I'm out of it. It all stops with you, and I won't have to answer any bullshit questions."

I sat still for a few seconds before replying, "So you want me to lie for you."

"Sweetheart," he pressed, "you said you weren't gonna tell them the whole truth anyway." Dad looked at me, his expression expectant. "Obviously if it made you uncomfortable, I wouldn't ask you to do it." He took a breath. "But I know things like that *don't* make you uncomfortable. Plus, you'd be helping me out." He smiled and gave me a wink. "But enough about that," he said, as we pulled to a stop. "It's showtime!"

I opened my mouth to respond but my door abruptly opened.

"Welcome to the Roxy," a valet said.

It took me a second to register what was happening. I shielded my eyes from the bulbs that flickered in the marquee. I'd had no idea we'd arrived. I felt disoriented. Disoriented and numb and now desperate to get away from my father, who was oblivious to the audacity of his request.

The valet offered me his hand and I got out of the car. Without looking back, I headed for the box office, passing a line of people that wrapped around the block. I nodded a quick hello to the doorman when he unhooked the velvet rope to let me in. Once inside, I was surrounded by people. I squinted in the darkness as I made my way through the lobby. I felt invisible, but not the way I preferred. I felt hazy. The ground beneath my feet was unsteady. Heading for the bar, I scanned the crowd for a face I recognized—or even one that would simply register my existence. But I was alone.

For a second I considered screaming. Or shoving the girl in front of me hard enough to make her head snap backward. Or yanking the hairpin out of her topknot and plunging it into the neck of the guy standing next to her. Anything to make it stop. The rising stress. The criminal numbness. The emotional poverty.

Then I saw him.

"David!" I shouted.

He was standing at a bar table, his elbow propped elegantly next to what I knew was his signature gin and tonic. "David!" I yelled again, nearly shrieking as I waved to him above the crowd. A crush of bodies knocked me off-balance, and I was swept sideways. But not before we locked eyes. He stepped forward and grabbed my hand. Allowing him to rescue me from the sway, I took a second to collect myself. Then I threw my arms around him.

Standing there, holding on for dear life, I said nothing. I just allowed myself to be held, plucked from the current and temporarily resuscitated by David's existence.

"Hey," he said after a few seconds. "Are you okay?"

"No," I whispered into his neck. "No. No. No. No." But the noise from the crowd drowned out my voice.

David pulled away to look at me. "Are you okay?" he asked again.

Gazing up at him, neon lights from the bar casting shadows across his face, it took all the strength in my soul not to confess. To fall into his arms and beg him to save me. To tell him the truth. That I loved him. Needed him. Ached for him. And not just because he was the only person who ever truly made me feel safe. And not just because being in his arms felt like home. But because he *was* home. David was the best person I'd ever known. The best person I would ever know. And who was I?

"I don't know," I said quietly. This was the problem. The reality

exposed. But as I felt his arms wrap tightly around my waist, I was confronted by a torrent of sadness. I rested my head on his shoulder and took several deep breaths. It felt so *good* to be in his arms. So honest. So safe. "I love you," I said, too quietly for him to hear.

It was a tranquility I was never able to sustain but could occasionally sense when he held me. A future with David was *my* version of phantom limb syndrome, at the same time so real and unreal that it was maddening. I wanted to stay there forever, suspended in that stillness. But I knew that I couldn't.

David, like everyone else in the world, needed more than stillness. He needed more than emotional poverty and mimicked responses. He needed someone for whom love wasn't just inherent but was all-encompassing, deeply rooted in the fabric of their being.

Summoning all my strength, I released my grip on him, signaling I was ready to leave. But he kept squeezing, challenging my bluff with one final act of affection. He almost succeeded. For a moment, I imagined what it might mean to never let him let me go, to yield to our dreams of a lifetime together, a lifetime of love and laughter, of music and books, and everything good in the universe. My resolve was fading—I wanted it so much—when something caught my eye.

It was a flash of movement from across the room, something my peripheral vision registered immediately but delayed incorporating into my reality until it was unavoidable. Max was there, staring at me. He stood lopsided, an arm draped haphazardly around the shoulders of a skinny blonde I'd never seen before. From the way he was looking, I knew he'd been watching us.

"Jesus Christ," I hissed. I dropped my arms from David's neck and took a step backward. "I'll be right back," I told him, then I stormed across the room.

"What the fuck are you doing here?" I said, making no effort to disguise my rage.

Max smirked. "I came to see a show," he drolled, raising a beer bottle in a toast to David across the room, "... although apparently it's already started." Max snickered and leaned forward, the blonde's neck twisting uncomfortably beneath his weight. He was clearly drunk.

I mustered a thin smile for his date and cocked my head toward the bar. "Can you give us a sec?" I asked. She nodded and took what seemed to be a grateful exit for the lobby bar. Meanwhile, Max had started a tirade.

"Was I *boring*?" he taunted. "Was that it? You got tired of fucking around with me so you're back to fucking around with Mr. Wonderful?" He made a show of pointing at me with one hand and raising the other in a pretend high five to David. Disgusted, I turned around just in time to glimpse the back of David's head disappearing into the crowd. His cocktail sat abandoned on the table.

"Fuck you," I hissed through clenched teeth.

"Nah," he said with a smirk. "I'm pretty sure that's off the table."

"It wasn't *on* the table, you bruised little bitch," I snarled. "Would you look at yourself? Jesus, I should have known you'd do something like this."

"No, *I* should have!" he yelled, attracting far more attention than I knew he wanted. "I don't know why I'm surprised," he said. "You told me from the start. You're a fucking sociopath!" He laughed. "You don't love anyone. You don't even *care* about anyone . . . not even yourself."

His attempts at provocation were pathetic. It was as if he thought that by baiting me, he could force me to act like his version of a sociopath. His pedestrian, banal, stereotypical version.

"Look on the bright side," I said, eating his insult, "at least you'll get some decent album material out of it."

He rolled his eyes and said, "Don't flatter yourself."

"Aww, poor baby," I replied in a playfully hideous singsong. "Flattery's *your* addiction, remember?"

"Fuck you," he spat, pointing his finger in my face. "I fucking *loved* you."

"Spare me." I shoved his hand away. "You knew *exactly* what you were getting into."

He leaned close enough that I could smell the scotch beneath the beer on his breath. "No, *you* knew," he rasped, his tone oddly level. He slowly shook his head. "You might suck at having emotions," he continued evenly, "but you're an expert at using them. You take what you see, and you use it. I've *watched* you." He pulled back so he could focus on my eyes. "You fucking *knew* how I felt about you," he said. "You knew where this was going, and you used me . . . like *all* sociopaths use people. But you weren't after cash or fame or power." He leaned in close again. "You were after *feeling*. And you fed on me like a fucking vampire."

I stood still as a strange sensation overwhelmed me. What was this? I couldn't place it. It was something from far away, an unexpected scent recalling some long-forgotten memory. I began a frantic spin through my emotional color wheel, desperate to find the correlating tile. I rarely discovered a perfect match but could usually land on something close enough to hide what was missing. I'd done it so many times. Why couldn't I find one now? And then, suddenly, I realized. I stared at Max as the understanding of remorse crashed into my consciousness. "I'm . . . sorry," I managed to stammer.

Max was right. I was culpable. I hadn't played the role I'd been assigned. I'd played the one that was most convenient for me. Just like I'd done all my life. "I'm sorry," I said again. I meant it.

He just stared back at me. After a few seconds, he looked away. He raised the bottle to his lips and drained its contents, then turned back to face me.

"Nah," he said quietly, looking me in the eye. "But you can fake it pretty good."

He walked away, leaving me alone to appreciate the irony of his final barb.

Somehow amid the swirling lights and the crowd, I managed to collect myself. I made a beeline for the backstage door, cutting directly through the crowd, brushing past people slightly harder than necessary as I went. I climbed the stairs to Everly's dressing room. She shot me an impatient look as I collapsed on the couch next to her makeup table. "Man," she said, looking me up and down. "What happened to *you*?"

I held up my hands. "I seriously cannot even begin to describe what just happened," I told her, shaking my head.

"Well, I'd love to hear *all* about it," she began, with benign curiosity, "except I have to play a rock show!" She bounced from her seat and beamed at me. "Wanna watch?"

With a deadpan expression I nodded toward an alcove in the hallway that overlooked the stage. "Can I do it from up here?"

Everly laughed. "Of course! I like having you up here anyway. You're like my guardian angel."

I rose laboriously from the couch. "I'm sorry," I said. "I don't mean to be a buzzkill on your big night."

"Don't be ridiculous. I'm ready to get it over with, really." She smiled. "The sooner I get done, the sooner we can celebrate."

I accepted a compulsory hug as Everly prepared to leave. That's when I caught my reflection in the vanity's mirror.

"Ugh," I said, recoiling at the image. "I look like I've been through an exorcism." I shook my head as I stepped closer to the mirror. "Seriously, I feel like I should get baptized or something."

Everly's face appeared over my shoulder. She cocked her head and grinned. "What a delightful idea."

Dorian's hillside pool floated on stilts above the Hollywood Hills, the city laid out like a blanket of inverted stars beyond the perimeter of an infinity deck. I took a deep breath and dove in, slicing through the surface of the water before finally coming to rest at the bottom of the pool. God, how I wanted to stay there.

I counted as high as I could and then broke the surface, swimming to Everly, who was sitting on the edge of the attached Jacuzzi. She looked sad.

"I can't believe you," she said.

I gave her a chagrined pout. It was nearly three in the morning.

Everly and I had driven up to her bandmate's house to celebrate the end of their residency. The atmosphere had been buoyant at first. Flying high on performance buzz, Everly and her band were celebratory and exultant. And I was happy to coast off the wake of their emotions. But as their adrenaline began to settle, so did my mood. Shortly after we jumped into the pool for a moonlight swim, I caught myself drifting back to a familiar state of apathy. So, I used the opportunity to rip off the Band-Aid and confess to Everly that I was going to quit.

"I knew you'd be bummed," I said, looking up at my friend. "But I just can't do it anymore." I paused, then added, "I understand if you don't want to be friends."

Everly looked at me as if I was crazy. "What the *fuck*, Patric? You think I wouldn't want to be friends anymore?"

She nudged me with her foot to get my full attention. "Be honest," she told me. "Don't you *feel* the way I feel about you? Don't you know deep down, that—more than anything else—you're my best friend and I love you?"

"It's not that I don't feel it," I told her. "It's that I don't trust it. You don't understand—it's not just *my* interpretation of love that's disjointed. It's other people's, too." I shook my head.

"People have never loved me, Everly. They love the darkness *in* me. They see the darkness and recklessness and emotional freedom, and they're attracted to it. They want it for themselves. So, they take it. They use me for it. Steal my ego strength. Ride my wicked coattails. And I use them right back."

I tilted my head. "But then, after a while, one of two things always happens. Either I get annoyed and cut the supply, or their guilt kicks in and I become the scapegoat." I scowled as I felt a subtle indignation churning at the base of my throat. I stared defiantly at her. "And you know what? I'm fucking over it."

"Over what?" she asked.

"I mean, I'm done being invisible," I continued, my ire continuing to rise. "Seriously. Why should I be the one hiding behind some fucking 'mask of sanity'? *I'm* not the insane one." I pointed to the city below. "Those people out there? *Those* are the insane ones. The ones who deny their darkness. The ones acting like sociopathy is some disgusting disease they couldn't possibly relate to. The ones talking shit about the word as if it's not the name of the standoffish girl in school they're all secretly trying to fuck. Or imitate."

I looked back at Everly and sneered. "I may be a sociopath, but at least I can accept it. And those people out there?" I pointed once again toward the skyline. "They don't get to have an opinion about it. Just like they don't get to have an opinion about depression . . . or anxiety . . . or PTSD. You know why? Because I'm not a fucking Rorschach. I'm not here to be a projection for their basic bullshit. I'm not a self-object for whatever crazy interpretation of love they've decided is the only one."

"But they're not all crazy, Patric," Everly insisted. "Believe it or not, there *are* people in the world who love you. People like me. People like David."

I lowered my eyes and contemplated this undeniable fact, momentarily distracted by the twinkling reflection of the moon on the water's surface. "I know," I admitted. "And in my heart, deep down, I do know you love me. And I know David does, too." I shrugged helplessly. "But he doesn't accept me."

"You said Max accepted you, though," Everly pointed out. "And that didn't work out."

"Because he only accepted my darkness," I replied. I held out my hands. "It's like David was too far left and Max was too far right." I paused then said, "I need to find the middle."

Everly looked confused. "And what's that?"

"I am." I fell silent as the weight of my statement settled. "I'm a sociopath," I continued. "I sit right in the middle of the spectrum. But my whole life I've been using *non*-sociopaths as compasses." I shook my head. "First, I wanted to be good for my mom," I said. "Then, I wanted to be good for David. But over and over, that strategy kept failing." I took a slow inhale. "The reality is that I need to want to be good for *myself*. I need to want to make healthy choices because *I* see the benefit in making them, not because someone else is pushing me to."

I turned my back to Everly and rested my head against the edge of the pool. I stared at the giant concrete slab that framed one side of the house and thought again of Rothko and his expressionist color fields.

"It's just like you said. I'm one person with David. A different person with you. And invisible to just about everyone else. That has to stop. I need to accept who I am all the time. I need to *be* who I am all the time. That's the only way I'll ever be able to stabilize my life." I paused, then added, "That's the only way I'll ever be able to share my life."

I looked down again at the water and realized: It was going to be hard to completely surrender invisibility. That ultraviolet aspect of my personality had, in so many ways, informed my existence. It had granted me access to people and places and adventures that most would give anything to experience.

A kaleidoscope of memories flashed through my mind. The texture of bricks in an underground tunnel, the view from the balcony of an abandoned hotel. I smiled as I recalled the time I ran my hand through Samson's fur, his head in my lap as we enjoyed a stolen afternoon. Or the nights I felt the reverb from Miles Davis's trumpet blaring from borrowed speakers and bouncing off the rocks of Laurel Canyon as I sped through her hills. I closed my eyes and begged myself to be grateful—for the fact that I was never bothered by the expansive stretch of solitude, or the feel of a stranger's dress against my skin. To be sure, it was an extraordinary existence. Unorthodox, but extraordinary.

"So, when do you think you'll start?" Everly asked, playfully interrupting my reverie.

"Tomorrow," I said. Then I belted out to Jane's Addiction, "Gonna kick tomorrow!"

Everly laughed. "Well, I've got news for you, sweetheart," she said. "It's already tomorrow."

I leaned defiantly over the side of the pool and flashed a mischievous grin. "Well, I guess I'd better get started."

Then Everly laughed and pushed me backward until I fell beneath
the surface.

I was already underwater before I remembered I'd forgotten to
breathe. A feeling, I realized, that had long ago become my baseline.
The water rushed over my face and into my eyes, obscuring my pan-
oramic view of the city. Beneath the surface the artificial landscape
flashed once more against my eyelids. Its edges sparked one last time,
then faded slowly into the aquatic darkness until it, too, was nothing
but a memory.

EPILOGUE

Modern Love

"Aunt Patric?" the little boy asked. "Can I ask you a question?"

More than a decade had passed, and I was at my sister's house. We'd just finished Thanksgiving dinner and Harrison, my nephew, had wandered into the dining room and taken a seat. He looked at me curiously, his wide eyes unable to conceal the same twinkle I'd seen in Harlowe's countless times over the years.

"I don't know," I teased. "*Can* you?"

He furrowed his brow, soft brown hair falling across his face like a scrim.

"Hello?" I nudged sarcastically. "I don't have all day."

"All day for what?" Harlowe asked as she and her husband, Gibson, joined us. She collapsed into the chair next to me and reached for my glass of wine. "What are you two talking about?"

"That's what I'd like to know," I said. "Your son says he has a question for me."

"Oh, yeah?" Gibson prodded.

Harrison, struggling not to smile, would only look at me sideways. His head was tilted ever so slightly. "Aunt Patric," he began, peeking tentatively at his mom, "are you really a thief?"

My jaw dropped in falsified shock as I placed a hand on my chest. "A *thief*?" I pulled him into my lap. "No, I'm not a thief!" Then, whispering into his ear loudly enough for only my sister to hear, I added, "But I *am* a liar . . ."

"Oh, good grief," Harlowe huffed, then took a long sip of my wine. She rolled her eyes and shot me a knowing glance as her son giggled and squirmed out of my lap. "It's the article," she explained. "Everyone keeps talking about it."

"The article" was an essay I'd written for the *New York Times* titled "He Married a Sociopath: Me." The piece, in which I'd disclosed my sociopathic diagnosis—along with an evocative glimpse into my marriage—had been published a month earlier and had caused a bit of a stir.

"Are you talking about the column?" asked my mother as she entered the room. My father, returning from the kitchen, appeared alongside her. Despite their divorce, I'd always appreciated that they'd managed to remain close. But never more so than the last few weeks. "I loved it," Mom said. "It was so interesting."

"Have you been reading all the comments?" Dad asked, taking the seat next to Harlowe.

I shook my head.

"You *haven't?*" Harlowe was incredulous. "There are thousands! It's all over Facebook and Twitter."

"Oh, I know!" my husband yelled from the kitchen. A moment later he joined us, slinging a dishrag over his shoulder. "I'm trying to stay cool," David said, "but I really want to beat the shit out of some of those assholes."

I smiled at him. "My sensitive guy," I said. "What would I do without you?"

It was a question, I'd realized a long time ago, to which I never wanted an answer.

"Fuck this noise," I grumbled.

It was a few weeks after Everly's last Roxy show and I was standing in my neighbors' backyard, staring up at their second floor balcony. I was in a furious mood. I'd recently discovered that the Mulholland cottage had been sold. I didn't know anything about the new owner, just that they had no intention of doing anything with the property other than letting it rot. (More than a decade later, in fact, the house remained exactly the way I'd left it: untouched and uninhabited.)

I knew my neighbors had recently left for a "last-minute ski trip."

The morning they'd left I'd made a point of smiling and waving as they drove away. Their house had been on my bucket list for years. I could see their bedroom's balcony from my bedroom window and had spent many nights imagining myself there. Just beyond the casement, a large citrus tree divided our properties. Late at night I could hear the branches brushing against the glass. *Tap-tap-tap.* It sounded like a lover gently knocking on my window, tempting me to surrender. And I wanted very much to comply.

My restlessness had been steadily rising. Despite my resolve, I was having a tough time maintaining discipline. A balcony trip, I figured, would have been simple enough—*harmless* enough. Nobody would get hurt and, once it was done, I'd have a clean space to work with, psychologically speaking. I flashed back to emptying my box of stolen trinkets as a child. Then, standing in the yard, staring at that terrace, it hit me. "I'm not a fucking child."

Annoyed, I turned and headed back to my house. I found my phone and dialed Dr. Carlin's emergency number.

A week later I was in her office. "I don't want to live like this anymore," I said. "I don't want to constantly feel like I have to resort to destructive prescriptions, behavioral solutions I came up with when I was a *kid*, for fuck's sake." I sighed.

"But, more importantly, I don't want to feel like things like relationships and love and family are out of reach just because I don't 'internalize emotions' the same way everybody else does. No one diagnosed as sociopathic should feel that way." I paused. "No one diagnosed with *anything* should feel that way."

I was done wasting time. I wanted to lead a "healthy" life. I wanted to help others like me do the same. So, we agreed. I signed a new "treatment contract" promising I would no longer engage in any illegal behavior whatsoever. Only this time I was eager to comply. I steeled myself to handle the weight of apathy and then we got to work.

Arms laden with books and copies of every research study I'd found related to the treatment of sociopathy, psychopathy, and anti-social personality disorder, I'd arrive at the therapist's office for our weekly (and sometimes twice-weekly) sessions. Together we pored over my findings, discussing various therapy methods and treatments.

Dr. Carlin, whose training was based in psychodynamics, believed that behavior is driven by our innermost thoughts, memories, and compulsions. "You can't alter your behavior," she'd say, "until you explore your unconscious."

Although effective, this traditional approach clashed with my own more than slightly impatient desire for a solution. I argued that reducing destructive behavior needed to be the first step in any sociopathic treatment plan.

"I agree with what you're saying," I countered, not for the first time, "but you can't reasonably expect a sociopath to sit through years of therapy. Hell, *I* didn't!" I lifted my palms toward the ceiling. "It's all fun and games until the stress spikes and then, I promise, it doesn't matter what you've agreed to or what contracts you've signed or blah, blah, blah."

I shook my head. "Therapy can take years. And that's fine, but only if the *behavior* is in check. Trust me," I insisted, "you have to address the behavior first."

With that in mind, I decided to investigate the field of cognitive behavioral therapy. Instead of merely identifying unconscious machinations, CBT patients are asked to address conscious thoughts and actions when they happen. It is a goal-oriented, real-world approach that calls for clear-cut objectives and well-defined tasks to minimize unhealthy coping mechanisms. CBT focuses on managing problematic behaviors first and saves understanding why they exist for later. "It's a commonsense approach to psychology," I reasoned, "perfectly suited for the sociopath."

Dr. Carlin was steadfast in her belief that examining the unconscious mind with a therapist was the best way to effectively treat sociopathy. Eventually though, she acknowledged that simultaneously addressing my immediate issues would be helpful. In the end, we combined forces.

Days bled into weeks. I packed my academic schedule with every class I could find related to cognitive behavioral and psychoanalytic training. This, combined with my independent research on sociopathy and work at the counseling center, left very little time for anything else.

For months I disappeared down this therapeutic rabbit hole. All I did was eat, sleep, and breathe psychology. When I wasn't busy with school or clinical training, I was in therapy. Dr. Carlin's psychodynamic techniques, in concert with cognitive behavioral interventions, were proving extremely effective in reducing my sociopathic anxiety. As I suspected, understanding the causes of and accepting my symptoms was a huge contributor.

Although I had long surmised that my "pressure" and the subsequent compulsion to commit destructive behavior was a common sociopathic cycle, I had never taken the next step and investigated its origins. With Dr. Carlin's help, however, I started unpacking my experiences. We began mentally retracing my steps, as I tried to remember the first times I felt the pressure. I recalled watching kids respond emotionally to things and feeling very much like I had to act the same way. This anxiety had been present as early as kindergarten. There had always been an uneasy feeling in my stomach whenever I faced a situation that assumed an emotional response. Milestones were especially difficult. Circumstances that for others would typically elicit extreme happiness came with the inevitable expectation of some outpouring of emotion. Continually disappointing those who wondered why I wasn't more excited (or morose) was frustrating. Worse, though, was repeatedly having my own hopes dashed.

In therapy, I recounted how I felt the day I graduated from high school. *Maybe today will be the day*, I remembered thinking. But it wasn't. When the ceremony was over, everyone wanted to know, "How do you *feel*?!" And I didn't have the heart to say, "Actually, I feel nothing. This whole thing has been little more than another sharp reminder that I will probably always feel nothing. So, if you don't mind, I'm going to skip the party so I can break into the abandoned mental asylum downtown that I've been saving for a special-occasion emotional jolt."

These recollections laid the groundwork for my growing understanding. I approached my memories as I would a research study,
compiling evidence and organizing it like a road map leading to who
I had become. Then I used cognitive journaling to help connect the
past to the present.

Cognitive journaling is a CBT technique that asks patients to keep
track of actions, beliefs, and reactions to isolate patterns, moods, and
urges. I used a notebook to keep a precise record, in real time, of when
I noticed feelings of anxiety, what preceded the feelings, and what
compulsions they triggered. The more aware I became of my own
destructive psychological patterns, both past and present, the more
adept I became at addressing them. CBT offered me better ways to
cope with my compulsions. On the (increasingly rare) occasions I felt
the sensation of pressure (and subsequent urge to act out), I was able
to employ healthier methods of stress reduction.

One CBT technique that was particularly helpful in this regard
was exposure therapy. This tactic encourages patients to consciously
engage with anxiety-inducing stressors by intentionally facing stressful situations. It is primarily used to help people explore the sources
of their anxiety rather than simply react to them. But I decided to use
this technique in a slightly different way.

I knew that anxiety was only one piece of the sociopathic puzzle.
My desire to act out (both voluntarily and compulsively) was something else I needed to understand and, better yet, to control. I figured
the best way to do it was through repeated exposure to places and
things that triggered my urges. Ginny's house, for example, was a
place where my compulsion to act out was easily activated. Dr. Carlin
disagreed with my desire to return there, but I was adamant that
re-exposure to that environment would allow me to witness my compulsions rather than be a servant to them. So, once again, I began
making weekly trips to Ginny's sleepy suburb.

From the very first visit, I was stunned by the things I observed.
I noticed my stomach start to flutter as soon as I pulled off the freeway. My hand instinctively reached to turn off the radio, allowing for

complete sensory focus. When I drove through the gates of the community, apathy washed over me as all traces of emotion disappeared. I pulled to a stop in the familiar parking lot and studied myself in the rearview mirror. The first thing I saw was the subtle prominence of my jugular vein. It was faint, but I could clearly see movement through my skin as blood pumped steadily just beneath its surface. My cheeks were flush with color. Inside the car, the only sound came from the space between my lips, as my breath moved quickly in and out. Although I'd previously never paid attention to it, I now saw that my physical response to the increase of apathy—and proximity to darkness—was arousal. *I was so busy reacting to it*, I thought, *that I never saw it.*

I let my hand fall to the driver's-side door and wrapped my fingers around the cold metal handle. "Sixty minutes," I said. "You will sit here for sixty minutes and then you will go home." And so I did.

Each second stretched into an eternity. I stared at the clock as the minutes ticked by, forcing myself to monitor my thought patterns and subconscious urges as they arose from the depths of my psychological abyss. The things I noticed, I wrote down in my notebook. After a while, though, I couldn't focus. *I can't do this*, I thought. I felt trapped and frustrated. I wouldn't do what I wanted to do more than anything, which was to get out of the car and eliminate the sensation of psychological claustrophobia with a trip to Ginny's backyard. The longer I sat, the greater the urge became. When the hour had passed, I couldn't drive away fast enough.

After repeated visits like this, however, I was relieved to find that reaction diminishing. The urges, though often present, registered more like hunger pains, benign biological tugs rather than complex sociopathic compulsions. Through cognitive journaling, I began to unravel my history of stuck stress and realized that the sensation of psychological claustrophobia (and the subsequent urge to act out) was a very, very old cycle. I had been reacting destructively to similar sensations for as long as I could remember.

So why am I still doing it? I wondered. I didn't need destructive behavior to neutralize my anxiety any more than I needed floaties to keep from drowning in a pool. *I just need to learn how to fucking swim*, I thought.

Learning to swim in apathetic waters turned out to be a critical aspect of my sociopathic treatment. My entire life I'd attempted to shun my apathy, this primary sociopathic trait, and for good reason. The more I paid attention, the more I noticed just how often "apathy," "lack of feeling," and the word "sociopath" were associated with evil. Everywhere. From celebrated books like *East of Eden* and *The Sociopath Next Door* to award-winning films like *The Silence of the Lambs* and *American Psycho*, the "sociopath" character composite was almost exclusively reserved for the "bad" guys (and girls). These one-dimensional portrayals weren't limited to fiction, either. Anytime there was a sensational crime that captured national attention, or a politician who displayed callous indifference for their constituents, even respected journalists would jump to invoke a diagnosis of "sociopathy." This despite having no training or qualifications to do so.

Sociopathic children were also condemned, even by many of my clinical colleagues, who were quite vocal about their "preferred" pediatric disorders. In a group supervision meeting, one of my fellow interns announced, "I'd rather my kid have cancer than be a sociopath." Others nodded in reluctant agreement. Meanwhile I sat frozen, overcome with an unfamiliar feeling: a profound sense of sadness.

Her admission was the *precise* sentiment I'd felt my entire life. Regardless of whether they realized it, my parents, my friends, my teachers, my lovers—everyone, on some level—was uncomfortable with my limited emotion. Because it meant something sinister. Because, along with the rest of the world, they had been programmed to believe that sociopaths were atrocious. A worst-case scenario for parents.

In that moment I wanted to race back in time to the child I once was and take her face in my hands. "You're not bad," I wanted to tell her. "I swear to God you're a good kid, a *kind* kid. Don't let anyone tell you different. Wait for me," I wanted to beg. "Wait for me and I'll prove it."

But I knew I couldn't go back in time. The only thing I *could* do was drive to my fellow intern's house that night to burn the letters "T-A-I-N-T" onto her front lawn with table salt. Then later at home, to take stock of my own self-perception. What I came to realize, after some reflection, was that I was often just as guilty of having repetitive negative thoughts about sociopathy as the people around me. I *need to be more conscious of the way I perceive* myself, I thought. It was the only way I would ever be able to reframe my adult sense of identity: by deprogramming a decades-old belief system, a false narrative that was built using all sorts of subliminal misinformation I had no say in receiving.

In an effort to do this, I turned to the CBT technique of cognitive restructuring, in which patients are asked to record unwanted negative thoughts and then refute them. I started logging every time I noticed one of these automatic negative thoughts and then forced myself to write down a fact-based counter-thought.

"I feel nothing," one entry read. "And if I don't do something to provoke a feeling, it will only get worse. The apathy will make me do something terrible."

"I feel nothing," I wrote as my counter-thought, "but there is no evidence that apathy is a dangerous state of mind. People go to yoga and spend thousands of dollars on meditation classes to learn how to let go and feel nothing. But I get to do it every day. For free."

"I hate people," another entry read.

"I don't hate people," I responded to myself. "I hate that people project their feelings and insecurities and judgments onto me. But I don't have to accept delivery of other people's projections, and I don't have to endure fake interactions to conceal my sociopathy. I am perfectly content being antisocial. Anyone who has a problem with that can go fuck themselves."

I smiled and crossed out the last four words. "Should hang out with someone else," I corrected.

The more I restructured these—and other—negative thought patterns, the better able I was to move through the world without the weight of negativity attached to my core identity. This self-liberation was delectable. It was like learning to walk after decades of crawling.

My trips to Ginny's complex were thus an evolving experience. I still didn't feel guilty about being there. Nor did I feel any shame or concern. I felt nothing. Only now, I *liked* the way that nothing felt.

"It's relaxing," I confessed to Dr. Carlin. "I just go and sit in the parking lot, and I feel nothing and it's wonderful, just like it was before. Only now, I'm not acting like a fucking lunatic." She pursed her lips and I laughed. "You know what I mean."

It had been six months since I'd returned to therapy, and I was having my regular late-afternoon session. She was pleased with my progress, but still unhappy about my visits to Ginny's.

"Which is why you don't need to go there anymore," she insisted. "I think we can both agree you've conquered that particular trigger."

I nodded. "But it's better than that. It's more like I've leaned into it." I stopped to think about it before continuing. "I enjoy feeling nothing. I really do. I think I always did. I was just so afraid of what feeling nothing meant, what being a sociopath meant. And the only reason I was afraid was because of *other* people's reactions to my apathy. My anxiety about *their* fear led me to do things I didn't want to do. Didn't *need* to do." I looked out the window at the familiar outline of the trees framing the park and shook my head. "What a fucking waste of time."

"Still," Dr. Carlin replied. "You've worked hard to overcome your challenges. You should be proud of yourself, Patric." She closed her notebook and asked, "*Are* you?"

I wasn't sure how to answer. For the most part I was thrilled with how far I'd come. I felt like I finally had a high-functioning grip on my personality disorder. I was able to effectively deal with the challenges of my symptoms through healthy coping mechanisms. The only problem was that I hadn't tested any of this progress in the real world.

My latest therapy experience was like a stint at a posh rehab. The environment in which I'd made all my recent progress was, in a psychological sense, hermetically sealed. Locked away in my own little bubble of school and research and therapy, I hadn't faced any of the temptations of day-to-day life or been forced to confront the demons that waited for me in the real world.

Dr. Carlin was quiet as I explained my concerns. "So, what's your greatest fear?" she asked when I was done. "What's the real-world test you are most afraid of failing?"

His name came out of my mouth before I had a chance to think about it. "David."

The more headway I made in therapy, the more certain I became: He was the man I wanted to spend my life with. I'd known I would return to David almost as soon as I'd stepped away from him. But I also knew that wanting to be "good" for someone else was the oldest—and by far strongest—trigger for my anxiety.

"That's why it's so critical to confront it," Dr. Carlin reassured me. "Give yourself a little credit," she added. "And David, too." She paused before asking, "Have you had *any* contact with him since that night?"

I shook my head. "No."

She smiled. "What do you think he'll say?"

The night I decided to find out, I arrived unannounced. After several days of reconnaissance, I waited until I was certain he was home alone. Then I walked up and rang the doorbell.

"Nice to meet you," I blurted out when he opened the door. David started to reply, but I cut him off. "My name is Patric, and I'm a sociopath."

He crossed his arms, but I caught a hint of a smile.

"I don't feel the way other people feel," I continued. "I'm not good at empathy, and telling the truth is something I have to work at. I enjoy being alone. I don't like affection that much. Or at all, really.

I get off on doing mischievous things, and I have to actively choose not to. Every day. Like an alcoholic. Most of the time I cry, I'm faking it." I held up my finger because I knew, with him, I needed to add, "Except for when I hear 'Sailing' by Christopher Cross because it reminds me of my first house in San Francisco that looked out over the Golden Gate Bridge." I took a deep breath.

"People who need to be liked annoy the shit out of me and, yes," I said, "I know you think that's most people, and I'm on the wrong side of the argument, but there's nothing I can do about it." I took another breath. "While we're on the subject, being friendly is not something that comes naturally to me. I can pretend, but not for long because it makes me tired. I don't really like dogs. Or kids. I'm never gonna be one of those women who wants to 'hold the baby'—if that makes sense." David bit his tongue trying to hide a grin.

I was on a roll. "Oh! And I get really impatient with people who base their decisions on everyone else's opinions. I have no shame, very little remorse, and feeling absolutely nothing is my default state." I swallowed nervously. "And there's probably a million other things I'm forgetting. But this is who I am, and I'm okay with that," I said. "I like *me*. And I'm hoping that maybe you can like me, too. Because I'd really prefer to not have to live the rest of my life without you."

David pulled me into his arms and kissed me. My body relaxed against his chest. Only seconds before, my thoughts had been a jumbled jigsaw puzzle. But now, everything fell perfectly into place. He pressed his forehead to mine as we stood there for a few seconds in silence. Then he wrapped me in another embrace, this one much tighter.

"I love you," he whispered in my ear.

I kissed his neck. "I love you, too," I said. I let him hold me for a few more seconds before adding, "But I hate hugs."

His arms went slack, but he didn't let go. He looked me in the eyes and asked, "Seriously?"

"Yes!" I said, trying to keep things light as I wriggled out of his grasp. "This is what I'm talking about," I explained. "I love you, but

there are things about me that are just different. Not *wrong*," I clarified. "And not less. Just different."

But David was looking over my shoulder, distracted. "Whose car
is that?" he asked.

I sighed. "Did you hear what I just said?"

"Yes. Whose car is that?" he repeated.

I glanced to the driveway and shrugged. "Some guy's," I said. "I
don't know, I grabbed it last night."

David glared at me. *"What?!"*

"It's mine," I admitted dryly. "I bought it a few months ago."

"Christ, Patric." He exhaled. "Why do you have to scare me?"

"Because I hate it when you change the subject like that! We were
in the middle of a conversation!"

He shook his head. "That's really not fair."

I sighed. "I know," I replied, taking his hand. "And I'll work on
it. But I need you to work on things, too." I took another deep breath.
"I think we're perfect for each other. But if we want to *be* together, I
think we need someone to help us."

"You mean, like, a therapist?"

"Yeah."

David raised his eyebrows dubiously. "What kind of therapist can
help me know whether you've actually stolen a car, or whether you're
just joking about stealing a car?"

"A very *special* kind of therapist," I told him with a sly smile. "And
I can't wait for you to meet her."

David surveyed the room. "I've heard a lot about this place," he said.
We were at Dr. Carlin's for our first couples therapy appointment.
She'd agreed to work with us together with a caveat.

"If I'm to remain your personal therapist, then David must also
make time for individual sessions," she'd said. "It's important for him
to not feel marginalized."

David was enthusiastic about the arrangement, confident that

Dr. Carlin would share his prosocial perspective. He jumped in with gusto that first day.

"I'm good," he said after Dr. Carlin asked him how he felt. "I love Patric so much and I want this to work. I see the good in her. I've *always* seen it." He squeezed my hand. "I'll do anything to help her see it, too."

She took a deep breath, and I bit my lip to stifle a sneer. I looked down at my lap but could feel David shifting his gaze back and forth between me and Dr. Carlin.

"What?" he finally asked.

She gave him a sympathetic nod. "I know how much you love Patric," she began, "but the purpose of couples therapy is not to help *Patric*." Dr. Carlin let this sink in. "We're here to focus on your relationship," she continued. "I want the two of you to thrive as a couple with a happy, healthy dynamic."

"Me, too!" David insisted. "That's all I've ever wanted."

"As long as I act like a good little girl," I said.

Dr. Carlin shot me a stern look. "David, you said you love Patric, and you see the good in her."

"Yeah," David replied. "I do. I always have."

She nodded and asked me, "So, Patric, what do you hear when David says that?"

I exhaled sharply. "I hear that you love me *in spite* of what you know about me. I hear that your feelings for me are conditional. That you love me for what I'm *capable* of or have the potential to be— according to *you*—and not for who I am right now."

"That's not true," he said. Then, to Dr. Carlin, "Look, I know she struggles. I want to help her. I want her to believe in herself the way I do—"

"I *do* believe in myself!" I exploded, startling him. "I just don't 'believe' the same way *you* do. I don't need your help to be good or better or whatever the fuck you think I 'should' be. I'm a sociopath, David. And no amount of 'support' or 'help' from you is going to change that. And even if it *could*, I wouldn't want to!"

He crossed his arms and stared angrily at Dr. Carlin.

"David," she asked, "what did you just hear Patric say?"

"That she doesn't need to change," he blurted out angrily. "And that what I want doesn't matter. That *I* don't matter. I'm irrelevant, and it doesn't make a difference how much I love her or how much I care. Because all that matters is that she *doesn't* care. She's a 'sociopath,' so she's just gonna do whatever she wants anyway."

Dr. Carlin looked for my reaction, but I was simply staring straight ahead. She looked back to David, and then to me again.

"Well," she said, "it looks like we've got our work cut out for us."

David reached across the couch and took my hand. "So, let's do it."

"Okay," I said, taking a deep breath. "Okay."

It wasn't easy. For months it seemed like all we ever did in therapy was argue. David, to his credit, worked hard during his private sessions with Dr. Carlin and became more cognizant of his own contributions to our previous dysfunction. He finally acknowledged his problems with my apathy, and admitted to often being condescending and critical when I didn't respond to his love the way he expected—and needed—me to.

"I think what happens is that I project my emotions onto you because you're a blank canvas," he confessed. "It allows me to avoid taking responsibility for how *I* feel. So, when I'm mad at you, I act like *you're* the mad one. When I'm upset, I ask *you* what's wrong." It was fascinating to see him processing these things. He told Dr. Carlin, "I think I use her personality type as an excuse. I want her to care as much as I do, so I get pissed when she doesn't."

"That's because you're still framing it as a *choice*," I said, "which makes *me* pissed. So I bait you into arguments. I know when you're not being honest with yourself, and I use it to pick fights. Then I get to go be destructive. Because I know you'll blame yourself."

David looked sad. "I *do* blame myself."

"I know," I replied. Then I promised, "So I'll try not do that anymore."

Confessions like this, although initially only ever sparked in session, eventually became a part of our everyday language. True to his word, David worked hard, not only to better understand my personality type but to empathize with others who struggled with it, too. On Dr. Carlin's suggestion, he began doing sociopathic research online. First, he volunteered to help me analyze the data for my doctorate. When I completed my dissertation, he proofread every single one of its hundreds of pages through countless edits. Once I graduated, he continued doing his own research.

As I'd long suspected it would, empirical data about sociopathy became David's gateway to understanding. The more he read and learned, the more supportive he became. Instead of seeing me as damaged, he came to see me as different. More importantly, he stopped taking our differences personally. His understanding of my personality type allowed him to navigate things from an impartial perspective. He became less reactive and therefore more empathic.

As for me, I doubled down on my efforts to become a prosocial partner. David, after all, was an emotional person. Social. Affectionate. Kind. So I did my best to match him as closely and authentically as I could. In doing so I became aware that I had my own set of biases, subconscious judgments of people who were *not* like me.

"I don't trust people who are overly nice," I remarked in therapy one day. "Like *really* don't trust them. When someone's super nice to me, I want to punch them in the face."

"Including *me?*" he asked.

"Sometimes," I admitted. "I think it's because my instinct is to perceive acts of kindness as manipulation."

David was patient and chose his words carefully. "But when I'm kind to you, it's because I *love* you. I do nice things for you because I want to show you that."

"No," I argued. "You do things for me because you want *me* to love you. It's transactional."

David looked helplessly at Dr. Carlin. "I don't know what to say."

She nodded. "This is an instance where I think both things can be true," she said. "Patric doesn't process kindness and trust the way most people do. It's a common sociopathic trait." She looked at David. "Remember, love is a learned emotion and Patric is *still* learning. Not only how to give that emotion but also how to receive it. To her, overt acts of kindness are only ever quid pro quo." She shifted her attention to me. "But that's not always the case. David does nice things for you because he genuinely loves you. His desire for kindness in *exchange* for kindness is not selfish. It's how most people give and receive love."

This was a revelation to me. "Oh," I replied.

David laughed. "Jesus, Patric!"

"What a fucking idiot," I said, marveling at my lifelong ignorance.

"No!" David said. "I'm just glad we're talking about it. I *get* it now." He looked at Dr. Carlin. "This is why she hates Christmas presents."

That was an understatement. "Ugh." I groaned. "He's right. Unless they come from someone I'm really close to, I *haaaate* them. The whole thing is just a guilt-currency circle-jerk." Dr. Carlin laughed. "Admit it! You know what your cousin who sends you a fucking oven mitt for Christmas wants? She wants *you* to feel obligated to send something back or to prime you for a future favor—whatever. It's completely transactional."

"But that's not always the case, Patric," Dr. Carlin said. "Sometimes people give you gifts because they love you, because they want to *connect*."

"Well, they can connect with someone else," I muttered.

"David loves you," she continued, "and being kind is one way he demonstrates that. I think you need to work on reframing your interpretation of kindness."

I agreed to try. I started paying attention to the way my muffled notion of things like trust and generosity informed my skewed perception of others' actions. I worked closely with Dr. Carlin to improve my sensitivity to things like empathy and shame. Such concepts might never come naturally to me but, with time and practice, I was able to better internalize them.

"I don't want Simon at the wedding," I declared a few months later, after we'd quietly gotten engaged.

David cautiously slid the guest list to me across the kitchen table. "Honey. I've known him since high school."

"Yeah, but his wife is a basic-bitch twat. I don't want any twats at my wedding."

He took a patient breath and asked, "So, what if I was like Simon?"

I raised my eyebrows. "A nice man married to a basic twat?"

He smiled. "What if I was being excluded from things because my wife is a sociopath?" I grimaced. "Do you think that would be fair?"

I didn't respond but glumly added Simon's name to the very short list.

David squeezed my hand. "That, my love, was an empathic response." Then he added, "If I didn't know any better, I'd say that you were becoming a sensitive little sociopath."

I wasn't so sure. During my self-imposed psychological rehab with Dr. Carlin, I had all the confidence in the world. But that conviction was inconsistent. David, with his seemingly endless supply of love, patience, understanding, and compassion, was a constant reminder of everything I wasn't—nor likely could *ever* be. I often found myself struggling to believe I could ever truly be a good person, much less a good partner.

Even after we were married, I continued to have my doubts. I wrestled with my desire for solitude. I grappled with David's preference for extreme affection. I fought against my periodic longing for invisibility and the occasional destructive relapse. These were the same issues I'd always had—*would* always have. Lucky for me, my husband was a fierce ally.

"It's okay that you're not like me, honey," David said, following a particularly rough setback. "I don't need you to be anything other than exactly who you are. I wasted so much time wishing you would change, but I was wrong. I was insecure." He poked me in the chest.

"But *you* aren't. You aren't like anyone else." He pulled me close and smiled. "So what if you don't like hugs? So what if you aren't bubbling with emotion? Who gives a shit?" he said. "You are a fierce, bold, intelligent, observant, brilliant fucking trailblazer. People meet you and they don't forget you, Patric. Because you *see* them. You're like Neo, only you've cracked the *psychological* Matrix."

David's ability to accept my sociopathic symptoms—to see the little girl still often retreating, lost and lonely in the empty house of her own mind—was nothing short of life-changing for me. Without my handy dose of behavioral prescriptions and psychological shortcuts, there were times I felt I might buckle under the apathetic pressure. My lack of feeling was like a pitch-black complex of caves accessible only by a steep psychological drop—the emptiest place on Earth. But then David's voice would echo through the chamber. "It's just darkness," he'd say. "Right now, you feel uncomfortable in your apathy. You're tired and you don't want to fight. It's okay. Just relax and let it pass."

In those times, it was David who would encourage me to keep journaling and, eventually, to keep writing. His confidence in me helped me navigate the darkness. He kept me believing that I could lead an emotionally full life, that I could be a good partner . . . a loving wife . . . an empathic mother.

Granted, my motherhood journey was not exactly orthodox. Nor was it anything like what I'd read about in books or seen on television. When our son was born, I was not overcome with emotion. I didn't get the profound surge of "perfect" love I'd been promised. And I was angry. Though I didn't realize it at the time, I'd been (once again) holding out hope that I, too, would be flooded with that overwhelming feeling at the first sight of my child. Throughout my pregnancy I'd been quietly dreaming that, unlike every other "important" life event, this most natural of human emotional experiences would not be robbed from me. So, when my son was born and, once again, I was unable to connect with my feelings—I was furious.

"Do you want to hold him?" asked the delivery nurse.

"No," I said, livid at the folly of my hope.

But David did. Moments after our son was born, it was David who removed his shirt so our baby could have his first skin-to-skin contact. It was David who learned how to swaddle and gave him his baths and took him on long walks and did everything those first few weeks of paternity leave. And it was David who convinced me that all was not lost.

"Patric, none of this is easy," he said, as he prepared to head back to work. "All the movies and books, none of it prepares you for this." He gestured around our bedroom-turned-makeshift-nursery. "If anything, being a sociopath is probably an asset right now. You're so fucking calm and organized. I'm so exhausted I can't even think straight." He offered a soft smile to the tiny boy asleep in my arms. "I know you love that baby," he said. "Just because your love is different doesn't mean it doesn't count."

When David left for work that day, I leveled with my infant son. "You have a weirdo for a mom, babe," I said to him. "So I can't promise your childhood is going to be entirely normal." I paused, then admitted, "I also can't promise that the next time we go to the grocery store, if we see that doggie locked in the hot car again, I'm not going to break him out, then tell Daddy we got him at the shelter." I gently placed his toy turtle on his little chest as if it was an oath. "But I *can* promise that I will never put you in danger. You will never be safer than you are when you're with me," I vowed. "And I'll never lie to you."

It was a promise I managed to keep.

Once again, at the precise point in my life I needed it most, David's faith in my capacity for love created the space for my own confidence to grow. It didn't come easily, but what I found over time was that those fundamental feelings for my son weren't nonexistent. They were simply non-*intrinsic*. I had to work to experience them. It took work, for example, to get to know my son's unique personality. Then I had to work some more once I realized how similar it was to my own. Before he even started preschool, he proclaimed, "I can get away with anything I want."

"Oh, yeah?" I asked. "And why is that?"

"Because I can just do what I want and say sorry and give love. Love makes people forget."

I gave him a kiss. "Love also makes people forgive."

Indeed, his mischievousness was just as dominant as his cunning. But I never worried that he might be a sociopath. Although blessed with my tenacity and remarkably fearless, our son also possessed his father's full range of deep emotions. I had to work to keep up.

Once he started school I had to work even more. Only then it was to keep myself from going after any classmate who gave him a hard time.

"Do you know how his leg got scraped?" I asked David, after a call from the school nurse. "That little shit Casielle pushed him off the dome climber." I fumed, "I swear to God I'm going to recess tomorrow so I can hip-check her."

"Please don't hurt a *child*," David responded dryly.

"I'm not going to hurt her. I'm just gonna knock her ass to the ground. It'll look like an accident." And it did.

When I got pregnant with our second child, I had to work all over again. Except then it was to imagine how I would ever possibly love another person as much as my firstborn. A concept that once seemed so alien to me was now as effortless as breathing. Yet fiercely less than perfect.

These days, I'm happy to report, I don't have to work so hard. I've come to accept that my version of love is a mosaic: tiny pieces of broken glass held together by fate so the light can shine through in different colors. It is not perfect. Perfect, I'm afraid, is far too tame.

The purest love is not born from bliss. It is pulled from the pyre. It is fierce and shape-shifted, slightly twisted and delicious. Accepting, forgiving, understanding, and relatably flawed, my type of love is the furthest thing from perfect. The closest thing to me.

"Mommy?" asked my oldest, as he joined us in Harlowe's dining room. "When are we gonna do the Turkey Bowl?!"

He was eager to kick off our annual family tradition, a game of football we played at the park every year after Thanksgiving dinner.

I smiled and pulled him into my lap. My child had grown into an idyllic combination of David and me: equal parts ferocity and unbearable compassion. I kissed the top of his head and inhaled. His hair smelled like sweat and magnolia trees.

"*Mommy,*" he whined, making his body go slack to slide from my grasp. "Can we please do the Turkey Bowl?" It was more of a command than a question.

"Five minutes," replied my sister, glancing at her own little boy. "You two get your brothers and report back here in five minutes. Then it's off to the park!"

They scrambled out of the room, yelling for their siblings to get ready. Harlowe finished off her wine and asked, "So what are you going to do?"

"You should write a book!" my mother suggested. "*Self-Help for Sociopaths!*"

It wasn't a bad idea. I knew nothing like that existed when I needed it most, and even now there was nothing like that I could find. I wasn't alone. When my essay was published, most of the messages I received were pleas for resources or help, and I had little to offer in reply.

"No way," my brother-in-law chided. "It would have to be a memoir."

"*Why?*" Mom asked. "That's so personal!"

"It would have to be," Harlowe answered for me. "It's the only way anyone would listen to her."

"Exactly," David added. "The honesty of it was why they ran the essay in the first place."

Dad asked me, "Is that something you'd ever want to do?"

I exchanged a quick glance with David. The truth was I'd already written one. It was, I thought, a very raw and very revealing narrative of my life, through which I'd managed to weave an assortment of psychological research and facts about sociopathy. My nearly completed memoir had been sitting on my computer for more than a year, only I didn't know what to do with it. I knew that my story had the potential to help many people. But I also knew that "helping sociopaths" wasn't exactly a welcome concept.

Despite the numerous advancements in mental health awareness and treatment options, sociopathy still seemed to be getting ignored. "Where are sociopaths supposed to go for help?" I still didn't have the answer, but I did what I could to fill the gap.

After earning my PhD, I continued to work as a therapist. Several of my classmates and colleagues knew about my diagnosis and my belief that sociopaths could be helped. So they started sending their problematic patients to me. I rented a private office where I earned a low-key reputation as "the sociopath therapist," willing and able to work with people who unnerved my cohorts. My practice was like a psychology speakeasy. Unlicensed and unorthodox, I welcomed the misfits nobody else wanted to see. David even helped me build a website where patients (and would-be patients who lived outside my area) could get access to research and essays I posted.

My decision to work in the mental health field did feel, at times, perversely counterintuitive. Therapists, after all, are expected to possess a rudimentary grasp of compassion. Despite my best attempts to access it, empathy (for the most part) had always been staunchly out of reach. But once I expanded my practice, things started to coalesce. After countless hours of listening to my patients' stories—many of which bore a striking resemblance to my own—I found myself flooded with understanding. And then rage.

"What the *fuck*?!" I would often complain to David. "People hate sociopaths for not having empathy and compassion . . . But who has empathy and compassion for *them*?" Sociopaths were villainized for failing to exhibit the very emotion they were denied. "How can anyone be expected to master a *learned* emotion they never get to experience for themselves?" The hypocrisy was maddening. These were human beings deserving of serious clinical attention. Instead, they were treated with malevolence and exiled.

I did my best to help, but I knew better than to think what I was offering was anything close to enough. My psychological interventions were just that: *mine*. They were a patchwork quilt of psychological swatches based on my personal hit-or-miss approach and anecdotal evidence—a Band-Aid on a bullet wound.

I knew the best way I could make an impact on any large scale was to share my story. This would allow people like me to see themselves in healthy, everyday situations, and provide the single thing I knew they needed most: hope.

I smiled at Dad and shrugged noncommittally. "Maybe someday."

David, seizing an opportunity to change the subject, rose to his feet. "Okay," he said with a clap of his hands. "We're running out of daylight. Let's get out of here."

Everyone agreed and we filed out of the dining room. I noticed Harlowe looked suspicious, so I asked her, "What's your deal?"

She ignored me and instead whistled to let the kids know it was time to go. A flurry of activity ensued as shoelaces were tied and jackets were demanded. The boys bolted out the door as if shot from a cannon, and a few minutes later the rest of us emerged from the house into the crisp afternoon. Harlowe stayed behind to lock up. When everyone was out of earshot, she turned to me and asked, "So can I read it?"

The question took me by surprise. Of course I knew what she meant, but I did my best to summon my most convincing "puzzled" look.

"The book," she clarified, cocking an eyebrow. "You've already written it, haven't you?"

Unable to contain my amusement, I responded with a Cheshire Cat grin. "Maybe," I purred, turning for the park.

Harlowe squealed behind me. "I knew it!" she said, running up alongside. "Who else knows?"

"David," I answered. "And Everly."

"Am I in it?" she asked excitedly.

"Of course!"

My little sister giggled and began jumping up and down. "Can I read it?" she pleaded. "And did you use our real names? If not, then I want my name to be Harlowe." She yanked playfully on my arm. "That's okay, right? I've always loved the name Harlowe."

"Sure."

"And can you include this scene?" She spoke quickly, excited by the prospect. "Where we're walking to the park and I'm asking you if my name can be Harlowe?"

"I'll consider it."

"Oh, Kaat," she said, adding a light skip to her step. "This is so exciting. Have I ever told you you're the best person at helping others out of the darkness?"

"You *have*, actually." I laughed. "Never fear!" I shouted. "Captain Apathy doesn't care!"

Harlowe threw her arm around my shoulders, and we made our way to the park. Beyond the trees, the moon peeked through the leaves. From the street ahead, I could hear the sound of our children's laughter. The autumn light cast long, delicious shadows, and the witching weather was cool and familiar.

"You care when it matters," she whispered. "That's all that matters."

Acknowledgments

Thank you to Dan Jones and Miya Lee at the *New York Times*. If not for you, this book would never have been published. Well, that's not true. It probably would have been (self) published, but certainly not with the guidance and wisdom of my goddess-agent, Melissa Flashman. Thank you, Mel, for taking me on this adventure and being the only person (besides my sister) to fully appreciate the Sears ladder reference. And to early champion Allison Hunter, for believing in me even *after* reading the first draft.

Staggering thanks to my super-editor, Eamon Dolan, for helping me find the clearest way to tell my story. Thank you, Eamon, for your pinpoint accuracy. It always sounds better the way you say it.

I am forever indebted to the gorgeous team at Simon & Schuster, including Paul Dippolito, Jamie Selzer, and Tzipora Baitch. Extra appreciation to Morgan Hart and Lara M. Robbins for your insane attention to detail. Bri Scharfenberg and Alyssa diPierro, your enthusiasm was infections from the jump and I remain so grateful. Thank you to Carolyn Levin for your legal genius, and Rodrigo Corral for the incredible cover.

Thank you to James Molesky, for keeping me out of (legal) trouble my entire life. If not for you, every step of this journey would have been much less entertaining. Cindy Farrelly Gesner, you didn't have the benefit of history tipping your scale. You met me through my pages and your faith has meant the world.

Special love and thanks to Pete Nowalk—who read every page of the unabridged version of this book (twice) and still invited me on vacation—and to Stan Parish, for the psychic introduction. I am so glad we met.

To my incredible steel magnolia Aunt Tricia "Daisy" Talley and Uncle Steve Lolli: Thank you for being there my whole life. And to David and Jenny Snyder, for helping champion every one of my creative impulses. Thank you, guys, for naming the guest room after me (not David—just me). Yours has always been the safest space to land.

Thank you to Michelle Gagne, for existing. Steve Ross, for showing me how to live. ESK, thank you for getting me out and lifting me up. Matt Cook, I am hopeful that by the time you read this you will have finished the fucking book. Regardless, thanks for being my friend even though I keep putting you in "crazy situations." Alison Dunbar, thirty seconds after we met, you asked me if I'd ever been arrested. You've been an ally ever since. Thank you for the early read and the unwavering encouragement.

Amanda, you have celebrated every step of this process (and served me Viktor Benês with champagne). I am so grateful. To Gilbert, thanks for the banter, bourbon, and posthumous letters from Pop-Pop. And your dad and I are the same age, and I'm rich and I have triples of the Barracuda. My oldest and dearest friend Ava: You have always set such a flawless empathic example. Thank you with every ounce. I'm sorry I took a chunk out of your knee that one time and ran you into barbed wire the other time.

RL. My darling freeeend. My gorgeous touchstone. I love you more than the marina. Thanks for the tuna-cone wishes and shame-alley dreams. To CB, for saving my life. MD, KAG, SP, FJS, and JCM: Thank you for being a part of my story and for letting me be a part of yours.

My parents have always been proud of me—even when it wasn't easy. Like now, probably. Dad, thank you for always including me in your adventures. I love you very much. Mom: The only reason I know anything is possible is because you taught me to believe it. This book exists because of you.

Deepest, endless, formidable thanks to my beloved sister. You are my alpha and omega. My wicked good witch and saving grace. There are simply no words to convey the depth of your current. I won the eternal lottery the day that you were born.

To my boys, thank you for allowing me the space and inspiration to tell this story. I know it hasn't been easy—especially for you, Bear. But I see you. And you see me. Better than anyone. As for you, little Pear, thanks for blazing your phosphorus trail. It's hard to get lost in the darkness when your shadow is a beam of light.

David. You've read every page. Every paper. Every joke. Every essay. Every story. Every word (including this one). You have been, are now, and will forever remain my true North. Thank you, my darling. I love you madly.